AF505940

The United Nations democracy agenda

Manchester University Press

To my parents

The United Nations democracy agenda

A conceptual history

Kirsten Haack

Manchester University Press
Manchester and New York

distributed in the United States exclusively
by Palgrave Macmillan

Copyright © Kirsten Haack 2011

The right of Kirsten Haack to be identified as the author of this work has been asserted by her in accordance with the Copyright, Designs and Patents Act 1988.

Published by Manchester University Press
Oxford Road, Manchester M13 9NR, UK
and Room 400, 175 Fifth Avenue, New York, NY 10010, USA
www.manchesteruniversitypress.co.uk

Distributed in the United States exclusively by
Palgrave Macmillan, 175 Fifth Avenue, New York,
NY 10010, USA

Distributed in Canada exclusively by
UBC Press, University of British Columbia, 2029 West Mall,
Vancouver, BC, Canada V6T 1Z2

British Library Cataloguing-in-Publication Data
A catalogue record for this book is available from the British Library

Library of Congress Cataloging-in-Publication Data applied for

ISBN   978 0 7190 7981 8   hardback

First published 2011

The publisher has no responsibility for the persistence or accuracy of URLs for any external or third-party internet websites referred to in this book, and does not guarantee that any content on such websites is, or will remain, accurate or appropriate.

Typeset
by 4word Ltd, Bristol
Printed in Great Britain
by TJ International Ltd, Padstow

Contents

Acknowledgements

There are many friends and colleagues who I would like to thank for their assistance and support in writing this book and the doctoral research it is based on, in particular Professors John Groom, Andrew Williams and Ruth Abbey for their comments and invaluable advice; my colleagues and students at the Open University for reminding me that the social sciences are eminently fun; Ina Klein, Christopher Macallister and 'Team Bear' for friendship in all aspects of life – professional and otherwise; the members of the small but very fine UN Studies Association, especially Henrike Paepcke, Julia Harfensteller and Kent Kille, whose ideas, advice and comments have had an important influence on my research in the last few years; my colleagues and friends at the Journal of International Organizations Studies; and Gita Subrahmanyam, Lynne Roberts, Chris New and Adél Pásztor for inspired enthusiasm, editorial and other support. The initial research for this book was made possible by the generous support of the University of Kent Alumni Association and I thank all those whose keen interest in their alma mater encourages them to support future researchers.

List of figures

List of abbreviations

ACC	(UN) Administrative Committee on Coordination
CCPOQ	(UN) Consultative Committee on Programme and Operational Questions
CEB	(UN) Chief Executives Board for Coordination
CSCE	Conference on Security and Cooperation in Europe
DPA	Department of Political Affairs
DPKO	Department of Peacekeeping Operations
HDI	Human Development Index
HDR	Human Development Report
HRBA	human-rights-based approach
ICCPR	International Covenant on Civil and Political Rights
ICESCR	International Covenant on Economic, Social and Cultural Rights
NGO	Non-governmental organisaion
SAP	Structural Adjustment Programme
SMG	(UN) Senior Management Group
UDHR	Universal Declaration of Human Rights
UN	United Nations
UNDEF	United Nations Democracy Fund
UNDP	United Nations Development Programme
UNESCO	United Nations Educational, Scientific and Cultural Organisation
UNGA	United Nations General Assembly
UNICEF	United Nations Children Fund
UNIHP	United Nations Intellectual History Project
UNPF	United Nations Population Fund
UNSC	United Nations Security Council
UNSG	United Nations Secretary-General
US	United States

Democracy ideas and practices

Democracy is a powerful idea with deep historical roots. Emancipatory in character, claims for democracy have instigated and responded to considerable social and political change, challenging established ideas of political rule and the nature of society. Yet active engagement in democracy support has long been anathema to the UN because democracy support in a world of sovereign states means intervention in domestic political affairs and, worse for some, the promotion of Western ideas. Despite this, today democracy has an international dimension. Some have claimed the existence of a 'right to democratic governance' (Franck 1992) in international law, while others declared democracy to be a 'settled norm' (Frost 1996) whose contravention requires justification. The promotion of this powerful idea is no longer confined to rhetoric or the realm of philosophy as international organisations such as the UN have created their own democracy agenda, adopting practices that support, or even promote, democracy. In the last twenty years democracy support has become mainstream UN practice, used in a variety of contexts from post-conflict state reconstruction to development aid. Indeed, as democracy has been part of most UN missions after the end of the Cold War, any intervention would, in one way or the other, be a pro-democratic intervention. With the widespread use of democracy, the question as to what kind of democracy the UN supports and implements is raised – a question particularly relevant for liberal peace-builders.

Following varying degrees of success in trying to implement democracy in the context of peace-keeping, post-conflict reconstruction and state-building in the last twenty years, both scholars and practitioners have realised the need for a moment of pause and a reconfiguration of existing strategies. Two schools of thought have emerged, which, while continuing to value democracy, approach potential solutions very differently. One school of thought is primarily concerned with the effectiveness of peace-building and seeks problem-solving solutions to the intermediate crisis of liberal peace-building (Newman 2009), an approach which Kumar and De Zeeuw (2006) consider a mismatch between strategies and goals in which technical solutions are used for essentially political problems. By contrast, 'critical' approaches question the ideas and assumptions of existing peace-building strategies, offering an alternative vision of peace-building processes and outcomes (Newman 2009). Critical scholars lament that liberal peace-building has become a 'system of governance', which does not support processes of reconciliation in post-conflict situations (Richmond 2010b). They criticise that the granting of political rights does not necessarily create a social contract, thus leading to a lack of legitimacy (Richmond 2009), or that the only social contract created is one between assistance providers and recipients, effectively creating a contract of dependency (Pugh 2010). Instead, critical scholars raise the question of 'welfare' and call for transformative, emancipatory approaches, which move beyond shallow uses of participation and the 'empty institutionalism' (Richmond 2009) of existing democracy assistance and statebuilding approaches. Instead, they call for participation which enhances local stakeholding, capacity buildin and most of all empowerment and welfare.

Despite their commitment to the ideals of democracy, be that as basic as 'ownership' and participation or as broad as social democracy and welfare, both sides of the liberal peace-building debate have yet to state which form their idea of democracy should take. Yet democracy, while 'known' to all, is notoriously difficult to define. 'I know it when I see it' was US Supreme Court Justice Potter Stewart's famous conclusion as he considered the issue of hard-core pornography in US law, battling with the question of what defines obscenity. The same can be said about democracy. Like obscenity, democracy is a moral concept, open-ended and value-laden, with each side of the argument defending an equally strong legal or philosophical position. What constitutes democracy depends on the context of its application, the ideological position and the lived experience of those defining it.

Conceptual historians have shown that ideas are always influenced by their social and political environment, which shapes their meaning over time (see Koselleck 1985). Thus, the role and place of democracy in the international system have been an expression of its time and the historic, systemic constraints placed upon it. For example, in the small city states of ancient Greece democracy was a form of equal and shared direct rule in a constitutional framework. This, however, was only accessible to 'citizens', a limited number of free, wealthy men, which left the majority of people – slaves, women, children, foreigners – excluded. In Greek democracy the 'rule by the people' was regarded as mob rule. This view of democracy was maintained throughout medieval times as feudal landlords, royalty and the church dominated political rule, and it was continued in parts well into the nineteenth century. A more general, positive view of democracy slowly developed in the eighteenth century, assigning democracy again to a more general political system. In the nineteenth century broader social and philosophical ideals became associated with democracy. For example, Kant connected liberal values and ideas of education and progress to both the democratic system and the democratic process. As a result, democracy and 'the democrat' became associated with specific political groups and social classes, and generally with liberalism. To maintain democracy's relevance even for modern, large-scale societies, the focus on direct democracy gave way to representative forms. At the same time, through increased emphasis on the democratic principle of elections and by disconnecting its meaning from a form of polity alone, democracy was made compatible with monarchy. It is only in the twentieth century that democracy became the kind of system that is today generally associated with a democratic state, extended in depth and breadth, including the entirety of the population and a number of areas of public life. This only happened by degree, stimulated by the end of both world wars. The demise of monarchy after the First World War went hand-in-hand with an extension of the voting population to all citizens, bar those under age. The end of the Second World War increased the number of democratic states, deepened democracy where it already existed and increased the role of the state in social and economic affairs through the introduction of the interventionist welfare state. Consequently, today democracy describes as much a state as a *society* (Conze 1972; Hanson 1989; Oppenheim 1971; Williams 1983).

While conceptual histories offer us an insight into different conceptualisations of democracy, their account remains focussed on general trends and broad brush definitions. They do not unpack the range of views and approaches contained within them. Thus, we apply 'democracy' in the workplace, in many places where groups come together and, of course, in states; and while we are sure what kind of ideals we want to promote in these different settings – legitimacy, accountability, fairness and the opportunity to participate – we are uncertain as to what the necessary criteria of a functioning democracy are. Is casting a vote enough? Do we need ballots if we have the rule of law? Do we need a state to provide services for its people to be called democratic? Is liberalisation essential or not? Even among states that are deemed to be democratic, the criteria of what constitutes democracy vary, as Carothers (2009) showed. According to Carothers, US democracy assistance focuses on the core *political* functions of states, centred around elections, while European approaches assume a broader perspective, including *socio-economic* dimensions.

Taking into account the multidimensionality of democracy, the question begs not only what a UN democracy agenda entails but what it ought to achieve. Without a doubt, democracy has come to play an important role in UN missions, both in practical terms and in the imagination of those aiming to maintain and uphold the values of the UN. However, UN missions have had varying degrees of success and commentators have been quick to deem a mission a failure, not only when violence returned to the region but also where elections held under UN supervision and the gaze of the world did not transform the state in question into the peaceful and prosperous society that is the (Western) image (and experience) of democracy. Thus, more important than understanding what the *minimum* criteria of democracy are, is understanding what the *maximum* criteria are. How does the UN conceptualise democracy? How far does a UN concept of democracy reach? How many principles, processes and institutions are considered important in achieving a functioning democracy?

Whose democracy?

In trying to understand the ideas which shape the UN democracy agenda, further questions arise as to how such a complex and controversial idea has come into being. Its association with the West too often implies imperialism for those who are at the receiving end of democratisation attempts from the outside. In trying to understand what democracy means and what it entails, a conceptual history therefore also needs to unpack the process of agenda-development and identify the drivers of the democracy agenda to understand the context in which an idea is shaped. Considering the variety of ways in which democracy can be approached and defined by focussing on views propagated by member states is unlikely to yield further insight than the realisation that Western, liberal democracy is a predominant feature and that within this dominant discourse exist different views on the scope of democracy. This dominant discourse is likely to follow general patterns of power and represent the relative influence yielded by those most heavily involved in providing assistance, a practice which carries ideas and ideology. Indeed, the provision of assistance is an important avenue in shaping ideas as the operationalisation of ideas explicates and makes real their conceptual cluster, as Carothers (2009) showed. Like member states, the UN as an organisational actor operationalises ideas and policies, and in doing so shapes a discourse of how democracy could or should operate. The ability, or authority, of the UN, in particular the Secretary-General as its representative, to act in this capacity is part of the prescribed role, not an assumed one. Focussing on the Secretary-General as norm entrepreneur (Johnstone 2003; Rushton 2008) in the conceptualisation of democracy therefore yields a sharper image of what UN democracy is.

According to Newman, the office of the Secretary-General is 'something of a chimera, with a tension between explicit administrative duties and an implied political role' (Newman 1995: 1). Accordingly, the United Nations Intellectual History Project (UNIHP) identifies the existence of two United Nations: the literal United Nations, an assembly of states and an arena for debate and decision-making; and the organisation as such, the leadership and staff of international secretariats (Emmerij et al. 2005). This distinction is maintained and justified by Rittberger, who differentiates between activities and the process by which they were brought about. Thus, policies are differentiated from operational and information activities by the fact that they rely on intergovernmental negotiation and majority based decision-making, while operational and information activities rely on rational choice, routinisation and bureaucratic politics (Rittberger and Zangl 2006). This distinction reifies the hierarchical separation of 'high politics' and 'low politics', and thus corresponds with a widely held view of the relative importance of peace-related functions and diplomacy over social and economic activities undertaken by the UN. Thus, conventionally the peace-related functions of the Secretary-General, of which Art. 99 of the UN Charter most clearly delineates a role in the policy-making process, are referenced to demonstrate the potential for influence and leadership (Boudreau 1991; Gordenker 1967; Johnstone 2003; Newman 1998; Skjelsbaek 1991; Zacher 1966). By being able to bring to the attention of the Security Council any matter that he regards as threatening to international peace and security, the Secretary-General influences the Security Council's agenda. This political dimension of the Secretary-General's role is further emphasised by tasks relating to fact-finding and the provision of good offices, and the Secretary-General is able to assume an important role in the policy-making process. However, the potential for the Secretary-General (and his administration) to shape ideas and discourses is in practice more explicit in Art. 97, which names him as the 'chief administrator' of the organisation.

A brief but not necessarily comprehensive list shows that he is responsible for tasks such as the administration of programme finances and the preparation of the budget, as well as the appointment of staff. He (or the Secretariat on his behalf) registers and publishes international treaties and accredits diplomatic representatives to the UN. Further, a broad duty relates to information management – documentation, information and public relations are part of the Secretary-General's duty, including the receipt of statistical information, the preparation of documents, reports, legal opinions or procedural advice for UN organs (see Simma 2002: 1191–1196, 1205–1216). These activities are complemented by coordination duties that require the Secretary-General to manage the communication between different UN organs to ensure the efficient working of the system. In this function, he assumes the role of chairman of the Chief Executives Board for Coordination (CEB) and, since 1997, the Senior Management Group (SMG), which includes agencies and programmes. Parallel to intra-organisational cooperation, the Secretary-General also manages communication between the General Assembly, the Security Council and the other principal organs. In this administrative capacity, the Secretary-General assumes a neutral role, solely focussed on the successful management of the organisation. Yet, at the same time, he has wide-ranging discretion in the exercise of his own decisions (Beigbeder 1997), and it is here that an important role in the policy-making cycle and the development and conceptualisation of ideas occur.

The Secretary-General not only has the right to speak and participate (albeit on invitation) in the various UN organs, he prepares the sessions by drawing up reports and documents. Here, the Secretary-General may communicate his ideas and understanding of an issue, which will then form the basis of discussion for member states. These powers assume considerable influence in an ideational framework, as Gordenker notes:

> members of the Secretariat who work on such [routine] reporting very quickly become the rare experts on what specific activities the UN and member governments undertake as a result ... They can consequently insert a particular tone in the proceedings and on many occasions quietly inject their thoughts or take an initiative in offering government representatives ideas and data for mapping an altered or, for that matter, unchanged course. They not only compile institutional memory but themselves embody the bureaucratic memory – the sum of their personal experience – of UN work for the general welfare. (Gordenker 2005: 59)

Some have recognised this process as an increased 'politicisation' of technical-administrative functions (Bøås and McNeill 2004), leading Simma (2002) to liken the Secretary-General to the Security Council's sixteenth member, albeit without veto or voting rights. Indeed, this influence, exercised by way of reports, has also extended to the area of peace and security concerns, as Rich shows. According to Rich, since 1989 the Security Council has increasingly relied on and utilised the Secretary-General's report of a conflict situation for its own decision-making and final resolution. As these reports have become more detailed, the Security Council has simply approved the report and used its recommendations as the Council's mission mandate. Seventeen out of nineteen missions containing a significant democratisation element were based on such a report (Rich 2004: 71).

The administrative function of the Secretary-General therefore offers important insights into how a UN agenda is constructed and how its meaning is shaped. The way in which the Secretary-General engages with ideas such as democracy plays an important role in the creation of a UN agenda and the final application of these ideas in the field. The process of policy-making does not start with negotiations but is precluded by a pre-negotiation stage in which (primarily bureaucratic) actors prepare proposals and therefore pre-structure not only discussion but the negotiator's (here: UN member states) view of the issue at hand. Thus, by taking the role of ideas seriously in framing the interest of member states, the two sides to the Secretary-General's role – political and administrative – converge. Consequently, the Secretary-General plays a more considerable role in the policy-making process than generally expected.

UN ideas and practices

According to the UNIHP, ideas may be the most important legacy of the United Nations (Emmerij et al. 2003). The UNIHP showed that the UN has functioned as a platform for the development of major changes in thinking about how we approach development, how peace could be achieved and conflict managed. It showed the shifts and changes in international law and how human rights have been protected, as well as how (statistical) data were collected and interpreted to solve global issues. The project's first book thus defined the agenda: the UNIHP showed how the UN was 'ahead of the curve' in developing or promoting ideas. Drawing on a range of methods and sources, UNIHP took an eclectic approach in trying to compile a comprehensive history of UN ideas, also compiling a rich archive of oral histories. UNIHP followed ideas from the moment they came into contact with the UN, through the process of promotion, adaptation, modification and, finally, institutionalisation. With this, the project's researchers emphasised the importance of seeing the UN not just as the sum of its members and in particular the decisions of the Security Council. Instead, it demonstrated the importance of individuals in creating and promoting ideas. As constructivism has shown, norms and ideas help to understand actors, their motivation and actions. Ideas are important in shaping interests and therefore policies. They encourage learning processes and therefore play an important role in the socialisation of states into the ideal of a peaceful international community and cooperative world society (see Checkel 1998).[1] Ideas highlight the interaction between and mutual constitution of structure and agency. Actively promoted by agents, ideas then assume an independent role that guides and constrains state behaviour, defining new interests and changing identities. However, while this expansive intellectual history highlighted the role of the UN as an intellectual 'actor', tracing changes in understanding over time, the conceptual-theoretical foundation of UNIHP's research also highlights the limitations of the study of ideas in understanding democracy and the role it may play as active UN agenda.

Emmerij et al. (2003) distinguished between three categories of ideational literature:

- institutionalist approaches, which are concerned with how organisations shape the decisions of their members for specific policies, highlighting structural concerns;
- expert-group approaches, which focus on the role of groups such as epistemic communities or transnational networks (non-governmental organisations (NGOs) or other activists) and institutional learning processes, therefore emphasising new aspects of agency beyond traditional UN actors, such as politicians and diplomats;
- constructivist approaches and critical theory, which address the meta-theoretical issues concerning the possibilities and limitations of change (see also Bøås and McNeill 2004).

While these approaches highlight the importance of ideas in understanding actors' behaviour, they treat ideas as one-dimensional objects, devoid of any internal contradiction or change across time. They focus on what ideas *do*, not what they *are*. Thus, we may learn why states or individuals think or behave in a certain way, but we do not understand the meaning of the idea itself. Understanding the meaning of an idea requires a deeper engagement with its conceptual cluster, that is, the different ideas that further describe it. This is especially so where an idea as complex and contested as democracy is concerned. Thinking about concepts, rather than one-dimensional ideas, helps to open up this complexity as concepts emphasise the compositional nature of the general idea of democracy, often implying a multitude of different compositions that can be expressed by users in different ways. The study of concepts and conceptualisation opens up an idea and makes explicit the shape of the conceptual cluster that actors hold. This highlights the question of how democracy is constituted, that is, which elements form the conceptual cluster of the specific composition. The analysis of the process of conceptualisation of democracy at the UN thus seeks to bring out the foundation of democracy. The study of concepts therefore makes explicit the shape a policy may take.

In undertaking a conceptual history of the UN democracy agenda, this book takes a practice-focussed view. In other words, it focuses on the operationalisation of ideas as an important avenue for their conceptualisation. This operationalisation forms the basis for the explication of a UN practice. The importance of this process is highlighted by Weiss and Carayannis (2001), who distinguish between normative and causal ideas. This not only highlights the compositional nature of ideas but also points towards the process in which the UN produces and processes ideas, developing ideas into practice. Weiss and Carayannis define normative ideas as 'broad, general beliefs' that describe a particular view of the world, or desire for how it ought to be. Causal ideas, on the other hand, are defined in more specific terms, detailing quantifiable targets, strategies or goals. According to Weiss and Carayannis, the UN often expresses causal ideas in an operational form. To illustrate the difference, Weiss and Carayannis quote 'equitable allocation of world resources' as an example of a normative idea, which can be expressed as a target or causal idea of '0.7 percent of GNP as contribution to development assistance' (Weiss and Carayannis 2001: 36–37), suggesting an increasing degree of specificity between the two types of ideas. Applying this hierarchy of ideas to democracy, a normative idea could entail the claim that democracy is good and that there should be more democratisation in the international system. On the other hand, a causal idea could be construed as '51% voter participation in elections to declare the election valid' or 'continual increase of states to become democracies'.

Interestingly, Weiss and Carayannis do not to make a distinction between normative ideas and the key ideas of the UN Charter which they call the 'four powerful ideas': peace, independence, human rights and development. As both the idea of 'equitable allocation of world resources' and the target of '0.7 percent of GNP as contribution to development assistance' can be derived from at least one of the UN Charter ideas, Charter ideas can be termed *root ideas*. Root ideas may be normative but are less specific than causal ideas. They thus literally form the root from which other normative ideas may branch out. A connection to root ideas enhances the legitimacy of any idea, normative or causal, as root ideas form the overarching goals of the UN Charter, to which the international community aspires. Whether and how democracy can be, or has been, connected to root ideas is a central question here, and it will be shown how this connection has enabled the creation and development of a UN democracy agenda.

Finally, in adopting a practice-focussed perspective, a distinction between policy and practice highlights the role of organisational actors such as the Secretary-General. While it is generally recognised that international policy is influenced by ideas promoted by norm entrepreneurs, an international policy-making perspective largely focuses on actors who either promote a particular idea or are at the receiving end of this pressure and have the ability to adopt the final policy, including diplomats, politicians or policy entrepreneurs such as epistemic communities (Haas 1992). This perspective ignores the relevance of organisational actors in the process of developing agendas by following too narrowly the prescribed role of the Secretary-General. Yet, the analysis of the legal-institutional powers of the Secretary-General, however, demonstrated that he is at the same time neither policy-maker nor simply observer. A practice-focussed approach recognises the unique role of organisational actors as it regards practices and those who create and develop them, like the Secretary-General, as influential variables. Practice, also often described as a 'programme', describes a pattern of UN activity. This practice is distinct from its application 'in practice' (implementation) as programmes may exist in theory, as a framework for intended implementation in ideal circumstances. Practices are thus forms of assistance available on request by member states. UN practices may include activities such as development aid that are part of those organisational activities which do not require or rely on continual approval by member states. They are part of the organisation, and through their development a considerable amount of conceptual development takes place within the organisation. In this sense, practices

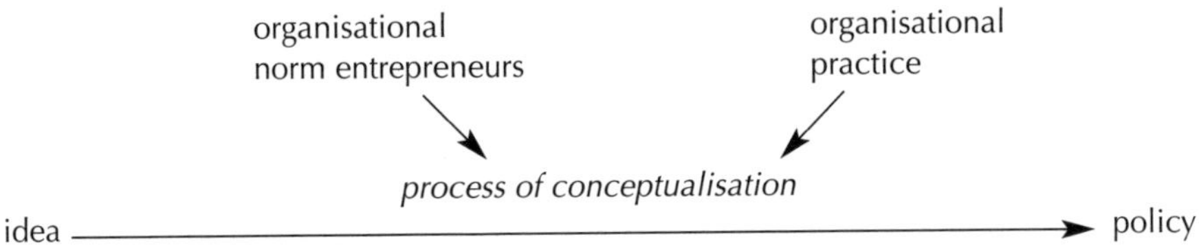

Figure 1.1　*Conceptualisation processes from idea to policy*

may also be seen as originators of ideas. Following this, the relationship between ideas and concepts, practices and policies, and the process of conceptualisation, can be summarised as in Figure 1.1.

While ideas may influence policy-making by member states, organisational policy entrepreneurs such as the Secretary-General influence the shape of these ideas. They do so through utilising organisational practices as well as creating a discourse that promotes a particular conceptual composition based on these practices.

Chapter outline

To understand the way in which democracy can be conceptualised, Chapter 2 draws on a 'democratic continuum' as a tool to locate different interpretations of democracy. The democratic continuum is conceptualised as ranging from minimal/procedural democracy to maximal/substantive democracy. While the former focuses on elections, the latter describes a comprehensive picture of processes, institutions, rights and policies which constitute a democratic society. This includes ideas of transparency, fairness, equality and accountability, as well as an 'ethics of care and responsibility' and community. Analysing classic definitions of democracy in political theory and juxtaposing them with applications in political practice it becomes clear that any conceptualisation will suffer from the open-endedness of the concept's nature. The problems influencing definitions of democracy are exacerbated by the different use and study of democracy by democracy theory and democratisation studies. The democratic continuum therefore aims to capture the nuances in defining democracy and draw out the lack of clearly set boundaries between definitions without imposing such boundaries.

Chapter 3 then turns towards the philosophical foundations of UN democracy, including the political discourse leading up to the creation of the UN, and its place in the UN Charter. In this period the idea of democracy features strongly as an essential element of the liberal internationalist politics out of which the UN grew. At this time, democracy is defined through its civilisational promise and its association with (Western) ideology. In this sense, democracy is divisive – the world is split between civilised, free and democratic states and uncivilised, colonial or authoritarian and undemocratic states. Chapter 3 thus shows that despite a central location in the philosophy of international organisations and liberal international relations, democracy was not included in the UN Charter but subjugated under the pragmatics of peace and the establishment of sovereignty in the decolonisation process. The loopholes that consequently emerged in the UN Charter as a result from the push and pull between this idealism and pragmatism led many to conclude that democracy is indeed present in the UN Charter, if only in spirit. These loopholes were closed only to a degree over forty years of UN practice (1945–1988).

The path of UN democracy after the Cold War and its transformation from idea to agenda form part of Chapters 4 and 5. By the late 1980s the moment was ripe for the development of a UN agenda of democracy. Chapter 4 shows how democracy emerged and was shaped by the increasing democratisation of member states. In this period democracy was conceptualised and defined through existing practices, such as the support and supervision of plebiscites, referenda and elections previously used during the decolonisation process. This interest in election observations expressed a wish to have validated both the results of democratic elections and the legitimacy of governments. Drawing on these practices provided the necessary legitimacy for the UN to engage in this new, controversial area. However, the enthusiasm to embrace democracy and the support for its implementation in member states was equally strongly met by hesitation and anxiety to reiterate sovereignty and principles of non-intervention. In this scenario democracy remained a limited practice that was largely based on the event of voting. Consequently, democracy was defined in very limited terms as elections. Democracy as elections proved only partially successful as a tool in UN missions where an elections-as-exit strategy soon came to dominate. As the democratic method became used for undemocratic means, leading to the stagnation of the democratisation process and the transformation of some states into 'authoritarian democracies', it became clear that elections had proved not to be a magic tool for conflict resolution. Democracy beyond elections became seen as increasingly necessary, as well as politically viable.

Chapter 5 explores an extended version of democracy beyond elections, focussing on governance. Democracy from the mid-1990s was understood not just as a process but as a system which supported the outcomes of elections between the casting of the ballot. Again, this vision of democracy was introduced through existing practices, such as the good governance agenda as used by the World Bank and the United Nations Development Programme (UNDP). The good governance agenda re-introduced the state into development and offered greater opportunity to embed democracy in post-conflict, failing or developing states. Increasingly, the democracy agenda became institutionalised by linking and embedding democracy with other UN agendas, such as peace-keeping, development and human rights, leading to its normalisation. Thus, democracy as governance was defined in increasingly broader and more substantive terms. The drivers of the broadening and institutionalisation of the democracy agenda were the Secretaries-General Boutros Boutros-Ghali and Kofi Annan, most notably Boutros-Ghali's trio of Agendas – Peace, Development and Democratization.

Chapter 6 then turns towards a substantive vision of democracy. This chapter is a change in direction as it explores the *potential* of a 'developmental democracy'. While the three visions of democracy explored thus far – civilisation, elections, governance – have all found expression at the UN in both ideational and practice form, the extent of democracy as governance did mark a conceptual and practical end-point for the UN democracy agenda. Despite some reluctance to extend democracy too far, the idea that democracy encompasses more than processes and structures has been expressed by the UN and its Secretaries-General on several occasions. Chapter 6 builds on ideas put forward by the UNDP, which outlined a 'citizen's democracy' for Latin America. Drawing on this report, recent research in democratisation studies and democracy theory, Chapter 6 develops a framework for a 'developmental democracy'. The chapter then explores to what extent the five dimensions of this developmental democracy have been addressed by the UN, and whether the individual parts of developmental democracy have become a greater whole or whether they remain fragmented in both theory and practice.

Concluding the journey through the conceptual history – and potential future – of UN democracy is Chapter 7, which looks again at different ways of defining democracy. Ideology, practice and vision (or envisioning) all form essential parts in understanding what UN democracy is and how it has become institutionalised. Finally, revisiting the process of developing the democracy agenda, Chapter 7 shows how intimately connected *thinking* (ideas) and *doing* (practice) are in the agenda-setting process at the UN, highlighting the role of organisational actors in conceptualising ideas and creating practice. This conceptual history thus clears the fog that is the essentially contested and highly complex nature of democracy, which we too often can only define 'when we see it'.

Note

1   Checkel criticises the tendency among constructivist scholarship to focus on 'ethically good' norms rather than utilisation of constructivism as a method for the development of any norm. Hence, the constructivist agenda can be summarised as a socialisation into a particular kind of society, in this case the liberal internationalist philosophy of international organisations (see also Chapter 3). It may, however, be suggested that ideas differ from norms in that they are morally neutral in character, whereas 'norms by definition embody a quality of "oughtness" and shared moral assessment' (Finnemore and Sikkink 1998: 892).

2

Framing democracy: the democratic continuum

In the twentieth century claims for democracy were made by many, yet few states became democracies. In the early twenty-first century democracy appears to be ubiquitous. Western European and North American states have been joined by former communist states and dictatorships in the 'family of democracies', while wars continue to be waged to depose dictators and to bring democracy and freedom to previously suppressed people. In addition to this, democracy can be found in classrooms or workplaces. Not all democracies are the same – a political system differs from a personal relationship – however, to deny the existence of democracy in either of these two would undermine the idea conveyed by it. This is the idea that social relationships and power within them are ordered in a particular way, which those engaged in these relationships value more than other forms because democracy ensures equality and freedom for all parties involved. Thus, when thinking about democracy, most people would claim to know what democracy means and what it should look like. Some might say that democracy means that the people rule, others would refer to freedom or equality, while some may call for the rule of law, or indeed state provisions such as health care and education, invoking the wealth and the kind of societies created by the democracies in Europe and North America. Yet others may counter this by pointing towards the city state of Singapore, which achieved development and wealth under an autocratic leadership. Considering such multitude of views and ideas, what then is democracy? How is it possible to define democracy? Is there a definition that clearly defines democracy or do we have to contend ourselves with Justice Stewart's conclusion that 'we know it when we see it'? If so, how could an international norm of democracy be conceptualised? What would an international practice of democracy assistance that aims to assist in establishing democracy in war-torn countries and failed states look like?

To answer these questions this chapter sets out a democratic continuum as a framework for the process of conceptualising democracy. The democratic continuum functions as a tool to locate mainstream theories of democracy theory, highlighting their methodological advantages and disadvantages. These theories are divided into broad categories of minimal/procedural democracy and maximal/substantive democracy to demonstrate the opposite ends of this continuum. Theories of democracy are examined in relation to existing states, and the question 'is this really democracy?' functions as a reminder of the possibilities and limitations international organisations may face in developing an international norm and practice of democracy. Analysing the quantitative core and the qualitative boundaries of various conceptions, it becomes apparent that the practical difficulties in defining substantive (or indeed genuine) democracy are all too obvious as the procedures and institutions of the democratic state have been found to be used without democratic content. On the other hand, conceptual difficulties arise from differences in disciplinary approaches, mainly those of political theory and democratisation studies. This includes a lack of definitional boundaries, in particular the question of whether democracy is to be described as political, social or economic. The democratic continuum allows for these different theories to be accounted for and viewed through the lens of quantity (scope), rather than the more elusive question of quality.

Defining democracy

Ambiguity is a key concern in any attempt to define democracy, not only within the Western democratic discourse but also in particular on a global scale where local traditions may add further dimensions to an already broad field of ideas and theories. This ambiguity, Gallie (1956) argued, is part and parcel of the concept of democracy itself. Democracy is fundamentally an 'essentially contested concept'. It is subjective and value-based, internally complex and open-ended. The individual criteria that are attached to any explanation can be given different weighting or interpretation, favouring at one time equality over freedom or participation, or vice versa. More so, the conceptual cluster of ideas that explain democracy (such as freedom and equality) further increases the complexity of defining democracy as each of these component concepts is equally complex and open. Any attempt to define the concept of democracy would therefore also require full operationalisation and weighting of all explanatory concepts (Connolly 1993). Proponents of the idea of essential contestability therefore stress that the study of democracy needs to take account of its different definitions. Histories of ideas, that is, the study of conceptual development over time as well as in time (Koselleck 1985), are one such method to recognise these differences. However, critics of essential contestability suggest that any definitive definition of a concept like democracy is futile, claiming that the label of essential contestability is conveniently used to disguise a theorist's attempt to convince readers of the superiority of their own definition. Thus, Saward (1998) pessimistically concludes that a retreat into essential contestability is 'to give up'. Indeed, the strategy offered by proponents of essential contestability, to scrutinise the differences and similarities in definitions and their historical use, merely demonstrates how democracy has been used and understood at a particular time, how popular it has been, how its use has changed throughout time and what this means for, and says about, this particular period of time. This kind of historical analysis does not necessarily provide an insight into the features of the concept. While conceptual histories in the context of the essential contestability thesis emphasise epistemological issues concerning the idea of democracy, conceptual analyses require further complementary approaches to gain additional insight into the ontological dimensions of democracy. These can be found in etymological, normative and empirical approaches (Saward 1998).

The starting point for any definition of democracy is etymological. Here the component parts of the word democracy are simply translated from their Greek origins. Democracy, or *demos kratein*, is the idea that the people (*demos*) should rule (*kratein*). The people, or citizens, should participate in the regulation of political life of the society in which they live. How this rule should be exercised, through which channels and in what way, however, depends upon further elaboration, hence a set of principles complements the literal translation in order to capture the idea of *demos kratein*. This, however, continues to ignore descriptions or prescription of any particular form of institutions. Beetham therefore concludes that

> democratic institutions are so termed in so far as they embody democratic principles; democratic principles in turn require practical institutional form for their realization. Of the two, however, it is the principles that are central to the question of definition; institutions are secondary and derivative, and may take different forms in different contexts. (Beetham 1999: 4)

Consequently, Beetham starts by outlining the 'sphere' of democracy. This sphere represents collectively binding decisions. From this he follows that a 'system of collective decision-making can be said to be democratic to the extent that it is subject to control by all members of the relevant association or all those under its authority, considered as equals' (Beetham 1999: 4–5). From this idea of people's rule the notion of equality is deduced. Equality embodies the idea that the demos necessarily includes all the people of the polity. Consequently, the core principles of democracy are defined as popular control and political equality.

While the etymological definition of democracy highlights the issue of popular control, it is the added notion of political equality which emphasises the foundations, the justificatory strategies adopted in the second, normative approach to defining democracy. Here, theorists start with the basic premise of equal human worth and human dignity. Humans are seen as self-determining, autonomous beings who are able of expressing themselves and taking part in the society in which they live. The idea of equality logically follows from this philosophical premise if effective people's rule is to be achieved. Beetham's definition thus claims to describe the function (distributional principle – political equality) and material (matter to be distributed – popular control) of democracy. Beetham leaves both of these concepts broad enough to allow their application in a number of spheres (public and private), but also to accommodate a multitude of institutional expressions. Beetham therefore emphasises the qualitative aspect of democracy, concluding that a key issue in a democracy is that 'associational life should be internally democratic' (Beetham 1999: 5). With this, Beetham goes on to widen his own vision of democracy to include economic and social rights as fundamental to democracy. Thus, the realisation of socio-economic conditions enables the realisation of political equality in practice – a view not shared by everyone.

In contrast to both the etymological and the normative approach, the descriptive approach examines existing political systems which are commonly called democracies and deduce from their political set-up the fundamental features that constitute democracy. Consequently, descriptive, or 'realist', empirical scholars offer highly reductionist definitions of democracy and democratic institutions, for example elections, to find an approximation of *demos kratein* in the real world. This approach, Saward (1998) argues, is highly arbitrary as the definition of core features is subjective to the observer, leaving the observation open to a 'definitional fallacy' in which democracies are those political systems that are commonly called democracies. On the other hand, the descriptive approach gains from recent research (and the practice) of democratic audits which aim to determine the depth and quality of democratic politics, as well as more global attempts to measure democracy. Beetham's audit of democracy in the UK, for example, starts with his basic democratic principles of popular control and political equality. The indices included in the audit's framework are:

1. reach of electoral process, its inclusiveness, fairness and independence ('free and fair');
2. open and accountable government in political, legal and financial terms;
3. the guarantee of civil rights and political liberties (which underpin points 1 and 2); and
4. civil society (Beetham 1994; see also Lane and Ersson 2003).

Although Beetham's audit claims to be based on principles which allow for institutionalisation in different ways, he similarly makes claims about what constitutes democracy through the choice of institutions and institutional indices. This, according to Beetham, avoids the problem of obscuring subjective interpretations inherent in 'apparently objective' numerical indicators as used in the Freedom House data (Beetham 1994: 33). Freedom House, despite surveying 'freedom' rather than 'democracy', ranks states from democratic to non-democratic, using a seven-point scale for political and civil rights. Thus, although Freedom House indices further reinforce reductionist definitions of democracy, they also highlight the advantages of conceptualising democracy as a continuum rather than a simple dichotomy (Bollen 1991). Crucially, the choice of indices highlights the importance of elections in defining democracy by emphasising political rights directly relevant to the electoral process (Gastil 1991; Haynes 2001: 209–218).

The analysis of these three approaches shows that the differences in understanding and defining democracy are not necessarily substantive but highlight similar points from different angles. While the etymological root of democracy informs both the normative and descriptive approach, recent democratic audits highlight that features beyond participation and political equality can be equally important in defining democracy. This diversity of approaches is emphasised by the idea of essential contestability. Following this, it is clear that the diversity of ideas of democracy and the democratic state are best conceptualised on a continuum (Figure 2.1).

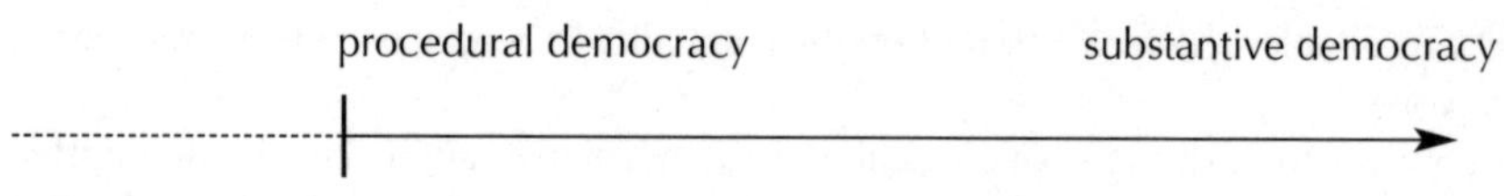

Figure 2.1   *The democratic continuum*

This democratic continuum, unlike the scales set out by Freedom House and Beetham described above, does not describe democracy in qualitative terms as 'better or worse' or 'more and less', but seeks to illustrate the breadth of application of democracy throughout the system. It reflects and represents the ideas and concepts of the existing canon of democratic theory.

Minimal democracy: processes and beyond

In the liberal, Western tradition of democracy theory the left-hand side of the democratic continuum starts with a minimal definition of democracy based on the literal definition of democracy as 'people's rule'. Outside the liberal tradition other definitions of (pseudo-) democracy to the left of this starting point may be possible. For example, these could be systems based on non-elected representatives where democratic decision-making is confined to the deliberations between representatives of specific groups. An example here would be recently used models such as the *loya jirga* in Afghanistan, where traditional leaders (clan elders or tribal chiefs) represent the interests of their clan or group in a central decision-making body. Other forms might include consultative processes or principles of accountability. In the liberal, Western tradition, however, the minimal definition of democracy here focuses on democratic procedures such as (universal) elections. This definition limits the people's involvement, their exercise of 'rule', to the event of casting a vote. Elections thus function as a transmission belt between the ruling and the ruled, working both ways to control and to legitimate. Thus, at the heart of procedural democracy is what Weber described as a 'plebiscitary leadership democracy', a modern state in which legal authority is *temporarily* held based on office (Held 1996: 165). Democracy defined in such procedural terms has the utility of being both comprehensive and functional, yet it also faces the challenge of being undermined by political leaders in non-democratic fashion.

In the democratic process elections perform the crucial task of establishing a connection between citizens and policy-makers by binding them into a relationship of mutual dependence, between and among them, as well as across time. The key in the electoral process is to enable the exercise of control and to confer legitimacy. The control function of elections is exercised both vertically (top-down and bottom-up) as well as horizontally (*ex post* and *ex ante*). Thus, elections provide opportunities to influence politics through an active choice of representatives, government and political agendas, enabling popular influence on politics, and determining, at least to a degree, the course of politics until the next election (*ex ante*).

Secondly, the control function of elections also provides the possibility for account-ability where participation is reduced to a simple procedure within a larger time-frame. Thus, elections enable the voter to hold governments accountable by dismissing from positions of power those who fail the voters' assessment of 'good practice'. In this sense, voters restrict policy-makers through the exercise of elec-tions (*ex post*). This bottom-up approach then most clearly demonstrates the idea of people's rule. Ginsberg (1982) emphasises that the bottom-up approach of control is matched by a top-down approach in which policy-makers use elections as a device to expand their power and authority through the incorporation of dissenters into the political system. Leaders encourage unquestioned obedience to state authority without reducing the state's autonomy as they substitute participation in the choice of government for a direct popular intervention (e.g. revolt). According to Ginsberg, elections thus have a clear conflict management dimension. In this sense, the institutionalisation of elections formalises influence in both a positive and negative way. On the one hand, 'even if rulers have the capacity to compel obe-dience, popular influence is not necessarily effaced' (Ginsberg and Stone 1991: 3). Instead rulers have been given the authority by the people to compel their obedi-ence and regulate them. On the other hand, institutionalisation creates other means to manipulate participation opportunities through the establishment of voting rules and procedures. As such, elections are 'an exchange of influence between governing elites and voters. Elites gain authority in exchange for respon-siveness to the voters; voters gain influence in exchange for obedience to decisions they only partly shape' (Harrop and Miller 1987: 245).

The legitimacy function of elections is equally as broad as their control function. Elections assign legitimacy not only to political outcomes (laws and policies) but also to a range of actors, such as the government and the opposition, and indeed the system and regime itself. Majority decisions engender legitimacy by expressing the 'will of the people' in elections both for those who govern and for the outcomes they produce. While the notion of legitimacy to govern rarely encompasses a specific, direct mandate, that is, an instruction from voters to follow a particular policy or programme which has to be obeyed, policy-makers do assume a general mandate to govern – an entitlement to impose policies with or without popular support. Thus, the ritual of voting, fair play and due process, through the representative nature of the democratic system and the general principle of participation, generates a 'gov-ernment with justification and authority, with a right to expect obedience and respect' (Harrop and Miller 1987: 258). Yet, it is not only policy-makers and policies that gain legitimacy through elections; the opposition also assumes the role of a legit-imate player in the game. Their tools as well as their existence in principle are justi-fied and legitimised by elections. Thus, as Ginsberg highlighted, elections serve an important conflict management function by institutionalising difference in opinion and the struggle for power. Finally, legitimacy is conferred onto citizens themselves. Elections based on universal suffrage serve as a means to ensure political equality, thereby decreasing at least partially the extent of social and economic inequality. In general, commanding political legitimacy on the basis of elections serves as a protec-tive function against undue intervention by both internal dissenters (including opposition, military, civil interest groups) and external actors (neighbours and the international community at large) (Harrop and Miller 1987: 259).

The classic definition of procedural democracy, indeed the definition most frequently used to identify democracy in general, was outlined by Schumpeter, who defined democracy, or more precisely, 'the democratic method', as 'that institutional arrangement for arriving at political decisions in which individuals acquire the power to decide by means of competitive struggle for the people's vote' (Schumpeter 1976: 269). This definition rests on three pillars. The first is the aim to develop a definition of democracy that is more representative, more descriptive of existing democratic systems, thereby avoiding unnecessary reliance on vague normative principles. The second pillar is the rejection of democracy as a universal value, that is, an end in itself, which Schumpeter called the 'classical doctrine'. The third pillar is the definition of democracy as a political method.

According to Schumpeter, the 'classical doctrine' had defined democracy as 'that institutional arrangement for arriving at political decisions which realizes the *common good* by making the people itself decide issues through the election of individuals who are to assemble in order to carry out its will' (Schumpeter 1976: 250). At the heart of this classical doctrine is the idea of a common will. Schumpeter denied the existence of such common will, which according to the classical doctrine can be achieved through rational discussion and decision-making. Schumpeter argued that this common will was impossible to realise because modern societies are too complex, incorporating a multitude of values and opinions. Moreover, Schumpeter claimed that occasionally decisions were made without the use of democratic means, which were fully accepted and even favoured by the people. However, most importantly, Schumpeter emphasised that it is the voter, the people, who are essentially unable to reach this common will by rational means. Drawing on research in crowd psychology and advertising, Schumpeter claimed that the voter 'drops to a lower level of mental performance as soon as he enters the political field' (Schumpeter 1976: 262), becoming emotional, irrational and prone to manipulation as his thinking becomes associative and affective. In Schumpeter's view the common will is thus a manufactured will, influenced by parties and leaders who offer an agenda on whose basis voters may form their opinion and decide which way to vote. Thus, the common will is as much generated through the democratic process as it is prior to it. Consequently, Schumpeter saw the idea of defining democracy in terms of popular sovereignty as unhelpful. The irrationality of the public and the lack of a common will have led Schumpeter instead to restrict his definition of democracy to elections. As such, leaders and voters are disconnected from each other, only to be joined when democracy is exercised: at the polls.

However, equating democracy with elections alone runs the danger of rendering the concept meaningless. Elections balance precariously between 'genuine' democracy in which the public exercises influence on political outcomes, and 'façade' democracy, that is, non-democratic regimes in which elections serve to create an image of participation. The problem is both conceptual and empirical. For example, democracy narrowly defined according to its literal translation ('rule of the people'), means that the definition of the people assumes a central role in defining what constitutes democracy in a particular state. In Schumpeter's view a *populus* should define itself. Following this, if democracy is defined as the method for producing a government, even a severely restricted franchise can be seen as democratic as long as competition determines the party to govern. Consequently, democracy would be compatible with almost any kind of society (Barry 2000). Dahl criticised Schumpeter for conflating the state of 'being democratic in relation to one's own demos' and 'being democratic in relation to everyone subject to its rules'. Instead, Dahl (1979) argued, it is inclusiveness that achieves a full procedural democracy. In modern Western democracies the question of inclusion and exclusion concerns primarily foreign nationals, the incapacitated, the young and other groups so marginal that suffrage can easily be seen as universal. Thus, while a demos narrowly defined could theoretically create a democracy, its quality would be questionable. This was not only highlighted by the experiences of the 'democratic' communist states – 'people's democracies' – but also the democratic state of South Africa under apartheid. As Brooker pointed out, South Africa under apartheid had considerably more multi-party democracy and competition than other 'joint-multiparty dictatorships' such as Colombia. However, the exclusionary policy of apartheid challenged the notion of semi-democracy conceptually (as well as ethically), and could only be summarised as a dictatorship of the white majority (Brooker 2000).

The case of South Africa highlights not only the difficulties of translating theory into practice, but also the problem of defining a cut-off point at which democracy can be said to exist. Research following the wave of democratising states in the 1990s had highlighted this fluidity of the concept of democracy and its expression in practice. As scholars reviewed the process of democratisation and with it the nature of democracy, previous dichotomous categories of democratic and non-democratic gave way to more nuanced continua and the idea of 'democracy with adjectives'. These adjectives signal the creation of diminished subtypes to overcome the methodological problem encountered in categorising the variety of democratic and non-democratic features. The labels thus created and assigned to political systems differed considerably: Collier and Levitsky (1997) identified electoral, limited, controlled, restricted, illiberal, guarded, protected democracy, while Brooker (2000), who focussed on democratisation processes, identified forms of semi-democracy, that is consolidated democracy, transitional limited democracy and transitional proto-democracy. Others devised continua highlighting the problems of identifying cut-off points between democracies and non-democracies. Haynes (2001), for example, distinguished between authoritarian rule, that is, systems in which the masses are denied a political voice and where power is held by a small elite and regime legitimacy is based on economic success (communist governments, non-communist single party regimes, 'personalist' governments including autocratic monarchies and military administrations), façade democracy (only elections are held), limited and full democracy. By contrast, Diamond, Linz and Lipset (1989) emphasised the autocratic end of the continuum, highlighting pseudodemocracies in which elections serve to legitimate authoritarian domination, hegemonic party systems (more institutionalised, less personalised and coercive) and semi-democratic regimes, in which electoral outcomes deviate significantly from popular preference.

What became apparent was that while a number of states featured democratic institutions such as frequent elections, parties, a broad, active civil society and the like, they could not be called in any meaningful sense democratic. Their undemocratic nature was seen either as part of a transition process or as a state of being an imperfect democracy, that is an unconsolidated or consolidating state, or a state in protracted transition (Ottaway 2004). Linz and Stepan (1996) argued that to see elections as a cut-off point for democracy in this context is an 'electoralist fallacy' which regards a necessary condition as sufficient. Democratisation scholars instead turned the political theorist's approach of defining democracy on its head by outlining the features a state in transition has to achieve in order to be consolidated. Consolidation then serves as a breaking point between 'theoretical' or 'developing' democracy, and 'real' democracy. Claiming that democratic consolidation requires more than simply elections and markets, Linz and Stepan stressed that a democracy can be seen as consolidated when it has become 'routinised and deeply internalised in social, institutional, and even psychological life' (Linz and Stepan 1996: 5). In other words, consolidation has taken place when the democratic system is no longer challenged but widely seen as the best way to govern political life, and both governmental and non-governmental forces are ruled and habituated to the democratic process. Democracy is considered consolidated when it is seen as 'the only game in town' (Linz and Stepan 1996: 5). However, Ottaway countered by pointing out that the key problem is that semi-authoritarian states in fact do know how to play the game. Their ambiguous character is deliberate: while they embrace liberal democracy rhetorically and allow for some formal institutions, such as elections, and limited civil and political liberties, semi-authoritarian states have mechanisms to prevent the turnover of power and allow no room for a debate of either the nature or place of power. Thus, balancing control and participation effectively, competition at the centre is a fiction in these so-called democracies (Ottaway 2004: 14–19).

The problem of identifying democracy with elections only and thus leaving democracy open for abuse is part and parcel of Schumpeter's definition as well as his subsequent reception. A number of elements, such as democratic rights and institutions, are left implicit in Schumpeter's definition as description and normative ideal mix. Formulating a descriptive theory of democracy, Schumpeter had to define a common ground between a number of very different forms of democracy that he observed. He therefore emphasised elections and competition as the smallest common denominator, which seemed to justify both the idea and reality of people's rule. As a consequence, other institutions were downplayed or ignored, a tendency which is most obvious in Schumpeter's reception where his view of democracy is equated with elections alone. Yet, Schumpeter never restricted his discussion of democracy to just elections. In fact, he focussed on elections to emphasise the idea of competition and the parallels between politics and the market system. Schumpeter not only pointed towards freedoms that are non-existent in semi-democracies or authoritarian regimes, but also focussed on the importance of both parties and parliaments (see Schumpeter 1976: 269–283). Parties and parliament serve as platforms for free competition, therefore implying both the existence of multiple free parties, government and opposition movements.

Further, not only are leaders free to compete, citizens are free to vote, choosing their preferred candidate and, as no leadership is absolute, ousting those of whom they disapprove. Thus, the crucial difference between democracies and non-democracies in Schumpeter's view was that leaders *propose* not *impose* themselves and that they do so on the basis of free and fair elections (Saward 2003: 40).

The second problem of equating democracy with elections is therefore that it reduces democracy to an event exercised solely at the moment of voting, thereby ignoring what happens between those moments of casting the ballot. Dahl stressed that for the democratic process to be free, that is to provide genuine choice and influence for the voter, citizen rights need to be applied not only during the process of voting but also before and after. According to Dahl (1956), polyarchies (democracies) are systems with a variety of citizen's rights inclusive of and beyond the opportunity to oppose government and vote leaders into and out of government. A number of institutions ensure the functioning of polyarchies:

1. elected officials: they have constitutionally vested control over government decisions about policy;
2. free and fair elections: officials are chosen in frequent and fairly conducted elections without undue coercion;
3. inclusive suffrage: nearly all adults have the right to vote in elections;
4. the right to run for office: nearly all adults may stand for office, although age limits may apply;
5. freedom of expression: freedom to criticise or appraise any party, official or institution without fear of punishment;
6. alternative information: those exist and can be freely sought by all citizens, they are protected by law;
7. associational autonomy: to achieve their rights, citizens may form independent associations including parties and interest groups.

Dahl claimed that the expansion of these rights in modern, increasingly pluralistic societies, where close social ties give way to increasing social distance, serve as a substitute for political consensus. They regulate interaction, especially conflict, and therefore provide a free space for the individual (Dahl 1989). While Dahl outlined a relatively broader version of democracy than Schumpeter, he, like Schumpeter, nevertheless remained election-focussed as the institutions he outlined served to bring about or support elections. Despite this emphasis on elections, Dahl's definition of democracy draws attention to the unexplored space of procedural definitions of democracy that match the image of today's systems only to the most minimal extent, ignoring a wide range of institutions and methods often regarded as part of democracy in the public discourse. Thus, Schumpeter's and Dahl's definitions need extension to include a number of these political institutions which today commonly describe and define democratic states. Lijphart's study of thirty-six countries, for example, described a number of political institutions and power relations, which are usually considered part and parcel of those states commonly called 'democracies'. These include the separation of powers at the national level as well as between the

1. **Citizenships and rights**
   - Citizenship and immigration laws
   - Protections for human rights (classic liberal rights and freedoms of individual citizens, group/community rights, economic and social rights)
   - Affirmative action (in favour of minority groups, women, and other groups who have experienced negative discrimination).
2. **Vertical accountability of state to citizens**
   - Independent electoral process (autonomy of national electoral machine from government, international monitoring of elections)
   - Forms of electoral representation (first past the post FPTP, proportional representation PR, mixed systems, electoral quotas, separate electoral rolls etc.)
   - Party systems (conventional criteria by which party systems are compared include: number of parties (multiparty, two party, single dominant, single and, non-party system), degree of ideological polarisation, degree of institutionalisation of the party system)
   - Devices of direct democracy (referenda & recall provisions).
3. **Devolution and decentralisation**
   - Federalism and other forms of spatial decentralisation (confederalism, federalism, forms of decentralisation and autonomy within unitary state)
   - Corporate (ethnic, religious, etc.) forms of devolution (power-sharing on a communal basis, ethnic etc. recruitment quotas in state and military bureaucracies, representation of groups in second chambers, electoral lists on the basis of ethnicity, or communal votes over policies which have negative impact on groups rights).
4. **Horizontal accountability I: relations between executive, legislature and parties**
   - Executive-legislative relations (presidential system, parliamentary system, semi-presidential systems)
   - Types of legislature (unicameral or bicameral, different systems of representation in upper and lower houses, corporate representation)
   - Legislative oversight (committee systems, White Papers, Questions, etc.).
5. **Horizontal accountability II: embedded autonomy of state decision-making**
   - Measures to strengthen the capacity of civil society/organised public opinion to influence government
   - Consultation/cooperation with policy stakeholders
   - Procedures to enhance capacity of state bureaucracies to act against vested interests (including those of ruling party/government of the day)
   - Procedures to ensure independent public service (public service commissions, auditor generals, human rights commissions, ombudspersons, electoral commissions)
   - Control of armed forces, police and intelligence establishments.
6. **Horizontal accountability III: constitutionalism, rule of law and judiciary**
   - Constitutions & constitutionalism
   - Rule of law
   - Judiciary & judicial independence.

Figure 2.2 *Inventory of institutional choices in democracies*

national level and subsidiary levels, one or two chambers of parliament, judicial review, mediating institutions such as civil society, and, a key part of Weber's concept of democracy, state bureaucracy (Lijphart 1999). Luckham, Goetz and Kaldor's (2000) inventory of democratic institutions outlined in Figure 2.2 demonstrates the breadth of institutions to which democracy could be applied and thus the space into which democracy could be spread. Following Luckham et al.'s inventory, Schumpeter and Dahl focussed on 'vertical accountability' between the voter and the government, while Lijphart drew attention to institutions of 'horizontal accountability', in particular the separation of powers and institutional checks and balances. This horizontal accountability extended democratic control to other spheres of political life and, at least partially, to other areas of society. Although the discussion of these institutions is central to democratic theory, they have, again, primarily only one aim – not to define democracy but to manage the outcomes of competitive elections. They manage the much-feared tyranny of the leadership, be that tyranny of the majority (e.g. Schumpeter) or tyranny of minorities (Dahl). In other words, they are instrumental rather than conceptual, although they form a considerable part of modern democratic states.

Maximal democracy: substance

Considering the difficulties of defining 'genuine' democracy on the basis of a number of procedures and institutions, the idea of substance could simply be interpreted as 'good', or 'genuine' democracy, in distinction to 'bad rule' or 'façade' democracy. Indeed, Dahl regarded the processes of polyarchy as substantive as they allowed the citizen to achieve the common good whose existence Schumpeter had denied. According to Dahl (1989), the common good required both an 'enlightened understanding', including the full knowledge of alternatives and outcomes, and the processes of democracy that is, the exercise of rights and opportunities. Dahl's institutions of polyarchy are thus part of this common good. However, unlike in democratisation studies, the issue of system failure or system abuse, other than by democratically elected majorities or minorities, is outside the immediate area of concern for mainstream democracy theory. Here, the emphasis of 'good' rule is on social and economic aspects, as well as procedural issues that may have an impact on and distort the exercise of democracy. Secondly, substance refers to a set of outcomes that, again, should enhance the enjoyment of the democratic process but also ensure the fashioning of a particular kind of society. Thus, while procedural theories focus on political aspects of democracy alone, theories of substance introduce democracy to varying degrees into other spheres of society, thereby making the personal political. In this sense, substantive democracy is a form of life, 'the good life', and at the heart of it are questions about equality, justice, human development and participation. Thus, contrary to realist scholars such as Schumpeter, who deduce a concept of democracy from the observation of existing states, theories associated with ideas of substantive democracy are essentially normative rather than descriptive in their approach.

Like Beetham, the starting points for proponents of substantive democracy are the principles of democracy, the literal idea of *demos kratein*. The idea of a common good that can and should be achieved is (re)introduced and the idea of community emphasised. In all this, ideas of substantive democracy draw on Athenian traditions of direct democracy, the Tocquevillian stress on the importance of institutions of civil society, but even more so on the Marxist tradition and its emphasis on participation and economic (re)distribution. Unlike the empirical, procedural tradition, theories of substantive democracy are broad-ranging, rarely presenting a unified picture and thus cover a considerable stretch of the democratic continuum. While some theories have strong procedural leanings, others are highly substantive and nearly utopian. Theories such as social democracy, for example, are both substantive and descriptive. Like procedural theories, substantive theories reach their limits where historical evidence shows the diminished return and potential abuse of democracy, as for example in Marxism and Soviet communism.

Located to the far right of the democratic continuum, Marx never explicitly developed his own definition of democracy. Yet, out of his critique of liberal democracy and his vision of the ideal, classless society came the notion of a perfect democracy, a state in which the people rule. For Marx liberal democracy was only one step of history's development and served primarily as a tool to further bourgeois interests. Because of liberalism's guarantee and defence of property as well as its emphasis on equality, Marx saw the liberal democratic state as effectively partisan to those who own the means of production. Like Tocqueville before him, Marx had realised that equality and the rights to property were in conflict with each other. Marx, however, highlighted the fundamental division of classes as central to politics and claimed that the liberal democratic state participated in the control and integration of class-divided societies. The dominant economic classes were able to rule without governing. On the basis of their economic power they were able to influence government. Thus, he concluded that the liberal democratic state failed to achieve the accountability and protection of the public interest to which it aspired (Femia 1993). Marx' solution was the class-free society in which not only the redistribution of the means of production would lead to more equality but the dismantling of the distinction between state and society would lead to the end of politics. This meant not only the full participation of the working classes in government but also the full determination of all affairs by every citizen, in other words, communal decision-making. The resulting 'state' was to be minimal, at first socialist, and finally a communist, revolutionary dictatorship of the proletariat in which the general will could be achieved because all government aspects are accountable to the majority (Marx 2008). In this, politics would no longer need elections because general agreement would eliminate conflict, while administrative tasks were rotated between citizens. At the heart of the state would be a pyramidal structure of direct or deliberative democracy (Held 1996). The future communist state would thus be accessible to all, fully transparent and open to change. In terms of democracy it would be the ultimate form of *demos kratein*. In this state the democratic ideals of equality and participation would be fully realised.

This democratic utopia suffered from two problems. First, the idea of direct and deliberative democracy, a system in which all decisions are made by all in each commune did not square with a large, industrial society, and thus central economic planning needed to supplant worker-directed economics. Secondly, the gap between theoretical ideal and the reality of the communist states of the Soviet Union and Eastern Europe proved to be too great. The so-called 'people's democracies' may have been based on systems of participation and equality, yet, like Ottaway's semi-authoritarian states, the elites of these states prevented the systems from being filled with their intended substance. According to Femia (1993), this was due to the appropriation of Marx' theory outside its own context. While Marx had highlighted, indeed *insisted*, on the developmental, linear character of historical stages, the van-guard parties and thinkers of revolutionary Russia aimed to bring about a change of history without consideration for 'correct' progress. Where Marx had called for the development of a worker's consciousness to facilitate the change to socialism, the vanguard parties of the Russian Revolution insisted that if the masses had not realised the true, authentic common will yet, a superior intelligence, that is the elite, may *impose* freedom and guide the masses to this 'true' common will. Democratic deliberation then was unnecessary and, as Femia stresses,

> the schizophrenia of communist political practice (democratic forms and dictatorial substance) reflected the schizophrenia of Marxism itself: the people must rule, but only if and when they can demonstrate a grasp of higher dialectical reality. Seen in this light, communist ambivalence towards popular participation becomes wholly comprehensible. (Femia 1993: 135)

The central ideas of Marx' theory – participatory, direct democracy, the merging of the personal with the political, and the importance of economic redistribution – continue to inform modern democracy theory albeit to a lesser degree. Although some of Marx' ideas have entered the democratic toolkit of Western democracies, a number of problems that plagued Marxist theory remain, rendering some of the theories in places utopian. For example, in his description of participatory democ-racy, Macpherson (1977) battled with the problem of the size of modern societies and participatory decision-making. He conceded that the Marxian idea of direct democracy needed to be amended and changed into a combined representative and direct democratic system in a pyramidal structure, central to which would be a system of accountability of each level to the one below. In contrast to Marx, Macpherson also saw a competitive party system essential to this combination of direct and indirect democracy. With class divisions gone, the task of parties to blur class divisions and reach compromise would make parties compatible with participa-tory democracy, the more so if participatory democracy was increasingly applied to parties themselves. Macpherson highlighted that potential problems with this system could be found in a threat to counter-revolution such as in the post-revolutionary turmoil of the Soviet experience, the reappearance of class divisions and oppositions, and apathy on the lowest levels.

Indeed, apathy, participation theorists argue, is an almost inevitable outcome of Schumpeterian elitism due to its restricted opportunities for participation. In the participatory view, the citizen is conceptualised as fundamentally politically active and politically motivated – the citizen *wants* to be political. What is more, the people are fundamentally *able* to participate in democracy. Unlike Schumpeter, democracy theories emphasising substance have an essentially positive view of the people as political beings. The democratic process is to emphasise and develop this human capacity, and to further people's enlightenment. Hence, democracy on lower, sub-national levels, be that the public sphere or the workplace, would enable the citizen to 'learn to participate by participating and [thus] feelings of political efficacy are more likely to be developed in a participatory environment' (Pateman 1970: 105). Consequently, the entirety of political structures in democratic states would function in a similar fashion as elections in a Schumpeterian procedural democracy – as a transmission belt. However, here the transmission belt would not connect the state and the individual, but the individual and society. Institutions and procedures in a participatory democracy therefore need to be extended beyond elections to fora that enable exchange (deliberation) between citizens and thus the formation of the citizen's interest[1], which would then be moved upwards within the democratic system. This needs to be supplemented by further processes of involvement such as referenda, but also by further insurance of equality for previously marginalised groups such as women and ethnic minorities (Young 2000). The issue of inclusion of previously marginalised groups indeed highlights the most important element of a substantive definition of democracy: the (re)distribution of power – political, social or economic. For participatory democracy the redistribution of power is a key agenda. If the citizen is fundamentally a political being, wanting to participate, then the citizen needs to be able to do so. Democracy would facilitate this as the democratic process is seen as promoting human development by maximising opportunities for self-determination, facilitating moral autonomy and providing for rights and liberties (Diamond 1999).

By remaining focussed on the democratic process as such, the participatory approach does not occupy a position to the far right-hand side of the democratic continuum as set out above, but further to the middle. In contrast to this, theories of democracy further to the right of the continuum redirect the focus away from political democracy, extending democracy into other spheres of society. This includes not only the physical extension of democratic processes into areas such as the workplace, but also a shift in focus from democratic processes to democratic outcomes. In this vision of democracy issues of social justice and the redistribution of resources signify the achievement of a substantive democracy. Democracy here is much more than the structures and processes of its state and the participation of citizens in the democratic process. Democracy in this vision is a good in itself, a form of life that enables citizens to live a better life in a more *just* society. For Marx the redistribution of resources, that is the ownership of the means of production, was a key element of the democratic society. He argued that the right to property contradicts the notion of free and equal citizens and that only the abolishment of property would free society and achieve a just outcome (see Held 1996: 130; Marx 2008). However, this radical view of redistribution through expropriation proved anything but democratic in its application, as the history of communism in the former Soviet Union showed. Despite this, the validity of claims for economic redistribution, be that directly through taxes or indirectly through state provision of a number of services, remains a powerful call for the establishment of substantive democracy. But, again, the extent of this redistribution, whether primarily instrumental to the enjoyment of the democratic process or as an end in itself, remains contested, and thus no single vision of a substantive form of democracy can be established.

The instrumental nature of redistribution for the enjoyment of the democratic process is also highlighted by more moderate voices. In this view, it is not the equalisation of society through expropriation that necessarily achieves substantive outcomes, but the provision of sufficient means and opportunities for the individual citizen to be able to participate effectively, freely and on an equal basis. Thus, according to Macpherson,

> as soon as democracy is seen as a kind of society, not merely a mechanism of choosing and authorizing governments, the egalitarian principle inherent in democracy requires not only 'one man, one vote' but also 'one man, one equal effective right to live as fully humanly as he may wish'. (Macpherson 1973, as quoted in Lane and Ersson 2003: 26)

And so, at a minimum,

> democracy requires neither opulence nor the material standards that today prevail in advanced industrial countries. It requires instead a widespread sense of relative economic wellbeing, fairness, and opportunity, a condition derived not from absolute standards but from perceptions of relative advantage and deprivation. (Dahl 1985: 46)

Substantive democracy thus aims to apply the values of freedom and equality, which underpin the political concept of democracy, beyond the right to vote. Instead, freedom and equality are applied to general life chances, which are seen as intimately linked to the political. Hence, the personal is political. However, the idea of a just and equal society faces a problem where the right to property and the market mechanism lead to outcomes which undermine the achievement of such a society by creating economic 'winners' and 'losers', and structures which perpetuate these positions over time, leading to highly stratified and thus unequal and unjust societies.

Tocqueville had highlighted the tension between equality on the one hand, and liberty and freedom on the other, especially the right to property, and squared this tension by stressing the need for four conditions that would reconcile equality and the right to property. These included the decentralisation of power and social functions, that is, a close relationship between democratic institutions and a pluralistic society and polity; constitutional decentralisation, in particular the independence of the judiciary; a vibrant political culture; and most importantly, the general diffusion of economic well-being, through active state intervention to break up privileged social positions (Dahl 1985). Proponents of equal opportunities, for example, may regard inequality based on social circumstances as morally wrong, but acknowledge and accept natural inequality. Hence, unequal performance based on difference in ability is seen as morally right. Thus, although proponents of the equal opportunities approach champion education and training to enable every individual to determine its own social position, unequal outcomes are justified and accepted (Heywood 1999: 291–292).

The collectivist principle introduced by the social democratic welfare state, for example, sought to combine the guarantee of essential freedoms with redistributive measures – to varying degrees – in order to achieve *relatively* more equality in outcome. It did so by providing equal opportunities for everyone, while balancing the effects of the market through state intervention. Social democracy therefore tried to balance the equality of opportunity with equality of outcomes, a balance that has changed over time. Early social democrats had focussed on the nationalisation of industries, while later social democrats associated social democracy more closely with Keynesian economics in which the state takes an active steering role, be that through macro-economic policies or the provision of services and goods. According to Plant, it was no surprise that due to this connection the demise of Keynesianism led to a crisis in social democracy, which the so-called Third Way sought to address (Plant 2002).

Proponents of the Third Way aimed to create a middle way between the 'humanism' of social democracy and the free market, seeking to make the values of socialism count after the fall of communism, even if socialism's economic programme had failed (Giddens 1998). It did so by providing more equality of opportunity through investment in individuals, for example through skills training and education. At the same time it left individuals exposed to the free, unrestrained market. Critics of the Third Way pointed out that the Third Way, contrary to its declared aims, was not a substantive democracy but merely the Emperor's new clothes, a disguised continuation of neo-liberal economics. While this new social democracy has increased substantive democratic procedures by providing more opportunities for participation and accountability, the focus on achieving substantive outcomes has decreased, reducing and undermining the communitarian responsibility which formed the invisible glue for substantive democracy. Indeed, Box et al. (2001: 613) claim that the market model of the New Public Management at the heart of this democracy prevents the establishment of substantive democracy because it undermines collective issues, converting, for example, questions of racism, poverty and disability into individual problems.

In the absence of a single definition substantive democracy could thus be summarised as a form of polity in which some degree of communitarian responsibility leads to policies, institutions and structures that try to ameliorate the effects of market activity and other social dynamics in general and particularly for those without a voice and conflict potential of their own. This form of democracy is essentially a developmental one. It is developmental in that it regards participation as an end in itself. It believes in a 'democratic humanism' that needs to be spread throughout society, into every part of the culture, because democracy is a 'way of life'. Developmental democracy combines the protection and regulation of the market by the state with a free market and the right to property. Indeed, developmental democracy and the developmental state, first expressed by John Stuart Mill, 'can be read as one of the earliest statements of the idea of the democratic welfare interventionist state and the mixed economy' (Green 1981, as quoted in Held 1996: 118). This concept of developmental democracy stands in contrast to protective democracy, as Macpherson showed. Protective democracy outlines a limited form of democracy focussed on the protection of the individual against the state. According to Macpherson, protective democracy does not include a vision of moral transformation, but is merely the 'logical requirement for the governance of inherently self-interested conflicting individuals who are assumed to be infinite desirers of their own private benefits' (Macpherson 1977: 43). Focussing on the individual as utility-maximiser, protective democracy provided the perfect rationale for the capitalist market society. In this the task of government was to establish and nurture a free market. This form of democracy expresses and subsumes in it a Schumpeterian model of democracy as a market, a model that I described here as 'minimal'. Developmental democracy by contrast describes a state that aims to foster the physical form of the state towards economic development and societal well-being beyond the opportunity to vote.

The democratic continuum – real or façade democracy?

The democratic continuum provides a framework for the UN's understanding of democracy by demonstrating not only the breadth and depth of potential interpretations along democratic theory's common definitions of democracy, but also by highlighting the potential problems in defining an organisational practice and organisational goals based on these interpretations. These problems relate to a number of tensions within the definition itself and between those who define democracy. These tensions are likely to be reflected in any definition of UN democracy, in particular in the process of defining and modelling a democratic practice. Questions about qualitative boundaries (the constitution of democracy and non-democracy) are as likely to emerge as questions of quantitative boundaries (what is included and what is not). The first problem of definition here is a methodological one. Here, a tension exists between the labels of procedures and substance, and the notion of quality and quantity attached to these labels. This includes the question of where to locate certain theories of democracy on the continuum. Participatory democracy is a prime example. Participation is a process, yet participation theorists claim that it is the extension into other spheres of life beyond elections that creates substance. Is participation then a substantive or a procedural form of democracy? Are procedures fundamentally non-substantive? And if so, does that mean they cannot achieve or result in a 'good' polity? Further, in the definitions outlined above, institutions tend to be either ignored or, at most, seen as subservient to elections. Yet, according to democratisation studies, institutions add substance to democracy. Outcomes, on the other hand, tend to be either overvalued, as in the Marxist case, or not specified in other theories.

This methodological problem of categorisation between process and substance leads us to a second problem: the tension between genuine democracy and façade democracy. As a number of scholars have shown, overlaying reality with the ideals of theory is problematic where authoritarian leaders allow for democratic institutions and civil society to exist, yet concede no power. Thus, although the observer might be able to tick all the boxes for the existence of democracy, assuming that the existence of institutions equals substance, or genuine democracy, is a fallacy. This fallacy is underlined by reading the classic Schumpeterian definition of democracy as elections without considering their context. The problem in finding a point where genuine democracy can be determined is therefore a result of ignorance on both sides, theory and practice: where democratisation scholars and practitioners emphasise structures over of social relations, which are more difficult to manage in post-conflict situations, democracy theorists ignore the possibility of abuse of structures. Situating genuine democracy on the democratic continuum is further complicated by transition periods in which the state of 'not (yet) being democratic' is part and parcel of the process. However, using criteria for the process and its result, for example Huntington's criterion of 'two turn-over' (Huntington 1991: 266), that is change of government to the opposition and back again through election, is equally unhelpful as a number of states generally regarded as democracies (such as Japan until the 1990s) would not fulfil these criteria. This has two consequences: First, the question of what constitutes 'real' democracy is ultimately a subjective one. Secondly, instead of utilising a linear continuum to devise qualitative categories for polities in general, and democracies in particular, a circle would more adequately represent the fine line between genuine and façade democracy. In this perspective, the labels 'process' and 'substance' would become empty categories for their purpose, losing meaning as a quantitative signal. Instead, to highlight the quantitative aspect of each definition, the scope of application, the labels 'minimal' and 'maximal' are more appropriate. Here, I use 'procedure' and 'substance' quantitatively. In other words, a focus on processes and procedures means minimal democracy, while substance refers to maximal democracy.

The third tension can be found between the empirical and the normative in democratic theory. The reductionism inherent in the act of defining leaves the work of realist, empirical scholars, in particular Schumpeter's minimal definition, incomplete. The observation of existing democracies as a basis for defining democracy means that common features are taken for granted. These features are consequently left unexplained as they are seen to be only a subsidiary part to the main event: elections. Thus, while existing democracies exhibit a number of institutions as part of their political make-up, scholars aim to find the closest possible approximation of *demos kratein*, the people's rule, in modern, complex societies. They thereby reduce democracy to an *activity* that roughly corresponds to this idea of rule. In doing so, they either ignore further institutional features of existing democracies as meaningful or exaggerate their usefulness as a solution to the undesired event of tyranny. Thus, realist scholars are ultimately normative in their selection of criteria.

Finally, a fourth tension in defining democracy can be found between political theorists and those studying democratisation processes. Political theory either follows a reductionist agenda, focussing on elections, or is highly idealistic in its approach, emphasising desired outcomes and widened processes. Thus, political theory either loses itself in utopia or, like empirical accounts, ignores institutions that are common to democratic societies. On the other hand, institutions constitute a central part in democratisation studies. Unlike political theorists who focus on the 'good' in their definition of democracy, democratisation scholars set out the 'effective', or 'necessary', to achieve the goal of establishing democratic societies. They outline features which can be observed in existing democracies, supporting their existence with reference to balanced power relationships, highlighting the possibilities of participation and equality between all citizens, while trying to avoid power accumulation in the hands of abusive leadership, be that minorities or majorities.

These problems or tensions lead to the confusion between democracy in analytical terms, that is, an interpretation or approximation of *demos kratein* for modern societies, and democracy in empirical terms, democrac*ies* or democratic states. Democratic states enjoy democracy, exercising people's rule through elections. Yet, democratic states also consist of institutions and particular forms of regulating social relations that are an essential part of their successful functioning. These institutions include the separation of powers, the rule of law, bureaucratic rules and procedures, rights and liberties, rules for campaigning and voting, civil society (including active support measures), media, rules for engaging in social relations such as rules regulating relations between ethnic groups and religions or simply civil law. Most of all, all (Western) democratic societies have some sort of distributory and developmental function, be that through the provision of (partially mandatory) education and training, social, medical and financial support for the poor and disadvantaged, regulated and socially accepted support systems such as pensions, health care and other forms of insurance. The confusion of democracy and democrac*ies*, method and systems, is common where a single, authoritative definition is absent and different actors are involved in its interpretation.

Although democratisation scholars are informed by political theory, therefore ensuring a basis of agreed definitional space in their work, their research questions and goals redirect focus away from the philosophical problems of democracy. Instead the research focus of democratisation scholars are practical problems where democracy, and the various institution of democratic societies, need to serve a particular function: the transformation of non-democratic regimes and societies, and their consolidation as *democracies*. The understanding of this process is informed by insights into the functioning and historical development of existing democracies, in particular the major Western donor states. Indeed, according to Ottaway, this discrepancy between the philosophical ideal, or standard definition found in democratic theory, and the definition applied in practice is obvious in the Western practice of democracy assistance. Ottaway demonstrates the implications of this translation of theory into practice by analysing the Western donors' model of democratisation. Democracy assistance programmes are based on particular ideas of democratisation processes which tend to be simplified interpretations of the academic discourse based on both a selective reading of the literature and the operational requirements of donor agencies in particular. The focus on short-term solutions, in particular the need to show results in a short period of time, means that a picture of the form and function of existing democracies is superimposed upon states and societies which may lack the requisite conditions. Not only are extended time-frames of historical developments and potential set-backs ignored but so are the particular set and constellation of social, economic and political conditions which have led to the development of democratic states elsewhere. Thus, 'the idea that there are virtually no conditions that preclude the possibility of democratization has become an article of faith among democracy promoters' (Ottaway 2004: 13). As a result, the intricate process of democratisation that developed in Europe and North America is reduced to a simple three-phase model of democratisation: first, a period of liberalisation lasting about three years or less; secondly, transition proper, which is achieved by holding multiparty elections; and, finally, consolidation, a protracted process of strengthening institutions and deepening democratic culture.

The democratic continuum – a research framework

Justice Stewart's conclusion on obscenity – 'I know it when I see it' – could be equally well applied to democracy. Democracy is an idea that excites many people and evokes just as many thoughts on what it is or ought to be. One may think that a definition of democracy is obvious, yet probing deeper shows that the concept of democracy overlaps with other ideas and concepts such as liberalism, welfare, governance, constitutionalism and human rights, all of which could be conceived of independently from democracy. Thus, it is tempting to reduce democracy to the process of voting alone, in order to establish an 'exact' definition. However, each of these ideas and concepts enhances the idea of democracy and enables the establishment of democratic societies. Democratic societies provide a greater degree of qualitative substance than democratic systems and processes alone. Analysing definitions of democracy also shows that different research foci lead to very different definitions of democracy. While democracy theorists focus on the philosophical ideal of what could and ought to be, therefore building up a definition of democracy from its foundations, democratisation scholars turn this analysis around and start with specific problems such as post-conflict situations that require a democratic solution. Attempts to define democracy may instinctively follow the approach taken by democracy theorists, be that through establishing key desired principles or reducing observable features to meaningful definitions. Yet, democratisation studies offer a very different view. Democratisation scholars paint a more elaborate picture of the institutional and cultural landscape in which democratic processes and systems operate. This scholarship provides detailed lists of elements that democratic societies exhibit and sees them as part of the wider concept of democracy. This then means a move away from the strong individualist and rights-based tendency that democracy scholars, in particular proceduralists, emphasise. Instead, democracy is viewed as a description of a political community, not only stressing the duties and responsibilities towards others, but also viewing democracy as a holistic solution, a new state *and* society.

Considering the essential contestability of democracy and the differences in approach relating to professional or scholarly context and interest, which affect the understanding and conceptualisation of democracy, it can be expected that a UN concept of democracy mirrors these problems. Here, the analysis of a UN concept of democracy is not based on the discovery of a number of terms relating to democracy but on the vision, or scope of democracy, which informs UN practice in the area of democracy assistance. The concept of the democratic continuum as outlined above guides the analysis of a UN concept of democracy. By focussing on 'visions' of democracy, the aim is to emphasise the problem of essential contestability not only in philosophical and analytical terms but also in our everyday understanding of what democracy is or ought to be. Any understanding of democracy is likely to be informed by observation and opinion formed from existing democratic systems as it is informed by discourses that filtered through from the academic domain into the lay discourse. While the lay discourse may ignore the finer details of the philosopher's view, it most likely covers a similar range, and it is this range, in other words the question of how far democracy extends into the political, social and economic system, that is central here. Consequently, the democratic continuum is conceptualised as an increasing scope of democracy criteria applicable in each theory – going from a minimal definition (scope limited to political democracy) to a maximal definition (broad scope with democracy extending into areas beyond the political).

The continuum represents the liberal democratic paradigm of Western democracy theory, and the numerous visions of democracy offered by it. The starting point of the democratic continuum is the procedural, minimal definition of democracy as offered in the classic Schumpeterian definition. It may be possible to conceive of political forms that embody the idea of people's rule and participation that are not based on elections, for example, representation through unelected community elders who deliberate and vote on a regional or national level. These forms would be located on the democratic continuum to the left of the starting point, here indicated in by a dotted line (see Figure 2.3). How and whether such forms are acknowledged and represented in the UN democracy agenda is indeed an important question, as the case of Afghanistan highlights. The continuum moves on to an undefined endpoint of substantive democracy, a maximal definition of a democratic society in which democratic processes are complemented by democratic outcomes to describe a functioning democracy. Again, substantive ideas of democracy, or more precisely the democratic *society*, go beyond elections and democratic institutions, focussing instead on 'true' democratic outcomes that could potentially be denied by democratic processes. These ideas put in question how far the outcome of political decisions and markets have to contribute to democratic equality and participation in a democratic *society*, which stands in contrast to the democratic *system* described by proceduralists like Schumpeter.

While the democratic continuum may have a starting point on the right (elections), the open end to the left highlights the lack of a definitive definition of substantive democracy. Instead, it indicates that substantive democracy can be achieved through various combinations of institutions, principles, rights and processes. The democratic continuum thus functions as a conceptual tool to compare mainstream democracy theory with possible interpretations used by the UN and to locate these interpretations between the poles of minimal-procedural and maximal-substantive. It acts as a template from which to interpret UN rhetoric and practice.

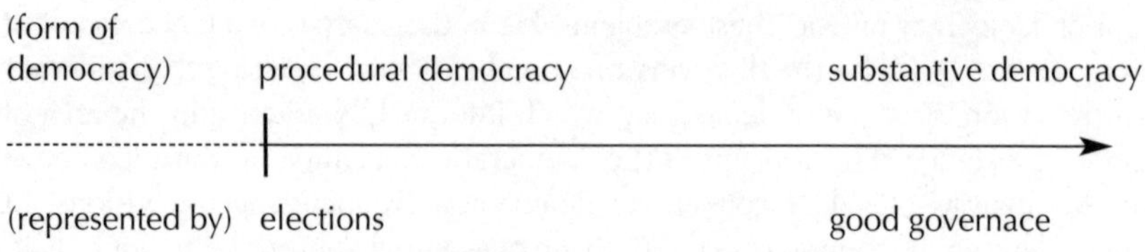

Figure 2.3   *Ideas and practices of democracy and the democratic continuum*

Since the 1990s, the guiding points for the analysis and evaluation of UN democracy are two UN practices that promote and implement democratic features – election support and good governance. These two practices highlight different but interrelated aspects of democracy and the democratic state. They are part of the democratic continuum from minimal-procedural democracy to maximal-substantive democracy and show an increased range of UN support activities. However, with an open-ended continuum to the right, the question arises how substantive UN democracy really is, and indeed how substantive it could be. Although UN practice may have some resemblance to the ideals of democratic theory, the organisation will construct its very own version of democracy, which may or may not vary under different circumstances. Addressing post-conflict situations in which such scholarship becomes relevant has been a major task for the UN in the last fifteen years. How do philosophical ideas of democracy and existing UN practice influence how democracy is viewed? To what extent is the UN influenced by its practice in conceptualising democracy, and to what extent is democracy developed as a theoretical construct without reference to existing problems? In other words, how does democracy fit in with existing UN ideas and practices?

Note

1   This is also expressed in points 3 and 5 of Luckham et al.'s (2000) inventory, see Figure 2.2.

3

Democracy under a veil: civilisation

As the previous chapter showed, the role and place of democracy have always been expressions of its time and the historic, systemic constraints placed upon it. To understand the limitations of democracy in today's international dimension, be that a 'right to democratic governance' or the promotion of democratic statehood through international organisations such as the UN, is to understand the limitations it faced in its historical development. As the UN is as much a result of its historical context and changes as it is a vehicle for them, many of these limitations lie in the philosophical or legal foundations of the UN. They are the result of the historical processes in which the UN was founded, through which it developed and which it helped to advance. This chapter shows how these processes have shaped the conception of democracy in the making of the UN, from the early planning stages to the writing of key documents, such as the UN Charter and the Universal Declaration of Human Rights (UDHR). What emerges is a view of 'us versus them', in which democracies assume a higher moral place than non-democratic states. The equation of democracy with civilisation is at once both teleological and exclusionary. The process of bringing into existence an international organisation like the UN started an intricate dance between philosophy, politics and law, between the concepts of democracy, sovereignty, independence and peace, and the question which of these elements is a sign of civilisation. Through the drafting of the UN Charter and the establishment of international law it becomes clear that in the first four decades of the UN, democracy existed under the veil of neutrality assumed by sovereignty in the context of ideological battles. Democracy was ubiquitous in thought but absent in fact. Questions of what constitutes democracy were of secondary importance as the label of democracy functioned primarily as an ideological identifier and classifier.

Democracy, civilisation, peace: philosophical foundations

The twentieth century can without a doubt be called the 'Democratic Century' (Freedom House 1999). Yet at the turn of the nineteenth to the twentieth century not a single democracy as we know it today existed. The democratic states which had come into existence could at best be called 'restricted' democracies in which women, racial minorities, the poor and the landless were not able to participate in the electoral process or indeed enjoy a number of rights (Freedom House 2004). The end of the First World War led to the introduction of full democracy in many European states. Suffrage was extended to a universal franchise in which leaders were to be elected through a multi-party, competitive election process. Fascism and militarism in the 1930s clearly dealt a blow to democracy, reducing the number of democratic states again, leaving only twelve democracies in the early 1940s. This amounted to less than a quarter of the total number of 61 sovereign states, down from nearly half of all sovereign states being democratic in 1922 (Huntington 1991). Yet, despite the limited presence of democracy at the turn of the century and the rather grim reality for democracy nearly half a century later, thinking about democracy and its international dimension had played a considerable part in academic and political circles for some time. This thinking had grown out of the social, cultural and military changes of the nineteenth century which saw the possibility of total war and its horrific consequences for entire populations as an ever greater possibility as technology advanced. Social engineering and the management of international politics through the study and understanding of the nature and dynamics of the balance of power became a key concern in an age where increasing industrialisation and the spread of the scientific method opened up new possibilities and threats (Olson and Groom 1991). These changes in thinking influenced the ideas of the planners of the new world orders (Williams 1999) following each of the destructive world wars, which led to the creation of the League of Nations and the UN respectively, infiltrating both their conceptualisation and negotiation phase.

Since the eighteenth century, when German philosopher Immanuel Kant outlined his ideas for a *Perpetual Peace*, democracy had become part and parcel of the liberal internationalists' agenda and their approach to the achievement of world peace and in some cases even world government (Heater 2004). The Kantian ideas of free trade, rule of international law and collective security, all in the context of international institutions, should serve to secure, maintain and enhance peace and international cooperation. In this framework, democracy is the means through which these aims could be achieved. Democracies, liberal internationalists claimed, are more cooperative than non-democracies, and the assumed similarities between democratic states would increase the chances for peace. Unlike authoritarian states, democracies would neither erect trade barriers, which are potential sources for conflict, nor would they rely on the fear-enhancing balance of power or secrecy used in traditional diplomacy. On the contrary, democracies, through trade, openness and a reciprocal recognition of democratic principles and institutions (e.g. a commitment to the rule of law, human rights, equality before the law and representative government based on popular consent), would find little ground for conflict. Public opinion, liberals contended, would prevent war, as the public in democratic states would not be willing to bear the costs of war, be that financial costs, human costs or other (Doyle 1997; Goldmann 1994; Heater 1996; Russett 1993). Following this logic, democracy is the elusive aim to which liberal internationalists aspire; moreover, to which reason and rationality would ultimately lead human kind.

Fukuyama captured this teleology well. Drawing on Hegelian historical dialectics, which saw history as ever progressive towards increasing reason and rationality, Fukuyama regarded democracy as a natural endpoint of human development. This endpoint, about which Fukuyama wrote in the early 1990s, was an *End of History*, the history of ideas, which saw liberalism as the winning ideology, embodied by democratic structures. As the end product and thus the supreme creation of the history of ideas, liberal democracy was seen as the only political and social form of life which would satisfy people's nature and basic desires, such as material wealth and the recognition of dignity by others, while guaranteeing people's rights through a reciprocal and equal agreement between the state and the people (Fukuyama 1992). A world consisting of democracies is thus the expression of the ultimate and perfect arrangement to achieve *Perpetual Peace* and the *End of History*. The inevitability and supremacy attached to democracy as a product of the highest rationality and the final stage of development have often led to accusations of liberal hegemony, which had also been expressed in the far more tangible practice of colonialism in the nineteenth century. Here, the distinction liberal internationalists made between the civilised, democratic world and the uncivilised, authoritarian and un-free world emphasised the value attached to democracy.

Thinkers such as Clarence Streit and Lord Lothian had drawn a clear line between the 'civilised world' (Europe and North America) and 'backward' people, who were not 'ready' for democracy and self-government (Bosco 1995). In the liberal internationalists' models of international union, world federation or international organisation this distinction was central to the construction of a successful alliance for the achievement of peace, and a state's placement in either group determined its opportunity to participate in international relations, and, in the case of the colonies, its international status. Many agreed that countries that were not 'ready' would have to be made so by the 'advanced' states, and until then remain under the control and rule of the advanced democracies, thereby justifying the lack of self-determination in colonial territories. Streit, for example, envisaged a Union of North Atlantic states with a core of fifteen states, consisting of those 'most politically advanced' countries, which he described as democracies. Streit equated democracy with civilisation, emphasising that 'democracy is based on faith in free and equal Man' (Streit 1939: 128). He found strong words for those states not possessing democratic features, claiming that

> Peoples that accept dictatorships must be classified, politically, among the immature, or retarded, or inexperienced, high as they may rank otherwise. In admitting to be governed authoritatively, they admit they are not able to govern themselves freely. While men accept being governed as children, they must be rated as immature. (Streit 1939)

As a lack of resistance thus signified consent in Streit's view, he did not see any problem or contradiction when he discussed the issue of colonies and democracies in his Union. Instead, his attention was on the question of whether the colonies should be transferred from the member states to the Union. Streit thus reinforced the idea of democracy as more civilised by ignoring the idea of a non-self-determining territory and the system of colonial rule. Even if Streit regarded his Union as not limited to existing democracies, emphasising that it was eventually to be built outwards, this was only to be attempted once those states had reached a sufficient level of maturity to join. For the time being, however, autocratic states as well as colonial territories were regarded as not strong enough to maintain and strive for the goals of the Union.

In his 1949 inauguration speech US President Truman outlined similar sentiments. In this speech, which today is best known for the creation of the underdeveloped world and the practice of development assistance, Truman presented the world as divided into three distinct areas and two blocs. On the one hand, he saw the areas of communist states and underdeveloped countries that neither possess democracy nor are ready to have it. Like Streit, Truman seemed to suggest that in communist states people freely gave their rights to the ruling communist party. According to Truman, communism was an obstacle to lasting peace and development due its oppressive nature, the suppression of its people, their freedom and initiative. On the other hand, Truman saw democracies that are free, advanced and industrialised. He stressed that it was these advanced states' duty to help those non-democratic, underdeveloped states by 'making the benefits of [their] scientific advances and industrial progress available for the improvement and growth of underdeveloped areas', on the condition that they would be 'peace-loving'. In so doing, democracy would form a vehicle as well as an incentive for the development process, as 'Democracy alone can supply the vitalizing force to stir the peoples of the world into triumphant action, not only against their human oppressors, but also against their ancient enemies – hunger, misery, and despair' (Truman 1949). With the goal of a 'perpetual peace' through some form of international association in mind, as well as the imperative to assist poorer states to achieve a certain stage of technological or economic development, the promotion of democracy had assumed the form of a 'white man's burden' or 'Manifest Destiny' for the 'civilised' world. These ideas eventually found their way into the UN Charter and the trusteeship system, where both decolonisation and development assistance were assigned a central place in the canon of goals, even if democracy and its benefits were dropped from this equation in the process of negotiating and writing the Charter.

In Europe, thinking about democracy had remained largely an intellectual exercise confined to academic circles. Scholars such as David Mitrany, Norman Angell, Lord Lothian and others developed ideas of peace, integration through trade, functional cooperation and in some cases world government, which expressed their expectations and dreams for what they hoped would be a better future for Europe and the world (Long and Wilson 1995). Yet, their ideas did not penetrate public policies beyond the construction of the League of Nations, a rather imperfect model of their visions. In contrast to this, liberal democratic internationalism in the USA had long found its expression outside the intellectual realm, too, and had been a considerable element of American foreign policy. Since Jefferson, it had been clear that for the USA a peaceful world would be constituted by democratic states. American interests and American security were seen as being protected by world-wide democratisation (see Smith 1994). In this tradition, President Woodrow Wilson had requested Congress in April 1917 to declare war on Germany to 'make the world safe for democracy'. In his subsequently issued *Fourteen Points* the idea of democracy had been absorbed into ideas of sovereign equality, national self-determination and the ideal of 'peace-loving' nations coming together in a 'general association of nations', a process of synthesis later to be repeated by Roosevelt in the planning of the UN. Yet, democracy, although highly desirable, had clear boundaries. Wilson's demands for self-determination (as a different expression of democracy), for example, was only to be applied in the reconstruction of Europe, not in colonial territories or other states (see Williams 1999).

In the 1940s Roosevelt's idea for the post-war world order had drawn on the same liberal internationalist foundations as Wilson before him – free trade, self-determination, democracy, international law, collective security and functional integration through an international organisation. However, Roosevelt, who had found himself constrained on the one hand by an American public (and Congress) in favour of isolationism, and, on the other hand, his deeply rooted internationalism, had ultimately taken a more pragmatic, 'realistic' approach in his foreign policy. As Smith points out, Roosevelt's realism 'was packaged as idealism: democratic government was not so much an end in itself as a way to limit Soviet expansion' (Smith 1994: 119). Thus, democracy had assumed second place as the USA supported non-democratic but self-governing, independent countries and the creation of 'spheres of influence' against rival powers and ideologies. As a result, despite Roosevelt's numerous pronouncements for democracy, the notion of democracy in declarations such as the Atlantic Charter was lost or clouded by the use of terms such as 'self-government' and 'self-determination'.

In January 1941, in his *Four Freedoms* speech, Roosevelt had successfully rallied Congress with a call for US involvement in the war in Europe, claiming that not only was the 'democratic way of life' in the world and thus the survival of democracy in America endangered, but that it was necessary to come to the support of freedom and those countries who had lost their freedom (and democracy) in this war. Despite this pro-democracy rallying cry, the first Allied pronouncement for a new post-war order, the Atlantic Charter, had not addressed democracy directly but declared that 'they respect the right of all peoples to choose the form of government under which they will live; and they wish to see sovereign rights and self government restored to those who have been forcibly deprived of them' (Atlantic Charter, as quoted in Russell 1958: 975). In the Atlantic Charter, as in Wilson's *Fourteen Points*, the precise use of democracy was circumvented and the sovereignty of the people emphasised. This tension between the ideal of democracy and the emphasis on sovereignty was most evident in the 1945 *Declaration on Liberated Europe*. Here, democracy as a structural prescription was eventually mentioned as an option for the peoples of Europe to pursue the 'government of their own choice' (Russell 1958). Of course, to the liberal thinker there was no question that a freely choosing and self-governing people would elect for democracy and that consequently the sovereignty of the people would be established. However, as in the American Draft Constitution of the UN Charter, which had provided that 'All self-governing States and Dominions, accepting the obligations of membership, shall be members of the International Organization' (as quoted in Russell 1958: 350), the free choice of government (self-government) became something different from democracy. Instead, it was understood as a form of self-determination, that is, freedom from outside interference such as imperial powers. In fact, when the term 'self-governing' raised question about democracy, the US drafting committee had insisted that 'self-government' referred to independence in external affairs instead of democracy.

In light of this interpretation of self-government it is indeed not surprising that it had not been the Soviet Union, the ideological antagonist of Western democracy at the time, who found this phrasing problematic but British Prime Minister Winston Churchill. Churchill saw in the American insistence on self-government a direct threat to the British Empire and British control over its colonies. Indeed, Churchill had to be convinced by Roosevelt to agree to the terminology of the Atlantic Charter. In fact, with this early terminological turn, it was easy for Stalin to agree on the increased emphasis on sovereignty instead of democracy (Luard 1982). Even if democracy had been spelled out, Stalin's understanding of what constituted democracy certainly differed from Roosevelt's, as a 'peoples' democracy' may have been democracy in name but not in substance. Thus, the emphasis on self-government and its interpretation as independence did in fact appeal to and connect with the revolutionary ideals of communism, as debates on the issue of decolonisation showed in the 1960s. However, Williams (1999) argues that when Stalin abrogated the agreements of the *Declaration on Liberated Europe* and the 1945 Yalta agreement by ignoring the promise to hold free elections in Poland (and Europe), it had become clear that democracy, despite declarations in support of it, had in fact no place in the reality of international politics.

As in the overall planning of the post-war world order, the USA took a leading role in the drafting of the UN and its Charter. Although democracy did indeed play a large role in European thinking prior to the war, it was in fact the USA that initiated conferences and meetings with their papers and proposals serving as discussion basis. At the same time, as the USA took the role of initiator, the failure of other participants, in particular the Soviet Union and China, to submit their proposals on time (Luard 1982), translated into an advantage for the USA in ensuring that its ideas for the future organisation would form the basis of the UN. Yet, according to Russell, smaller states did have considerable leverage on the drafting of the UN Charter when they were in agreement (Russell 1958: 6). Thus, the input of others in the drafting of the UN Charter was not negligible, as for example Chile had requested democracy to be a defining criterion for member states. The result of these negotiations was an organisation and a Charter, which recognised the need for pragmatism to achieve peace but left a few doors open which allowed those ideas of democracy that the USA had so openly declared from the time of Jefferson to creep in.

Democracy and the UN Charter

The UN Charter has often been said to be a patchwork of principles due to the rush in which it was drawn out. Negotiating the Charter was a complex process with drafts passing through several committees and several stages of drafting, correcting and approving. The time allocated for negotiations was short and debating took place under great pressure as the Red Army had surrounded Berlin. Many contradictions in the text of the Charter, which came about as part of the negotiation process, were not smoothed out by lawyers as would usually have been the case for (international) legal documents. The result is a document that is in many ways imperfect. However, as Nicholas points out, these imperfections may be found acceptable as otherwise filibusters and utopians would have taken over and agreement would have been 'sacrificed on the altar of perfection' (Nicholas 1959: 9). Thus, although attempts were made to include mention of democracy in the Charter, it was manifest more in spirit than in textual evidence, often leading to differing and controversial interpretations of ideas relating to democracy.

A central theme running through the negotiations was the issue of improvements on the League of Nations that were regarded as necessary if this new organisation was to be successful. Where the League had failed, the UN should now provide a structure of cooperation and security that was to prevent future conflict. The problem of membership had been seen as crucial to the League's lack of success. Reconsidering membership – who to include, when and how – also gave the opportunity to question the nature of the future members' polity. Thus, the question of democracy and membership became intimately connected from the start. Now universality was a key idea to determine membership of the UN and intended as a direct improvement on the experiences of the League of Nations. The League of Nations not only had limited membership with the US remaining in isolation and both the USSR and Germany initially kept out, but by defining members as 'civilised nations' it had created an elitist club which certainly no colonial territory could join as they, the 'savage nations' of the colonial dominions, had not yet reached a stage of maturity to be called civilised.[1] This new organisation, however, allowed not only for universality as such but also explicitly built expansion of membership into its Charter to remain responsive to the reality of disintegrating empires (whether through internal or external pressure) and with it a rise in state numbers. Thus, the UN Charter was drawn up with two forms of members: 'original' members, that is the 'UN' or the three allies who gave the UN its name, and subsequent members, which were to apply to the UN and which had to be deemed acceptable by the Security Council and General Assembly.[2]

At the drafting conference in San Francisco, opposition to universality had come from those states who favoured provisions for membership beyond 'peace-loving'. Suggestions such as Chile's that states should 'love the democratic system' as well as peace, or the French motion that peace-loving should be demonstrated by a state's internal structures, institutions and behaviour as well, were dismissed (Russell 1958: 844). Instead, the British proposal was adopted, subsequently becoming Art. 4(1) UN Charter. Requirements for membership were spelled out as statehood, acceptance of the obligations of the Charter, as well as the ability and willingness to carry out those obligations. Finally, the key to qualify for membership was the above-mentioned requirement for states to be peace-loving, a description fairly apt considering the aims of the organisation were to secure peace by foregoing war (see Simma 2002: 177–184).[3] Adopting this criterion was to allow for maximum flexibility. In other words, not only was the British proposal to satisfy universalists but established some, however superfluous, conditions of membership (Russell 1958: 845).[4] To make membership conditional, despite aims of universality, was necessary to shape an organisation whose emphasis and sole *raison d'être* was peace in opposition to the experiences of (yet another) world war, which, again, had been instigated by fascist and militarist powers such as Germany and Japan. As a result, the only amendments concerning the quality of member states was a statement aimed at these former enemy states.

At Dumbarton Oaks the Soviet Delegate had suggested the inclusion of a provision stating that fascist states or states of a fascist type did not meet the conditions of membership and should therefore not become members. While the USA and Britain agreed on this in principle, they rejected any such provision because they felt it could not be defined satisfactorily (Russell 1958: 811). In the San Francisco drafting process Mexico raised this issue once again, suggesting a provision which stated that 'states whose regimes have been established with the help of military forces belonging to the countries which have waged war against the UN' should not be accepted as members 'as long as these regimes are in power' (Russell 1958: 845).[5] This provision was finally agreed upon. Thus, although universality was deemed as highest priority, the fight against Nazi Germany and Imperial Japan, and the exclusion of enemy states, was not secondary to it.[6]

Although Mexico's proposal was initially aimed at Spain, this would also apply to puppet governments in China and Manchukuo (Russell 1958: 845). Franco's Spain, which had received help from Nazi Germany, was condemned by the General Assembly and requested to leave all technical UN organisations. In April 1946 the General Assembly declared that it hoped that the Spanish people would soon regain freedom, adding later that if a democratic government was not established within reasonable time, the Security Council should consider adequate measures to remedy the situation (Luard 1982: 363–364). However, as Kelsen (1951) emphasises, the issue of Spain's membership was more political than legal in nature, as were most other membership issues at the time, reflecting the East–West confrontation at its early heights. Thus, while the resolution was successfully applied for some time, the international condemnation of Spain soon abated and the resolution was revoked in 1950. Spain eventually joined the UN in 1955, like a number of other countries who had been judged on their war-time behaviour and had been deemed as not peace-loving.[7] In the case of Spanish membership the insistence on democracy was thus more of symbolic value, a case in which an ideal (democracy) was applied to oppose the current system. In this sense, any system but the current one was deemed more appropriate.[8] In similar fashion democracy was promoted as a yardstick for membership in the case of Korea. While the question of legitimate representation by either North or South was hotly debated, it was agreed that membership of the South was favoured *after* it had democratic elections, as the 'lawful government' was that which was based on elections, 'a valid expression of the free will of the electorate'[9]. But again, other issues soon diminished the importance of democratic legitimacy and both Koreas joined without a test of democratic legitimisation (see Luard 1982: 365–372).

If universality was vital to achieving the aims of the new organisation, this also meant that the reality of non-democratic states had to be acknowledged. To make democracy a standard by which to judge its members would have meant to compromise the central achievement of this new organisation, which was the promise of equality of sovereign statehood of all its members, or universal equality, defendable in a system of collective security based on the principle of non-intervention. Universality was central as it stood in clear contrast to a two-tier system of civilised and uncivilised states, democratic and non-democratic. Every document in the planning process of the UN, from the Atlantic Charter to the Moscow Declaration, therefore had emphasised sovereignty and the sovereign equality of states, thereby creating a tension between the ideal of democracy as promoted by the USA (and Britain) and the reality of the possible minimum (see Smith 1994).

With questions of official membership solved, the negotiating parties in San Francisco created another issue of membership that, unintentionally, should prove to be more contentious for defenders and opponents of a right to democratic governance today. This was based on the question of reading legal texts positively and consequently denying the right to democracy. It is in the opening words of the UN Charter which affirms 'We the peoples of the UN' as the authors of the document, that the founders of the UN left open a door for interpretation, introducing a democratic ideal which has led to much contention about the reality of democracy in the Charter. At the heart of this contention is the importance which the position of this phrase is afforded as the preamble performs an important role in the interpretation of the following Charter articles (Goodrich et al. 1969). In the drafting process of the Charter, the preamble was left till the very end. It was only on the insistence of South African Field Marshal Smuts that a preamble was considered in the drafting committee. The aim was to create a document whose introduction appealed to the 'hearts and minds of men' and outline the 'nobility of the intentions' of the founding members (Russell 1958).

In elaborate language Smuts' original draft outlined the intentions of the founders to work together to avoid future wars. It was the US delegation, however, which insisted on redrafting Smuts' version, not only for brevity and beauty, but primarily to include the phrase which features so prominently in the US constitution. The USA aimed to express the notion of popular sovereignty and the democratic basis of the UN, hence US Representative Bloom insisted on the inclusion of the phrase 'We the peoples' in the preamble of the Charter (Russell 1958: 913–915). This phrase had found support among a number of Latin American countries as well as China, Soviet Russia and the Ukraine[10], although the overall reception remained cool (Goodrich et al. 1969). Yet, even if this phrase conveyed the meaning that many had in their minds at the time, it remained unclear to what this 'democratic basis' actually referred. Who are *the peoples*? Understanding 'we the peoples' in terms of popular sovereignty, for example, meant defining peoples as individuals. The delegation of the Netherlands objected to an understanding of peoples as individuals as they claimed that in the Netherlands sovereignty did not rest with the people but with the Crown and therefore it was the Crown that was represented in San Francisco (Kelsen 1951: 7). Probably sensing these problems at the time, the Coordination Committee at the San Francisco conference had made no changes to the suggested initial wording. However, on the insistence of the Advisory Committee of Jurists, it had amended the preamble, including a second part which had to be read in conjunction with the first. This second part reads 'Accordingly, our respective Governments, through representatives assembled in the city of San Francisco', which made clear that the peoples referred to are governments (Russell 1958: 917–918). This phrase highlighted the character of the Charter as an international treaty between the states represented in San Francisco and thus constituting their relationship as contractual. Accordingly, the democratic notion of popular sovereignty was subjugated to the neutrality of legal sovereignty. Hence, as Simma points out, the uncertainty in the concept of 'peoples' should not be over-emphasised considering that suggestions to include a provision of democracy in the rules regarding membership were rejected (Simma 2002: 34).

Although the UN Charter did not explicitly mention democracy, it clearly contained a number of points where the phrasing of the text left an open door for interpretation, and the question of democracy therefore became a matter of reading the text in one way or the other. To be sure, in relation to the preamble these problems of interpretation could have been avoided if Field Marshal Smuts' earlier draft had been accepted instead of redrafting it according to American wishes. Smuts had used a standard international legal formula, as was used in the League of Nations Covenant. Smuts used the phrase 'the High Contracting Parties' to denote the members of the League (Russell 1958: 912–913), thereby clearly emphasising the contractual character of the document while losing the contentious notion of popular sovereignty. Problems of interpretation such as this were ultimately a failure of the USA to be explicit about its intentions as minutes of a Hearing of the Committee on Foreign Relations in the USA Senate on the issue of the Charter of the UN showed. The US delegation had assumed that it was generally understood that it considered the phrase 'we the peoples' to be popular sovereignty, yet it relied on this assumption alone:

> A Senator asked: 'Was there any sort of agreement or understanding about what "We the peoples of the UN" meant?' Whereupon the representative of the Department of State answered: '*I think* it was clearly understood that the phrase "We the peoples" meant that the peoples of the world were speaking through their governments at the Conference, and that it was because the peoples of the world are determined that those things shall be done which are stated in the preamble that the governments have negotiated the instrument.' Then the Senator asked: 'And that the governments represented at the Conference were actually the agents of the peoples of those countries represented there?' To this the answer was: '*I do not know that that question was discussed in that particular form,* as a matter of political

institutions. The document, being in the form of a treaty, had to be negotiated by governments.' Finally, the representative of the State Department declared: 'The phrase itself, "We the peoples" is borrowed from a well-known document.'. (as quoted in Kelsen 1951, p. 6, footnote 4, emphasis added)

From this excerpt of the hearings it becomes clear that not only was the USA, the proponent of this contentious phrase, not explicit with regard to its intentions but that it was also not always clear to the US government itself what exactly it intended to convey. While at times it appeared that the US understood the democratic basis of the UN to be the political make-up of member states, at other times this seemed to have been democracy within the UN, that is, between member states. It was clarified that governments were the negotiating parties in San Francisco, yet the relationship between those ruling and those ruled, and the relationship between the ruled and the international, remained undefined and most of all, it was not specifically addressed and questioned.[11]

Self-government and self-determination

Democracy, it has become clear, is both ubiquitous and absent in the foundations of the UN. Although this may seem contradictory, this quandary is indeed at the heart of the international dimension of democracy. Democracy is ubiquitous as an idea and as a concept that underlies the liberal foundations of this international organisation. Yet, the term itself is completely absent from the central text, the UN Charter. Democracy is not mentioned in the Charter. Where the issue of democracy arose in the negotiating process of the Charter, legal comments soon clarified a meaning which always explicitly moved away from democracy. In the conceptual triangle of democracy, sovereignty and independence, emphasis moved away from democracy and towards (external) sovereignty and independence, neutralising the question of civilisation. Now the question was how democracy was applied in practice. It is clear that the Charter as a text does not stand in isolation from its application and the practice the organisation engages in. As suggested above, one reason for the absence of democracy in the UN Charter was the need to give primacy to peace at the time. This was to ensure cooperation to achieve the minimal aim of establishing the organisation as such. This emphasis on peace and security, however, most prevalent in the first decade of the UN, was soon challenged. The dominance of the Cold War in the first decade of the UN's existence had led to a stalemate in questions of membership, with East and West divided about what a state's political make-up should be, and how a state should have gained independence. Democracy was used as an ideal but in the end not pursued, and instead dropped for political reasons. With a growing membership of developing countries, however, the demand for further decolonisation grew, requiring further conceptual clarification. This further shaped the way in which democracy was conceived of.

Issues of decolonisation had been part of the planning stages since the Atlantic Charter. However, while the US considered independence, 'self-government' or 'self-determination' as essential to the post-war world, Churchill had resisted this move. The compromise that was eventually agreed upon continued the principle of old mandates of the League of Nations system and provided a trusteeship system for ex-enemy territories occupied by the Allies during the war as well as for existing colonies voluntarily designated by the colonial powers. Questions regarding self-government and independence dominated the UN from the late 1950s onwards. The resulting independence of colonial territories not only increased the member-ship of the UN and changed the power balance within the organisation, but also meant that issues relating to the specific problems of those countries dominated the UN agenda in the 1970s and 1980s, creating a division between North and South. Through this, the ambivalent place of democracy in the UN was further enhanced as the understanding of self-government and self-determination changed and the demand for human rights increased. With this, the maintenance of the status quo as the primary goal of the UN, that is, the goal to restore and secure peace, was joined by another goal: to stimulate and encourage change of the status quo through the recognition of the right to self-determination and human rights.[12] This process was further complicated due to the changing meaning and application of either concept.

The concept of self-determination assumed four different meanings over time and between different ideologies. At the heart of these different interpretations lies the problem of interpreting the political–philosophical dictum of 'determining one's own political future' in either its external way or its internal way (Cassese 1995); in other words, to view self-determination as either independence or democracy. First, self-determination was seen as a means of territorial change, the transfer and secession of one part of a country to unite with a neighbouring country based on the holding of plebiscites. Secondly, it was defined as a democratic principle for people to choose their own government and thus legitimise the state's rule. Thirdly, self-determination became a principle of anti-colonialism to secede from a colonial power, that is, the right of peoples to be free from outside rule. Finally, it was regarded as a principle of freedom for minorities within a sovereign state. In its modern form, the debate within the UN displayed a clear distinction between Western liberal understanding of the concept and Soviet ideas (later backed by Third World countries).

The idea of self-determination has been generally dated back to the French and American Revolutions in the late eighteenth century, although some writers find its origins even further back in time (Franck 1992). The time of the French and American Revolutions established a number of key concepts of the modern understanding of democratic politics, and it was here that the concept of self-determination achieved particular importance. The idea of self-determination drew on a particular philosophical ideal, which aimed to counteract actions that were typical for feudal rule. The idea that everyone, not only those of noble birth or wealth, was able 'to determine one's own political future' carried with it a legal-pro-cedural dimension. The philosophical ideals and the legal, practical considerations were as much in accordance with each other as they were pulling apart to denote different practices. Philosophically, the revolutions had introduced a new concep-tualisation of sovereignty by establishing the idea of a political contract in which the free and independent individual transferred his sovereignty to the state, rather than have freedoms and rights bestowed upon him by a sovereign. Thus, the basis for this new state legitimacy was the free individual. This freedom was gained through their humanity and from birth, not through royal decree. Consequently, people were free to choose their own political constitution as a human being and with it their nationality (Grewe 2000: 251–252). This new political understanding of the individual implied new restrictions for rulers. Whereas previously sovereigns were largely free to rule over their people as they chose to, the French and American Revolutions deposed (the idea of) the omnipotent ruler and set in their place the people. Hence, the philosophy of self-determination gave birth to the practice of democratic rule.

To the *idea* of self-determination was added the *practice* of self-determination, which was applied in the specific context of territorial transfer. Territorial transfer between rulers, be that as a gift or as a ceding of a post-war settlement, had been common practice of a change of power at the time. With this new understanding of sovereignty and self-determination, rulers were no longer seen as able to exchange territory solely on the basis of their own interest and according to their political strategy. With governments now seen as responsible to their people, territorial transfer had to be made with the consent of the people in the territory. To ensure consent and full exercise of self-determination, plebiscites served as a means to establish the will of the people in the affected territories (Cassese 1995). Consequently, the practice of self-determination had a distinct territorial aspect and with it an international dimension which would dominate the debate of the legal concept of self-determination in the second half of the twentieth century. At the same time, the entanglement of the idea with procedures such as plebiscites (elections) and political forms such as democracy further complicated the definition of self-determination and its relationship to a potential international norm of democracy.

In the early twentieth century, contradictory interpretations by Lenin and Woodrow Wilson added to these complications in understanding and applying self-determination. For Lenin self-determination meant the liberation of oppressed peoples (colonies) as a prelude to class struggle. To achieve self-determination, Lenin claimed, the possibility of violence and secession should not be excluded, although federations should be favoured over independence. Lenin employed the philosophical idea of self-determination as a tactical, strategic weapon for socialist change. By contrast, Wilson favoured an orderly, non-violent approach to the exercise of self-determination. Wilson's initial conceptualisation of self-determination, which he set out before the First World War, strongly favoured the internal dimension of self-determination, emphasising an understanding based on Western political thought. This idea highlighted self-government, popular sovereignty and consent, or in other words, a democratic state. Wilson's vision of self-determination later shifted towards the external dimension of self-determination as the US administration was faced with the realities of the European post-war order and the restructuring of Europe after the First World War. Self-determination became the guiding principle for recognising territories and calling for new territorial arrangements for victors and losers alike. However, these arrangements were made inconsistently, following the political interests of the major powers, not following evenly applied principles and rules. This practice was seen by many as undermining the concept of self-determination, which highlighted some of the fundamental problems inherent in the idea of self-determination and the potential of its application.

The UN Charter had introduced self-determination as a fundamental principle on which international society should rest by stating that it was the organisation's purpose to 'develop friendly relations among nations based on respect for the principle of equal rights and self-determination of peoples, and to take other appropriate measures to strengthen universal peace' (Art. 1(2)). However, it failed to define further the concept of self-determination. In addition to Art. 1 further links were made to human rights in Art. 55 and to decolonisation (Art. 73), which provided that 'self-government' in dependent countries should be developed and assisted. Following the anti-colonial movement in the 1950s, self-determination assumed not only an increased political importance but also a more distinct legal definition as its spectrum and application were elaborated in a number of resolutions. Resolution 1514 (XV), the 1960 *Declaration on Granting of Independence to Colonial Countries and Peoples*, made decolonisation an issue relevant for UN support and elevated self-determination to a right; according to Art. 2, 'all peoples have the right to self-determination; by virtue of that right they freely determine their political status and freely pursue their economic, social and cultural development'. Resolution 1541 (XV), issued later that year, stated that a non-self-governing territory under Chapter XI of the UN Charter can attain 'a full measure of self-government', which could be achieved either by the establishment of a sovereign and independent state, by the free association or integration with an independent state or by the emergence into any other freely determined political status. Despite these attempts at delineating and defining self-determination, the concept continued to be compromised by the use of the phrase 'peoples'. The concept of 'peoples' proved to be too vague as to find agreement in practice, and the question whether peoples referred to nations, states or any other group showed that further legal clarification was necessary to apply self-determination effectively.

The key problem associated with the term peoples could be found where states were multi-national. Applying 'peoples' and thus self-determination to groups within states meant to justify and legalise secession. As most countries carried within their territory several nations, the consequence of their exercise of self-determination, that is secession, would be infinite divisibility of existing states. Therefore, only groups possessing territory (in other words, states) were awarded the right to self-determination. Instead of a right to political self-determination, minorities were given only a right to cultural self-determination within the existing state (Rady 1996: 381). Resolution 1541 (XV) consequently emphasised that the right was only to be applied in the context of peoples fighting against a colonial government and to peoples subject to 'alien subjugation, domination and exploitation'. Similarly, the Human Rights Commission interpreted Art. 27, which granted members of ethnic, religious or linguistic minorities the right to enjoy their own culture, religion and use of their own language, as to be applicable to individuals of these groups only (Cassese 1995: 61). Self-determination was thus defined territorially rather than nationally. It was limited by and subordinated to the territorial integrity of the state, the preservation of peace and the prohibition of intervention as mentioned in the UN Charter. Resolution 1514 (XV) clearly stated that 'any attempt aimed at the partial or total disruption of the national unity and the territorial integrity of a country is incompatible with the purposes and principles of the Charter of the United Nations'. The exercise of secession by a group from an existing state, as envisioned by Lenin, was therefore ruled out.[13] Instead of secession, independence was the logical result of exercising the right to self-determination, as the subject that had the right to self-determination was defined as an entire population of a state or colonial territory.

Thus, as the international community tried to deal with the political situation and the conceptual-legal issues with which it was confronted, self-determination moved further away from its original philosophical meaning and became a concrete legal concept applicable in a specific context. In this process the idea of democracy and popular sovereignty increasingly diminished as external sovereignty and the territorial integrity of states were reaffirmed and strengthened. Again, the necessities for preventing conflict and chaos prevailed over democracy. Moreover, the gap between the idea and the possibilities of its application, between rhetoric and practice, widened while the legal codification cemented this gap. In this gap the possibility for internal self-determination existed only for racial and indigenous groups. Although this right was described as (and limited to) *participation* in government (Cassese 1995: 112,131), this had no bearing on the political make-up of the state in question, as in typical legal fashion participation was to be interpreted as *non-exclusion* from government.

When regional agreements such as the 1975 Conference on Security and Cooperation in Europe (CSCE) Helsinki Final Act suggested a move towards an emphasis on the internal dimension of self-determination, linking both internal and external self-determination, many legal commentators were hopeful about the prospects for a renewed interpretation of self-determination as democracy, that is, internal self-determination. Considering the continuity of the right ('when and as they wish') and the link between human rights and self-determination, Cassese (1995), for example, argued that self-determination in this context was explicitly anti-authoritarian, aiming at democracy. More recent developments suggest that the interpretation of self-determination had again taken a further turn away from or even against, democracy, discouraging states from adopting particular federal structures (Thornberry 1994). For example, the Badinter Commission, which was established to guide European Community policy on the recognition of the republics of Slovenia and Croatia in the Yugoslav conflict in the early 1990s, had to consider the preservation of the federal state or the republics. It concluded that the Yugoslav state was in a state of dissolution and that therefore the republics could be recognised as independent states (Radan 1997: 382). The Commission argued that the central power had ceased to function effectively and power had devolved to the subunits. The fact that power had not broken down but had devolved was a crucial element for the 'effective control'-test of state recognition (see Roth 2000: 137–142). Thus, the internal, federal borders had gained international status. As the Commission refused to recognise the validity of claims to self-determination outside the context of *uti possedetis* (the sanctity of state borders), those internal borders could be afforded protection according to international law (Radan 1997). The only concession the Commission made was to acknowledge a right to individual self-determination, leaving the choice of nationality to each individual (Rady 1996: 384). By applying the right to self-determination to the constituent units of a sovereign state, the Commission's decision thus undermined the territorial integrity of the state and especially those states based on federal structures (Thornberry 1994), a feature common to democratic states.

Human rights, the machinery for democracy

Self-determination, as has been shown, carried within it the key principle of democracy, that is, the idea of a right to chose one's own political destiny. Yet, UN practice based on international law so far has focussed on the external dimension of self-determination, primarily in a colonial context or cases of foreign military domination. This understanding gave ontological primacy to the state, focussing on the international position of the state in relation to other states. Internal self-determination, the right to chose one's own government through democratic process, was significantly absent in international law. Where internal self-determination had been recognised, as in the case of racial and indigenous groups, it had been severely limited in scope. Limiting self-determination to the colonial context and expressly excluding secession on the basis of minority rights thus did not restrict its fuzzy conceptual boundaries and its connection to democracy. In fact, the meaning of self-determination was further complicated by its indeterminate legal relationship to human rights. The 'inextricable link' between human rights and self-determination was central to the individualism of the Enlightenment and both marked the overlap of individual and national sovereignty (Williams 1999). Yet, with the increasing legalisation of concepts like self-determination, the concept of human rights, too, was questioned and subsequently bound in legal terms.

Human rights had been a key interest for the USA and its allies in the planning phase of the UN. Driven by the need to prevent a repetition of the horrors of Second World War and the Nazi regime, an international bill of rights for the protection of human rights had been the most widely promoted war aim of the USA (Russell 1958: 323). Roosevelt's *Four Freedoms* speech had outlined four essential freedoms: the freedom of speech and expression, the freedom of worship, the freedom from want and the freedom from fear. These were as much a guideline for US interests as the USA's own Bill of Rights, which declared that 'Governments exist for the benefit of the people and for the promotion of their common welfare in an interdependent world' (Russell 1958: 325). However, as the UN Charter did not mention democracy, so the 1948 Universal Declaration of Human Rights did not mention self-determination. As Morsink (1999) pointed out, the drafting process of the UDHR had left the final document without any mention of either the 'winning' ideology of the Second World War (democracy) or the losing one (fascism), creating an 'ideologically bare' document. This was as much a result of political-ideological problems of the immediate post-war period and the early Cold War, as a bargaining problem of the documents' drafting process.

Although the UDHR was restrained on the question of democracy, it provided the machinery for democracy. Direct references to democracy were made only in Art. 29(2) with regards to the limitations of rights and duties within 'democratic society' (Morsink 1999: 63). Overall, the UDHR sets out a number of civil and political rights, as well as cultural and social rights, of which Art. 21(2) most clearly emphasises the notion of popular sovereignty by guaranteeing that everyone has the right to participate in the government of his country, directly and through freely chosen representatives: 'The will of the people shall be the basis of the authority of governments; this will shall be expressed in periodic and genuine elections which shall be by universal and equal suffrage and shall be held by secret vote or by equivalent free voting procedures'. The principles set out in the UDHR were subsequently taken up and manifested as rights in the Covenants on Civil and Political Rights. In 1966, with the decolonisation movement at its height, the International Covenant on Civil and Political Rights (ICCPR) and International Covenant on Economic, Social and Cultural Rights (ICESCR), linked self-determination to human rights. Together with resolutions 1514 (XV) and 1541 (XV), they shared Art. 1, the application to colonial peoples only and a reference to 'all peoples'. In particular, the link to 'all peoples' had been interpreted by many authors as a transcendence of the colonial context. Yet, the principle of *uti possedetis* and the application of self-determination as a group right – the group being people of an already existing state – prevailed over individual human rights.

With the Cold War cementing the ideological divide between the liberal West and the communist East, and with the increasing membership of developing countries, political rights, as well as social and economic rights, were relegated to second place. Instead, civil rights were emphasised, including, for example, the freedom from racial discrimination, torture, forced disappearance, summary execution, and arbitrary detention. As Weiss et al. (1994) argued, these civil rights were essential to the protection of the right to life and personal integrity and could thus be seen as more fundamental than any other right. Liberalisation was thus regarded as more important than democratisation. As Third World problems such as development, poverty and disease dominated the UN agenda, the issue of human rights moved further towards socio-economic and cultural rights in the 1980s. These developments included regional human rights charters and, most importantly, indigenous rights. It was not until the 1990s that the human rights agenda expanded to integrate political, civil, social, cultural and economic rights. It is only through the debate concerning the 'right to democratic governance' that individual political rights such as the right to political participation and free elections had been revived and the right to self-determination interpreted to apply outside colonial situations, emphasising democratic legitimacy and autonomy beyond the group (Alston 2001).

Four decades of UN democracy ideas and practice

Between 1945 and 1988 democratic principles became in one way or other embedded in a number of UN practices. Following the goal to help states exercise 'self-determination' and to achieve 'self-government', the UN supported the decolonisation process through the monitoring of electoral processes. Authorised by the General Assembly, the Security Council or the Trusteeship Council, the UN conducted in total thirty missions monitoring plebiscites, referenda, elections and acts of self-determination between 1956 and 1988. The UN was active in both election and pre-election processes, yet at the same time sought to ensure that missions remained comparatively small with only approximately 30 observers present. While the scope and shape of the task of each UN mission differed considerably, the 'ultimate objective in all cases ... has been to ensure that the people make their choice and determine their future in complete freedom' (UNSG 19 November 1991, A/46/609). In other words, UN activity focussed on certifying 'correct' democratic practices. Until 1977, UN activity in national democratic practices through election monitoring was strictly limited to the decolonisation context. In 1977 the UN became involved in the voting process of a plebiscite in an independent, sovereign state for the first time. Invited by the government of the Republic of Panama, to

> see how the people of Panama freely decide whether or not they approve of the new [Panama Canal] treaties. [Panama hoped] that [the UN] representative will inform [the Secretary-General] and the international community of the freedom with which the Panamanians exercise their right to determine their destiny. (Beigbeder 1994: 150)

UN Secretary-General Kurt Waldheim sent a 'witnessing mission' to Panama without prior debate or approval by the General Assembly or the Security Council. This was despite the General Assembly being in session. As Beigbeder pointed out, the willingness and cooperation of both parties to the treaties in question, Panama and the USA, facilitated this unique practice. Beigbeder concluded that 'this small, discreet and successful "witnessing" operation created an informal precedent, a successful test-case' (Beigbeder 1994: 151).

The 1970s also saw the introduction of quasi-democratic elements through development practices. Participatory development strategies encouraged the involvement of those affected in the formulation and execution of development policies and projects. These strategies worked hand-in-hand with the contemporary focus in development policies that aimed at targeting development aid where underdevelopment was experienced – at the individual level. These new strategies moved away from a focus on economic aggregates towards human needs, concentrating on poverty reduction programmes and strategies to generate employment. This 'Basic Human Needs' approach advocated by a number of international organisations thus not only aimed to improve the grass-roots levels but also encouraged a form of 'self-determination' by giving people the opportunity to shape their lives more productively and to take part in the decisions and processes of implementing this change.

The philosophy of equity which permeated this 1970s approach also sought to integrate groups previously excluded from these processes, and in particular aimed at supporting the organisation of the poor and women to participate in the political process (Jolly et al. 2004).

Despite these 'appearances' of democracy in UN practice throughout these 40 years, in the first four decades of UN practice undoubtedly democracy existed under a veil. Democracy had been a central element for those who conceived of the new post-Second World War world order, be that academics or politicians. American presidents at the forefront of promoting democracy often led American public opinion into the international arena with democracy as a rallying cry, and so did the rest of the Western world when war had yet again engulfed the world. The call for 'making the world safe for democracy' could also have been 'making democracy safe for the world', to ensure that democracy would take a place in the new world order after the Second World War. However, pragmatism and the overarching goal of conflict prevention relegated democracy into second place while peace through cooperation as the minimum requirement for the new world order was maintained. Not only did the ideological conflict between East and West prevent democracy from developing any further than declaratory status, but even more so the legal and conceptual development of the ideas of self-determination and human rights, used as surrogates for democracy, made it even more difficult for supporters of democracy to press for their cause. Democracy, it seemed, needed to have an environment that was friendly for its achievement in the first instance. Thus, for many newly independent states the establishment of their full, equal sovereignty in an international system of states was more important before any consideration of democracy was made. Indeed, not many states who gained independence after Second World War became democracies or remained so. Democracy was thus marginalised as rhetoric.

The question of what constituted democracy in the eyes of the UN was irrelevant as a distinct UN democracy agenda did not exist, nor had the development of a democracy agenda been attempted beyond suggestions to include mention of it in charter provisions regarding membership. However, at this time a distinct face of democracy was shaped which demarcated an ideological ideal from which structural prescriptions could be deduced. As the analysis of liberal internationalist writing demonstrated, democracy not only became a 'good' with a teleological function for both economic development and the process of 'civilisation', but its close association with Western, that is European and North American, forms of democracy, supported a liberal vision of democracy. Hence, democracy here had to be understood as an ideological identifier rather than a distinct definition of, or structural prescription for, a particular polity. As the demise of colonial empires did away with the grand narrative of the civilising mission and the cultivation of the 'savage in nature', that is, colonial peoples (Salter 2002), the notion of civilisation served as a justificatory strategy for representatives of both liberal democracy and Soviet-style 'people's democracy'. However, the demise of the Soviet Union by no means signalled the end of civilising mission of democracy, or more generally, the association of the concept of civilisation with democracy. The rise of the Democratic Peace theory in the early 1990s signalled another variant of the civilising mission that implicitly borrowed on the UN membership debate of the early UN years. To be democratic was to be 'peace-loving'. If the UN was to fulfil its goal of creating and maintaining peace, democracy could be the solution. How the UN addressed this relationship and in which form will be addressed in the following chapter.

Notes

1 This did not apply to Class A mandates, which were seen as being close to full sovereignty.

2 As Art. 4 had become a major battle ground between East and West, effectively grinding the admissions process to a halt, the International Court of Justice had ruled that Art. 4 alone and no further interpretations or conditions were necessary for the admission of new members (Luard 1982: 63–65; Simma 2002: 179).

3 The origins of the term 'peace-loving' seem unclear; as Russell points out, it was added by the British to the 1943 Moscow Declaration to qualify the notion of 'sovereign equality' (Russell 1958: 134). Luard, however, insists that it was the Soviets who insisted on it in order to exclude the enemy states of the Second World War, Germany and Japan. This was despite the fact that it had already been mentioned in the 1941 Atlantic Charter in relation to the sovereignty of states (Luard 1982: 64).

4 As Dutt points out, classifications of 'peace-loving' and 'war-loving' are meaningless because instincts hardly ever cause war. At the same time, aggressors believe their cause to be right and thus to be justified in a war-like act (Dutt 1990). In this sense, peace-loving must be understood in a very loose sense of claims to adhere to principles set out in the UN Charter – sovereignty, non-intervention – while the existence of the system of collective security itself proves that the possibility of war exists and states may behave in a non-peace-loving way.

5 The 'United Nations' here refers to the Allies (the USA, Britain, the Soviet Union and other signatory states of the 1942 Declaration by UN), not the international organisation.

6 This also found its expression in the 'enemy clauses' of Art. 53 and 107 UN Charter (Luck 1999).

7 Bulgaria, Finland, Hungary, Italy and Romania were admitted in 1955 although the Allied had already declared that upon concluding peace treaties these 'recognised democracies' would be eligible for UN membership (Goodrich, Hambro and Simons 1969: 90).

8 Spain was a special case as both East and West agreed on the way to deal with 'enemies' in general and Spain in particular.

9 The General Assembly agreed to this wording on suggestion of the USA (Luard 1982: 237).

10 Russia initially insisted on having a vote for each of its republics, therefore Ukraine, like Belarus, was represented as an individual voice (see Luard 1982: 14).

11 This is in fact mirrored by several authors writing about and commenting on the UN Charter and its history, for example Kelsen (1951).

12 For example, the Security Council in its earlier years was ready to act against colonial conflicts based on the understanding that these formed 'threats to peace' and in so doing took sides with those in conflict against colonial powers (Luard 1989: 10).

13 Although secession is not an option, the partition of a country, as for example in Czechoslovakia, is possible. The difference between both concepts is a matter of degree and the line often blurred, as Heraclides (1991) points out. It can be found in the criteria of consent – partition refers to a mutual understanding of all groups involved to break up the existing state; secession, on the other hand, usually involves the (violent) struggle of one group against another (ruling) group which does not consent to partition.

4

Lifting the veil over democracy: elections

In the 1990s democracy gained an international dimension. Democracy became part of the UN agenda as the end of the Cold War promised not only an end to the stalemate between East and West at the UN, but also the possibility to pursue the liberal ideas which had underpinned the very idea of international organisation itself. Disregarding any explicit mention of democracy – indeed steering away from democracy – had served a vital political function during the Cold War, while interpreting principles such as self-determination in terms of sovereignty instead of democracy proved important for the identity construction of former colonies in the process of gaining independence. In the same vein, choosing peace over democracy served to reinforce sovereignty and possibly prevented the failure of the UN and its ideals as the Cold War heated up. Yet, with large scale international wars no longer the primary focus of international relations, and former colonial states now fully sovereign, that is, with the issues and problems that had prevented the emergence of democracy as an international norm in the first four decades of the UN diminished if not solved, the legal and political foundations of the international system were reinterpreted in order to achieve a democracy agenda.

The second vision of democracy – elections – which emerged in the late 1980s/early 1990s, not only describes a historically distinct phase of the creation and legitimisation of a 'new' UN idea (and agenda) which had hitherto been seen as too controversial, that is, too ideological to address, it also represents a particular institutional as well as ideological practice and understanding. To understand this meaning and the philosophical trajectory of this second vision of democracy, it is necessary to understand the dynamics of the agenda's creation, its place in the UN system as well as its application in the field. This chapter analyses the reason why and how democracy became defined by a limited, procedural definition. It traces the philosophical foundations of the new democracy agenda, as well as the political and social changes that provided the impetus for a new international dimension of democracy, which enabled the creation of a UN democracy agenda. Analysing democracy in relation to developments in the areas of human rights and peace shows how a move away from a technical, legal interpretation towards the liberal ideal of popular sovereignty served to create elections as a crucial link in the relationship between states and their people. Moreover, it highlighted the relationship between the people and the international community by raising questions of international assistance, if not intervention.

Foundations for democracy in a new world order

The political changes of the 1990s allowed the Western liberal agenda, including democracy and human rights, to flourish. This change, conventionally marked as 'the end of the Cold War', that is, the demise of the Soviet Union and the socialist project and the end of superpower confrontation, opened up a window for the creation of a UN democracy agenda. However, despite its significance the metaphor of the 'end of the Cold War' offers only a limited explanation for the emergence of the UN democracy agenda. It hides a more complex situation, the foundations of which have been laid in the 1980s by academia, development politics and the dynamics of the so-called Third Wave of democratisation (Huntington 1991). The 'end of the Cold War' suggests not only a discrete event, usually signified by the collapse of the Berlin Wall, but also implies a highly limited picture of power wielded by the USA and the West. In this picture the emergence of a democracy agenda may be seen as a demonstration of 'rationality' or way of 'seeing sense' on the part of non-democratic states to embrace democracy as the 'right' and only form of government – a Fukuyama-esque 'End of History' that marked the ideological victory of liberalism and its ultimate political expression, democracy (Fukuyama 1992). Instead, the foundations of democracy and the UN democracy agenda extend beyond such a simplistic view of 'liberal victory' and structural change. The mechanics of change that led to the UN democracy agenda are multifaceted, drawing their energy from a number of ideas, actors, events and processes. They are structural as well as philosophical, and they are at least in part mutually constituting and reinforcing each other.

First, while the practice of political conditionality in development aid and the pro-democratic rhetoric of the USA and Western Europe were renewed or intensified after the end of the Cold War, their influence would have been weaker if not for the increased strength of the movement of the 'Third Wave' of democratisation. Following Huntington's image of successive waves of democratisation, the democratisation process had now reached its third distinct stage. According to Huntington, the first wave of democratisation was a long period of nearly 100 years, lasting from 1828 to 1926, in which 33 states became democracies. This was a slow process that had its origins in the French and American Revolutions. Following waves, including reverse waves, were much shorter and an integral part of the history of the twentieth century. The first reverse wave between 1922 and 1942 occurred as a result of fascism and communism. The second wave from 1943 to 1963 was a result of democratic state-building by Allied administration after the Second World War as well as part and parcel of the process of decolonisation, while the second reverse wave from 1958 to 1975 signified a 'relapse' or exhaustion. According to Huntington, the Third

Wave started in 1974 with the end of the Portuguese dictatorship and included not only the fall of communism in Eastern Europe but also the re-democratisation in Southern Europe, Latin America and Asia. However, despite a rise in numbers, in 1990 democracies accounted for only 45% of all independent states, the same share as in 1922 (Huntington 1991: 26). This share only increased in the 1990s, finally leading to an 'international' dimension of democracy. This was further supported by the efforts of democratising states to find recognition for their progress. For example, at the first height of the Third Wave in 1988 and before the fall of the Berlin Wall, fifteen 'newly restored' democracies[1], or countries who had become democracies between 1973 and 1988, met in Manila at the invitation of the Philippine government, to share experiences and discuss the challenges they faced in their democratic development. Meeting again in Managua in 1994, in Bucharest in 1997, in Cotonou, Benin in 2000 and Ulan Bataar, Mongolia in 2003, these countries not only tabled the issue of democratisation at the UN but their support gave legitimacy to a UN agenda of democracy. Their support undermined potential questions about ideological hegemony of Western countries. Only with the support of these formerly non-democratic and largely developing states could the Western rhetoric of democracy become an *international* agenda of democracy.

The second significant impetus for the creation of a democracy agenda emerged out of development practice and research. The connection that was made between democracy and development was a direct outcome of the economic experiences of the 1980s, resulting in a review of the role of the state in development and its achievement of development goals. The neo-liberal, anti-statist policies of the Reagan–Thatcher era had resulted in what was commonly called a 'lost decade' for development. The mantra of free markets and individual enterprise had demanded a rolling back of the state in terms not only of economic intervention but also in welfare programmes – a strategy that had a severe impact on developing countries, in particular African states. Programmes such as the World Bank's Basic Needs approach were dropped and replaced by Structural Adjustment Programmes (SAPs), which forced aid recipients to adopt liberalisation measures (e.g. privatisation, currency devaluation, fiscal austerity, and deregulation) and to drop state supported development programmes such as food and health schemes, as well as education. Although positive results from SAPs could be found in Latin America, in Africa the implementation of SAPs led to a debt crisis, increased poverty and structural inequalities. Thus, for the Third World, especially the African state, the neo-liberal economic model proved to be highly inadequate. As Rapley (1996) noted, neo-liberalism not only failed to see the limits of liberal individualism and its rational actor model in the Third World market, it also ignored the structural differences between the economies of the First and the Third World. Most importantly, neo-liberals too readily accepted the resulting inequalities as an inevitable outcome of free market forces as a given, placing the responsibility for development outcomes on each individual. For the development community these results were unacceptable. With the IMF and the World Bank dominating development politics in the 1980s, it was UNICEF that in 1987 highlighted the need for 'Adjustment with a Human Face' (Cornia et al. 1987), placing human concerns squarely back at the centre of development. This turn towards human development led to the re-introduction of the state into development and a reconsideration of the relationship between democracy and economic development.

Whereas modernisation theory had placed democracy at the end of development, in the new development paradigm democracy was seen as a motor for development. For modernisation theory development was instrumental to the achievement of democracy. The more developed a state, the more likely democracy was to survive (Lipset 1959: 75). While modernisation theorists regarded authoritarian systems as an acceptable, if not inevitable, preliminary stage, they argued that democracy would sooner or later replace an authoritarian system as the state developed. They argued that authoritarian states would be better equipped to deal with the pressures of implementing development policies and pushing for radical changes, whereas democracies would face too much pressure from particular interests which inhibited change. In this view the question of economic development and democracy was thus a trade-off, a 'cruel dilemma' (Bhagwati 1995; Sen 1999a). In contrast to this, the new orthodoxy of the 1990s embraced democracy as compatible, even beneficial to development, although empirical evidence showed inconclusive if not negative results for this approach (Sirowy and Inkeles 1991). Leftwich, who built on the 'strong state' image of the previous developmental state discourse, asserted that sustained and strong economic growth would only be possible in 'democratic developmental' states, or as he called it, 'authoritarian democracies' (Leftwich 1996, 2000). This new form of the strong state in development, although built on a pluralist political environment with competent and relative autonomous state institutions, relied on a single dominant party and most of all on the relative repression of civil society and individual human rights. In marked contrast to both modernisation theorists and supporters of the strong state, Diamond found that *any* form of democracy was indeed compatible with development. He therefore concluded that 'in fact the causal trend *can* be reversed, with democracy leading to development' (Diamond 1992: 127).

Irrespective of the form democracy should take – explicitly developmental and quasi-authoritarian or fully democratic and free – proponents of democracy agreed on one crucial variable: sustained economic growth. Only with sustained economic growth would democracy in a developmental state be able to survive. This growth, however, could not simply be expressed in terms of GNP but had to include a general form of human development in which growth was spread across society, in order to sustain the legitimacy of the democratic state. For example, focussing on the socio-economic factors outlined by Lipset, Diamond (1992) showed that the application of the UNDP's Human Development Index (HDI) instead of GNP, resulted in a more profound relationship between democracy and development. He concluded that democracy could occur even at lower levels of economic development *if* it facilitated conditions such as universal literacy and autonomous private organisations. From this he followed that the implications were obvious: prioritising human needs was not only economically imperative but also 'intrinsically humane'; it was essential for democratic development and more (cost) effective than strategies which delayed human needs until democracy had been achieved.

A third strand supporting a new democracy agenda could be found in empirical research showing democracy to be beneficial for both international peace and the protection of human rights. Liberal internationalists had long claimed and promoted this relationship. However, this liberal internationalist philosophy was now supported by empirical findings to substantiate its claims. Researchers proved that the 'spirit' of democracy (in other words, the norms of the populace), as well as the distinct structures and processes of democracy, ensured that power, control and violence would not be used in an arbitrary way to achieve particular ends, be that internally or externally. Thus, the ideas which Kant and liberal internationalists like Wilson had promoted became empirical fact in the 1980s as Michael Doyle reinvigorated Kant's idea of Perpetual Peace, leading to a body of research that came to be known as 'the closest [there is] to an empirical law in international relations' (Levy 1988: 662). As the number of democratic countries increased, the Kantian First Definitive Article – 'The Civil Constitution of Every State Should Be Republican' – could now be subjected to a more meaningful historical analysis, and the conclusion was a positive one. Supporters of the Democratic Peace Theory showed that democracies did not go to war with each other. The reason for this was seen not only in the structural constraints decision-makers face (e.g. the separation of powers, multiple decision-making arenas and bureaucracies) when contemplating a decision to go to war, but also in the normative constraints of a populace which does not want to bear the burden of a war and may withdraw its support in elections (Doyle 1996). These findings proved so convincing that even the criticism levelled at the Democratic Peace Theory did not undermine the strength of its claims, which indeed became the strongest foundation of the UN democracy agenda.

Critics attacked the Democratic Peace Theory on methodological as well as historical grounds, questioning whether the states analysed had been democracies at the time, and pointing towards evidence which suggested that democracies did indeed go to war in the twentieth century. Instead, they suggested that peace between democracies was based on their territorial contiguity rather than on a shared political–philosophical base and that democracies do indeed wage war as much as non-democratic states (Layne 1994; Maoz and Russett 1992; Ray 1995; Schwartz and Skinner 2002). Proponents of the Democratic Peace Theory conceded that the Democratic Peace was indeed to be understood in relative terms. In other words, democratic peace would only be realised between democracies whereas relationships with non-democratic states remained war prone. This difference was seen to be based on an implicit understanding of similarity and difference in the use of violence. Politicians as well as the people understood other democratic states and their political culture as similarly peaceful and structurally constrained as themselves. Thus, the same peaceful conflict resolution methods used in domestic conflict situations were seen as adequate in relationships with democratic states, ruling out war as a last resort. At the same time, democratic leaders regarded the lack of these structural constraints in non-democratic states and cases of state violence used against citizens in non-democratic states as evidence that peaceful conflict resolution will ultimately be inadequate in dealing with non-democratic states (Doyle 1996; Huth and Allee 2002; Ray 1995; Russett 1993).

A similar positive relationship was established between democracy and human rights. Scholars analysing political repression found that the higher the level of democracy, the greater the level of human rights protection. This was independent of its historical duration. Again, the particular structures of a democratic polity and the constraints they place on decision-makers and those involved in the political process were found to prevent an unjustified and excessive use of violence. The possibility to be held accountable and to be removed from office would prevent leaders from either adopting repressive strategies or pushing citizens towards actions that would subsequently warrant the adoption of politically repressive strategies. At the same time, police and the military would be less likely to choose repressive measures as they would have less power over decision-makers. Moreover, it was expected they would have also been trained to use different measures of conflict resolution (Davenport 1999).

These empirical studies were complemented by philosophical and legal efforts to reconceptualise the relationship between democracy and human rights. These stressed that the connection between democracy and human rights was not limited to a better guarantee of human rights through democracy, but that human rights in fact underpin the democratic process. This suggested that if democracy was viewed not just through its practices and institutions but also through its principles, human rights would form the basis for citizens to exercise democracy (Beetham 1997). Indeed, the most significant re-interpretation of human rights in the early 1990s was Franck's equation of democracy as a right in the existing legal canon of human rights. Franck (1992) based this new right to democracy, or 'democratic entitlement', on the right to self-determination, the right to freedom of expression and the right to free and open elections. This further validated the connection between human rights and democracy (Crawford 2000a, 2000b; Fox 2000).

As a result, these new empirical findings significantly supported the change towards democracy as an international norm and UN practice as they turned the ideal of democracy into fact. The causal arrow no longer pointed towards a remote *telos* in which democracy would be a civilisational end-stage. In other words, democracy was no longer seen as a political order which would only come into existence after development had reached a certain stage, human rights had been fully implemented and observed, and peace established. Instead, it now pointed in multiple directions. This emphasised the mutuality of its dynamics with UN root ideas – peace, human rights and development. Democracy, peace, development and human rights were seen as 'interdependent and mutually reinforcing', connected by an 'indissoluble link'. The triangulation of democracy with these UN goals was crucial in creating a UN democracy agenda.

The path to the democracy agenda

The UN democracy agenda began to take shape in the late 1980s in the context of this new understanding of democracy and its benefits. The agenda took off in the mid-1990s with strong support from a number of recently democratised states. The backbone for the developing democracy agenda was the UN practice in decolonisation. Involvement in the process of decolonisation, of which election monitoring formed an essential part, had always been part of the UN's concern to ensure and promote peace. In accordance with Art. 2(4) of the UN Charter, decolonisation aimed 'to develop friendly relations among nations based on respect for the principle of equal rights and self-determination of peoples', while Art. 75 connected the aims of the Trusteeship System to develop self-government with the goal of furthering international peace and security. According to the founders of the UN, international peace would only be assured if people were free of external domination and oppression. Elections, plebiscites and referenda served as the means to ensure that the will of the people in a given territory was consulted concerning their political future. Once this will had been established, the people were regarded as self-determining and sovereign, and the UN trust administering powers would leave. The developing democracy agenda built on these democratic processes to create a UN democracy practice of election assistance.

The first indication of a future democracy agenda was to be found in the General Assembly's resolutions on *Enhancing the Effectiveness of the Principle of Periodic and Genuine Elections* that were issued annually between 1988 and 1994. The first 'Enhancing' resolution drew on the General Assembly's annual condemnation of racial discrimination and apartheid in South Africa. The 1988 resolution was innovative in that it connected a single cause of human rights violation to the general principle of democracy, emphasising that 'periodic and genuine elections are a necessary and indispensable element' for the protection of human rights. According to Beigbeder (1994), this allowed for an extension of democracy towards all members of the UN. The last two years of the 1980s thus witnessed a number of 'firsts' concerning both UN ideas and practices relating to democracy. First, the request to the Secretary-General in March 1989 by the Nicaraguan Minister of Foreign Affairs to carry out an election observation in order to verify that the Nicaraguan February 1990 elections would be 'genuine during every stage', constituted the first election observation in an independent state. Despite question marks about possible interference in national affairs, the operation found support through a previous Security Council resolution that had set out support for Central American governments to achieve regional peace. It was further supported by the fact that it was organised in cooperation with a regional organisation, the Organisation of American States (OAS), and as part of a wider peace and security plan. In contrast to normal practice, the Secretary-General established the mission himself as it was considered a technical operation, not a peace-keeping mission. Both the General Assembly and Security Council were informed later and consequently endorsed the mission *post facto*.

Despite this member-led demand for election assistance, the General Assembly took great care to emphasise that this mission did not set a precedent. Following this, another first was the observer mission in Namibia, established in March 1989, which saw the first integration of election activities – election supervision and control – in a larger, more extended peace-keeping mission. Thirdly, the UN operation in Haiti from November 1990 to January 1991 signalled another development. Neither part

1956	Togoland unification and future Togoland under British administration: plebiscite supervision
1958	Togoland under French administration: election supervision
1959	British Cameroon (northern part): plebiscite supervision
1961	British Cameroon (southern and northern parts): plebiscite supervision
1961	Western Samoa: plebiscite supervision
1961– 1962	Ruanda-Urundi: election supervision (including referendum on the Mwami)
1963	Malaysia: inquiry on future of Sabah and Sarawak prior to establishment of Federation of Malaysia
1965	Cook Islands: election supervision
1967	Aden: election supervision (mission was not permitted to achieve fulfilment of its mandate
1968	Equatorial Guinea: referendum/election supervision
1969	West Irian: act of self-determination
1970	Bahrain: ascertain wishes of people of Bahrain
1972	Papua New Guinea: election observation
1974	Niue: referendum observation
1974	Gilbert and Ellice Islands: referendum observation
1975	Mariana Islands, Trust Territory of the Pacific Islands: plebiscite observation
1977	French Somaliland: referendum/election observation
1978	Trust Territory of the Pacific Islands: referendum
1979	Marshall Islands, Trust Territory of the Pacific Islands: referendum
1979	Palau, Trust Territory of the Pacific Islands: referendum
1979	New Hebrides: election observation
1980	Turks and Caicos Islands: election observation
1983	Palau, Trust Territory of the Pacific Islands: plebiscite observation
1983	Federated States of Micronesia, Trust Territory of the Pacific Islands: plebiscite observation
1983	Marshall Islands, Trust Territory of the Pacific Islands: plebiscite observation
1984	Cocos (Keeling) Islands: act of self-determination
1986	Palau, Trust Territory of the Pacific Islands: plebiscite observation (February and December)
1989	Namibia: election supervision and control
1990	Palau, Trust Territory of the Pacific Islands: plebiscite observation

Figure 4.1   *Plebiscites, referenda and elections held under the supervision or observation of the UN in trust and non-self-governing territories*

of a larger, multilateral peace process like the Nicaraguan operation, nor a decolonisation process like the Namibian mission, nor indeed related to issues of international peace and security, the goals of the Haitian operation were the consolidation of Haiti's democratic institutions through the provision of electoral assistance and training, election observation and verification, and assistance in maintaining public security (Beigbeder 1994).

In light of the changing attitude towards democracy, as well as the UN's early experiences in election assistance, the General Assembly subsequently developed its position on the importance of elections and requested the Secretary-General in February 1991 to report on measures undertaken by the UN so far and how the practice of election monitoring could be improved (UNGA 21 February 1990, A/RES/45/150). Secretary-General Perez de Cuellar reported subsequently under an item of 'Human Rights Questions' how the UN had so far engaged in election support and which UN bodies had been involved in these activities (UNSG 19 November 1991, A/46/609). Perez de Cuellar showed that, based on decolonisation practices, the UN had taken part in two acts of self-determination, seven referenda observations, ten election supervisions and thirteen plebiscite supervisions between 1956 and 1990 (see Figure 4.1). The two forms of assistance available were, broadly speaking, election verification and election assistance. The former consisted of the adjudication or certification of the election processes and its results; the latter entailed technical support to enable the conduct of 'proper' elections. Secretary-General Perez de Cuellar emphasised that the key objective of UN involvement should be to ensure that the people could make their choice and determine their future freely, clearly recalling the principles of self-determination in decolonisation practices. Perez de Cuellar noted that the presence of the UN should thus increase the confidence in the electoral process. Despite this strong emphasis on the electoral process, the Secretary-General also hinted that democracy goes well beyond the simple act of elections, and included all forms of participation in political life. The report showed that election monitoring and election assistance was a system-wide endeavour with some organisations, like UNDP, having undertaken similar activities since 1976. To reflect the growing organisational involvement, the report also called for the establishment of a Focal Point, and a unit to deal with these activities.

The first report by the Secretary-General remained rudimentary, showing the limited experience both in ideas and practices so far. It also demonstrated the role which the out-going Secretary-General Javier Perez de Cuellar played in the creation of the UN democracy agenda. Issues of conflict and security in the Cold War world dominated Perez de Cuellar's term in office. While he may have made tentative steps towards envisioning democracy, his understanding of the place and shape of democracy within the normative and operational framework of the UN was a continuation of the ideas prominent in the Cold War context. In his memoirs, Perez de Cuellar wrote:

> As the great global confrontation between East and West – between communism and democracy – diminished, the problems that must be dealt with in the new era emerged with sometimes daunting clarity. These are the problems inherent in the triangular relationship among development, freedom (democracy) and peace. The three are interdependent. If the United Nations is to lead in the pursuit of peace, it also must be able to promote the growth of democratic societies and encourage the

development of economic well-being on which both democratic governance and peace ultimately depend. At the end of my second term as Secretary-General, this is what I saw as the major challenge facing national governments and the United Nations. (Perez de Cuellar 1997: 18)

While he may have presaged the debate concerning the relationship between governance, economic development, peace and democracy, it is clear that he continued to equate democracy with freedom. This shows an understanding of democracy that is primarily in opposition to non-democratic, controlled communist states. With this, Javier Perez de Cuellar maintained democracy's character as an ideological identifier, which had so far undermined the idea's potential for success as an agenda. The task to re-envision democracy as a UN practice in the post-Cold War world then fell to Boutros Boutros-Ghali, who assumed office in January 1992.

Boutros-Ghali followed Javier Perez de Cuellar's report nearly two years later with his own report in which he showed that considerable changes and adjustments had been made to enhance UN capacity to address election monitoring requests. New developments included a Trust Fund for Electoral Observation and an Electoral Assistance Unit in the Department for Political Affairs, established in 1992, with the Under-Secretary-General for Political Affairs serving as Focal Point. A roster of experts had been created as well as mechanisms for institutional memory (UNSG 18 November 1993, A/58/590). These early activities in support of democracy through election assistance remained uncoordinated, that is, not supported by and anchored within a broader strategy. Moreover, they were only cautiously welcomed by the General Assembly, which was reflected in the Secretary-General's repeated insistence on the principles of sovereignty and non-interference. The activities were explicitly connected to the UN mandate in observing plebiscites in the process of decolonisation. At the same time they were regarded as a temporary measure. Thus, resolutions by the General Assembly stressed the importance of sovereignty on a regular basis, while the 1993 resolution 47/130 emphasised a limited time frame of two years in which the Secretary-General was to engage the UN in election activities. Considering these limitations it needed the active support by non-Western states to provide the necessary impetus for the creation of a democracy agenda. This push and support came in 1994 from the Second International Conference of New and Restored Democracies, held in Managua, Nicaragua, on 4–6 July 1994.

Although the declaration of the fifteen 'newly restored' democracies who met in Manila in 1988 had been transmitted to the UN Secretary-General, the UN took no further action at the time. In the Manila Declaration, the participating countries reaffirmed the 'indissoluble link between peace, democracy and development' and stressed their commitment to democracy, the legitimacy and 'moral superiority' of power derived from popular will. Declaring this commitment, they also reached out to 'older democracies' and 'advanced economies' to support their efforts in consolidating their democracies. This support, the declaration stressed, should address two points of fragility in transition countries. First, recognising the obstacles to democratic stability formed by socio-economic underdevelopment, the conference participants asked for the removal of protectionist measures and for the introduction of debt servicing mechanisms that would be compatible with development. Secondly, they highlighted the internal dangers posed by terrorism and external interference as potential factors of instability affecting the process of democratisation, again requesting assistance and understanding for the intricacies of the democratisation process (UNGA 16 August 1988, A/43/538).[2] However, while the General Assembly and the Secretary-General welcomed the efforts of the conference, it was only after the Managua conference that the proposals of the Plan of Action led the General Assembly to include a permanent item concerning democracy on its agenda, and to encourage the Secretary-General to consider how support for countries in the process of democratisation could be shaped (UNGA 22 December 1994, A/RES/49/30).

In meeting the challenges of the post-Cold War world, UN assistance increased and the democracy assistance increasingly reflected the variety of circumstances in which it was applied. By 1994 the number of election assistance activities had increased to over 60. Consequently, the 1994 report on *Enhancing the Effectiveness of the Principle of Periodic and Genuine Elections* presented a much more refined picture of UN election support activities than previous reports. Now the Secretary-General distinguished between seven basic types of assistance with considerable variations in terms of time limit, commitment to financial investment, degree of intrusion in national structures, and balance between political and technical elements:

1. *Organisation and conduct of elections.* These were the most complex missions, requiring a long lead time and high investment. This form of support required a Security Council mandate (e.g. Cambodia).
2. *Supervision of an election process.* These missions included the certification of all stages of the process. They were usually deployed in decolonisation processes or as part of peace-keeping operation. Supervision missions were long term and required both a high investment and a Security Council mandate (e.g. Namibia).
3. *Verification of election process.* In these missions, the UN verified that elections undertaken by national bodies had been conducted freely and fairly. These missions needed a Security Council mandate as they were usually part of a peace-keeping mission (e.g. Angola, El Salvador, Haiti, Nicaragua, Mozambique, South Africa).
4. *Coordination and support for international observers.* These missions did not need a Security Council mandate as they were primarily technical operations based on a short term, low cost framework.
5. *Support for national observers.* Again, this needed no mandate, although this technical operation format had a long term capacity orientation.
6. *Observation.* The smallest in scope, this form of activity was based on a single UN representative compiling an internal report to the Secretary-General. Its limited scope led to questions regarding its viability and its limitations.
7. *Technical assistance.* The most frequently requested support, usually employed as part of a larger mission or individually.

The 1994 report also added an eighth form of assistance, which the General Assembly had recommended a few months earlier – post-election assistance to support the success of democratisation processes. The report thus reflected the changing context in which it was conceived, and a new perspective which Secretary-General Boutros-Ghali had introduced, which will be further shown below. The report, however, remained vague as to how the task of post-election assistance should be fulfilled and merely pointed to the existing activities of other UN agencies such as UNDP or the Centre for Human Rights (UNSG 17 November 1994, A/49/675, annex III). An accommodation of organisational structures reflected these changes, yet also showed the uncertainty in the 'proper' contextualisation of democracy. For example, the Electoral Assistance Unit was renamed Electoral Assistance Division in 1994 and moved from the Department of Political Affairs to the Department of Peace-keeping of Under-Secretary-General for Peace-keeping Kofi Annan. This was to reflect the growing use of election monitoring as part of peace-keeping missions. However, the Unit was moved back to the Department of Political Affairs only in 1995 when this type of large-scale mission appeared to decline in numbers (UNSG 8 November 1995, A/50/736). Despite such uncertainties about the nature of election support practices and a clearly evolving organisational dimension, the extension of election assistance beyond the event of elections signalled the institutionalisation of a democracy agenda.

Democratic legitimacy, sovereignty and human rights

If the international community and the UN were to be able to make qualitative judgements about member states' rule by supporting democracy, then an answer to the question of what constitutes legitimate or 'good' political rule was key to creating a democracy agenda and, moreover, to locating democracy within the normative framework of the UN and international law. Thus, the first step towards creating a democracy agenda was by necessity a reconsideration of the principles of sovereignty and its corollary, non-intervention. In 1945, when negotiating the UN Charter, and again in the 1960s when dealing with the process of decolonisation, sovereignty had prevailed over democracy. Choosing peace over democracy in 1945, the international community had realised the potential for ideological conflict inherent in recognising a term that had essentially come to denote Western liberal democracy instead of communist people's democracy. Again, when in 1960 the process of decolonisation was cast in legal terms, sovereignty prevailed. Formulating an international legal norm of self-determination as an expression of freedom from foreign rule and outside intervention instead of an expression of democracy, meant that sovereignty restricted the idea of democracy. This assertion of sovereignty and non-intervention was reinforced by the recognition of existing borders as well as the denial of minority group rights. Reasserting sovereignty and non-intervention in the 1960s, and denying the possibility of a qualitative judgement of member states, the existence of democracy as an ideal had thus reinforced UN neutrality, its role as an arbiter and provider of assistance rather than an ideologically independent actor. In the new political context of the early 1990s the UN General Assembly and the Secretary-General dealt with the question in similar uneasy ways, torn between embracing the qualitative norm of democracy and reasserting the neutral criteria of sovereignty. The importance of democracy was not discounted but translating this importance into policy proved to be difficult. The strategies to solve this contradiction with positive results for the idea of democracy drew on a new understanding of sovereignty as popular sovereignty, as well as a reconceptualisation of governmental legitimacy and human rights.

Central to the development of the democracy agenda was the reinterpretation of sovereignty as popular sovereignty based on the reinterpretation of the concepts and terms such as 'we the peoples', self-determination and human rights. A reinterpretation was made in favour of their philosophical meaning rather than their legal manifestation. This was based on an imagined consensus. It was imagined in that this consensus did not factually exist because deliberate decisions against such interpretation had been taken in the process of writing the UN Charter. Yet, legal scholars such as Franck (1992) supported this reinterpretation by claiming that the increasing practice of election monitoring confirmed the emergence of a 'democratic entitlement' or right to democracy. In other words, Franck squared a circle by stating that what was meant to be reinterpreted in order to justify a practice relied on the existence of said practice. Thus, the existence of a right to democracy was justified through its observation.

The foundation for this new custom was found in the opening words of the UN Charter, which, it was suggested, supported the idea of legitimacy through the people. Moreover, the accepted principle of self-determination and the practice of plebiscites in relation to self-determination, various human rights such as the right to freedom of expression and the right to free and open elections, and indeed the General Assembly's own resolution on *Enhancing the Effectiveness of the Principle of Periodic and Genuine Elections*, were seen as evidence of the right to democracy (Crawford 2000a, 2000b; Fox 2000; Franck 1992). In other words, proponents of the right to democracy claimed that custom had created a new legal fact. Franck also claimed that the presence of a right to democracy was supported by an increased rhetoric of governments to justify the validity of their rule according to such a newly emerging global standard.[3] Governments, in particular those threatened internally, increasingly sought validation for their rule. To do so they drew on democracy to provide evidence of legitimacy. Therefore, Franck argued, the legitimacy of governments and the legitimacy of international rules to validate governance increasingly converged. Legitimacy, when achieved through electoral validation, was crucial as 'in the legitimacy of national government resides the legitimacy of the international regime' (Franck 1992: 91). In other words, the

> capacity of the international community to extend legitimacy to national governments ... depends not only on its capacity to monitor elections or to recognize the credentials of a regime's delegates to the UN General Assembly, but also on the extent to which such international activity has evolved from the ad hoc to the normative: that is, the degree to which the process of legitimation itself has become legitimate. (Franck 1992: 51)

With this, Franck extended his initial claim for legitimacy, denouncing the entire international system as illegitimate if based on non-democratic rule, thereby increasing the pressure to democratise. Franck thus argued that as international law had achieved a certain level of maturity, a new discourse of effectiveness and fairness needed to be opened, both on a procedural (right process) and substantive (distributive justice) level, to determine the legitimacy of rules. The 'democratic entitlement' constituted this fairness to persons, as elections were the key instrument for the validation of governments and their rule (Franck 1995). This was echoed by Boutros-Ghali, who in a lecture in 1993 conceded that the principle of democracy is the 'most modern aspect of the nation', explaining that

> with the legitimacy conferred by history, and a common purpose, the nation provides a structure more favourable to democratic participation than a world Government could ever be. The second fundamental [principle of the international system] then is democratization. (Boutros-Ghali 2003b: 665–666)

The evolution and active promotion of the UN democracy agenda, as well as member states' acceptance of democratic principles as universally recognised values was linked to the slow progress of the UN human rights programme. Resolutions such as the 1992 *Declaration on the Rights of Persons Belonging to National or Ethnic, Religious or Linguistic Minorities* similarly stressed the relationship between democracy and human rights, encouraging states to accommodate the diversity of multiple ethnic groups through *democratic* governance. The resolution emphasised the functional dimension of democracy, that is, its role in preventing conflict. According to Singh (2000) the resolution therefore viewed democracy as 'pragmatism in the face of challenging relationships between different people'. Because conflict is often inherent in the discrimination of minority groups as well as in attempts at their assimilation, the declaration not only assumed diversity to be a given but also assumes that 'the intellectual and political pluralism inherent in democracy goes against the assimilationist logic of the nation-State' (Singh 2000). By linking peace and conflict to questions of human rights, the nature of democracy as a mediating force only gained in importance. The conceptual and empirical linkages worked both ways and in making these linkages an ever tighter net of importance, relevance and necessity was woven.

The 1993 Vienna World Conference on Human Rights' embrace of the interdependence and mutual reinforcement of democracy, respect for human rights and development, provided an important platform for further development and integration of democracy in other areas of UN activity. At Vienna representatives called for national and international actions to promote all three. In his conference opening statement Boutros-Ghali emphasised that

> only democracy, within States and within the community of States, can truly guarantee human rights. It is through democracy that individual rights and collective rights, the rights of peoples and the rights of persons, are reconciled. It is through democracy that the rights of States and rights of the community of States are reconciled. (Boutros-Ghali 2003g)

Thus, the consideration given to human rights reflects the level of democracy in political regimes, which could be seen in the evolving language and discourse at the UN, for example, in the changing notation of the UN Yearbook. The Yearbook reflected these developments by describing the right to democracy, or the individual rights it subsumed, in increasingly specific terms. While Yearbooks before 1988 did not include references to democracy or democratic rights, the 1988 Yearbook introduced under the heading '*Protection* of Human Rights – Civil and Political Rights' items including 'Electoral Processes'[4], which was changed to '*Advancement* of Human Rights – Electoral Processes' in 1993, demonstrating an increased sense for positive protection based on active promotion. By 1995 this had changed to 'Democratic Processes' and was finally named 'Right to Democracy' in 1999, which included the key civil and political rights outlined in the International Covenant on Civil and Political Rights (ICCPR).

This reinterpretation of sovereignty in favour of democracy, a new understanding of legitimacy and the growing importance of human rights was part and parcel of a wider debate concerning Art. 2(7) UN Charter. The questions of intervention and the accountability of war criminals and heads of states (Ratner 2000) became more contentious and were vigorously debated, with the role of individuals and 'the people' central to the conclusion of this debate. As sovereignty became popular, in other words was seen to rely on the will of the people, the question of what to do when this connection broke down and people were ruled without their consent connected smoothly with the problem of (gross) human rights violations, which were increasingly seen to make international intervention logically viable. Indeed, as Boutros-Ghali argued in his Agenda for Peace, 'the time of absolute and exclusive sovereignty … has passed' (Boutros-Ghali 1992, para. 17). While the absence of democracy was not necessarily seen as sufficient for intervention, the disruption of democracy, as for example in Haiti, became seen as a credible threat to peace upon which the Security Council could act – provided that mass killings and refugee

---

- Rights to freedom of opinion and expression
- Rights to freedom of thought, conscience and religion
- Right to peaceful association and assembly
- Right to freedom to seek, receive and impart information and ideas through any media
- Rule of law
- Right to universal and equal suffrage
- Right of political participation
- Transparent and accountable government institutions
- Right of citizens to choose their governmental system through constitutional or other democratic means
- Right to equal access to public service in one's country.

Figure 4.2   *Right to democracy/rights to democratic governance*

flows added to the threat of peace (Byers and Chesterman 2000: 283, 284–288). Thus, while democracy could not directly lead to intervention, it became another element for consideration in the question of intervention. Although this type of pro-democratic intervention had been limited, the growing acceptance and endorsement of limitations to state sovereignty in the case of human rights violations opened up further opportunities to develop the idea and practice of democracy.

While the case of the pro-democracy intervention in Haiti remained an historical exception, democracy was increasingly regarded as necessary to judge the legitimacy of political rule. Hence Secretary-General Boutros-Ghali stated that 'the only legitimate source of authority lies in the people. And the only legitimate way for people to exercise their authority is democracy' (Boutros-Ghali 2003c: 1305). The application of this was, however, inconsistent. The UN Credential Committee may have started to use democracy as a guiding principle for decisions to accredit government representatives at the UN; however, it did not adopt this strategy as a rule. While the test of effective control had been consistently applied since 1945, in the 1990s it no longer played a role where the government in question had assumed power through a UN supervised election as in Cambodia, for example (Griffin 2000: 742). Analysing the committee's decision, Griffin demonstrated that between 1991 and 1999 five governments were accredited despite lack of effective territorial control when elections had taken place. Thus, democracy 'established' through UN election assistance became a stamp of approval, whether the democracy in question had been consolidated or not.

Despite the growing acceptance of democracy and the wide use of election support in several areas of UN activity, the General Assembly was uneasy about its own courage to embrace this change in ideology. Regardless of the spread of democratisation, if half of all states had become democratic or were ready to accept democracy, the other half was not. At the same time, fear of Western dominance and usurpation of indigenous processes resulted in hesitant action. After all, the possibility of specific cultural interpretations could not be ruled out, as protest by those who saw primary value in the community rather than the individual demonstrated. This hesitation resulted in a schizophrenic approach in which rival, contradictory and thus (seemingly) superfluous resolutions were issued soon after each other. For example, 'Enhancing' resolutions emphasised the importance of human rights documents and their affirmation of the individual's right to participation in its state's political affairs and stressed the General Assembly's conviction

> that periodic and genuine elections are a *necessary and indispensable* element of sustained efforts to protect the rights and interests of the governed and that, as a matter of practical experience, the right of everyone to take part in the government of his or her country is a crucial factor in the effective enjoyment by all of a wide range of other human rights and fundamental freedoms. (UNGA 8 December 1988, A/RES/43/157, para. 2, emphasis added)

At the same time, the General Assembly hastened to pass resolutions in *Respect for the principles of national sovereignty and non-interference in the internal affairs of states in their electoral processes*, occasionally only days apart from resolutions in support of elections.[5] Here, the General Assembly emphasised that states should refrain from interfering in the free development of election processes of other states and from providing financial or other support to political parties or groups. Most importantly, it stressed that the choice of electoral institutions and processes lies solely with the people as there is 'no single political system or single model for electoral processes equally suited to all nations and their peoples, and that political systems and electoral processes are subject to historical, political, cultural and religious factors' (UNGA 18 December 1990, A/RES/45/150). This initial hesitation led the General Assembly to emphasise that UN activity in election monitoring was to be limited, and indeed, to declare in February 1993 that further activities should be seen as 'provisional for the next two years' (UNGA 22 February 1993, A/RES/47/130).

These insecurities concerning democracy's place in the UN framework was mirrored by Secretary-General Boutros-Ghali's simultaneous promotion of democracy and his repeated reassurances that democracy, or a specific model of democracy, could not be imposed by the UN but that democracy was instead 'a goal to be achieved by all people'. Speaking frankly, he stated at the 1993 Vienna World Conference on Human Rights:

> When, like so many others before me, I stress the imperative of democratization, I do not mean that some State should imitate others slavishly, nor do I expect them to borrow political systems that are alien to them, much less try to gratify certain Western States – in fact, just the opposite. Let us state, forcefully, that democracy is the private domain of no one. It can and ought to be assimilated by all cultures. It can take many forms in order to accommodate local realities more effectively. Democracy is not a model to copy from certain States, but a goal to be achieved by all peoples! It is the political expression of our common heritage. It is something to be shared by all. Thus, like human rights, democracy has a universal dimension. (Boutros-Ghali 2003d: 681)

These retractions often appeared circular. For example, Boutros-Ghali recognised the growing importance of human rights to judge governmental legitimacy, thereby highlighting the permeability of sovereignty and the principle of non-intervention. Yet, he argued that this should be seen as a call for international co-operation rather than intervention. Ultimately, the state should be the best guarantor of human rights (Boutros-Ghali 2003d: 678). These early insecurities in locating (and accepting) democracy, as well as any suspicions regarding UN activity in election assistance, faded away as the democracy agenda developed through the integration with a variety of UN practices but in particular peace-related activities.

Democracy, peace and a new agenda for conflict management

As Boutros-Ghali assumed office in 1992, one of his first tasks was to revisit and revise the organisation's framework for conflict management to address the changing political landscape which was characterised by a decline of international conflict and a rise of intra-state conflict. Since 1988, six peace-keeping missions had been established which addressed national issues, primarily involving transition periods such as in Angola, Namibia, Nicaragua and El Salvador, or more traditional decolonisation issues such as in the Western Sahara. Encouraged by the success of intervention against the Iraqi invasion of Kuwait, the international community sought solutions to the developing atrocities in the civil wars of Yugoslavia and Somalia. Part of this solution was the reconfiguration of existing conflict management tools such as peace-keeping. Thus, in his *An Agenda for Peace*, issued in June 1992, Boutros-Ghali acknowledged the unique changes that the Third Wave of democratisation had brought about, highlighting new forms of insecurity, primarily non-military in nature, and the demise of absolute sovereignty. Key to this agenda was his framework of UN practice conceptualised as a cycle of UN intervention that mirrored the different stages of conflict. In this, traditional peace-keeping formed but one tool to be utilised in these new conflicts. In *An Agenda for Peace*, democracy assumed a key place and function. Democracy, Boutros-Ghali stressed, was needed to address the new non-military security issues as it promised political, economic and social stability. Addressing the underlying causes of conflicts was thus essential to their solution. Democracy would function as the institutional framework through which grievances that would otherwise lead to conflict could be mediated.

This new framework then saw the democratic institutional framework at the juncture between the prevention of conflicts and post-conflict peace-building. Although primarily part of the last stage of Boutros-Ghali's conflict cycle, post-conflict peace-building – including the promotion and institutionalisation of democracy – would also function as a preventive measure. From this Boutros-Ghali deduced a 'duty' for the UN to assist member states in their democratisation efforts in order to achieve international peace (Boutros-Ghali 1992, para. 81). This support would include assistance in the transformation of 'deficient' national structures and capabilities, and the strengthening of democratic structures (Boutros-Ghali 1992, para. 59), next to more general post-conflict peace-building measures such as the disarmament of parties to a conflict, the restoration of law and order, the repatriation of refugees and the protection of human rights. Crucially, however, elections and election monitoring were used to enhance the promotion of all 'formal and informal processes of political participation' in order to facilitate a solution to conflict (Boutros-Ghali 1992, para. 55). The integration of democracy into existing UN practices and its actual implementation in member states was therefore most easily achieved through peace-related activities. By connecting democracy to peace and peace practices, the new agenda delved deep into the key principles and root ideas of the organisation. The changing political context which required new, innovative ways of dealing with increasingly localised and complex wars, as well as organised violence, provided a framework for democracy to be utilised and institutionalised.

Despite strong Kantian notions of democratic peace in the philosophical underpinnings of the UN, the concepts and ideas of the Democratic Peace Theory had found very little explicit expression in the discussion leading to the creation of the UN, nor in its texts. The only attempt to recognise the importance of this connection had been made in the 1945 constitution of the United Nations Educational, Scientific and Cultural Organisation (UNESCO). UNESCO, dedicated to facilitating and enhancing mutual knowledge and understanding of peoples through collaboration in 'intellectual enterprises', emphasised that the 'great and terrible war [the Second World War] was … made possible by the denial of the democratic principles of the dignity, equality and mutual respect of men'[6]. In other words, the absence of democracy, in particular the refusal to adhere to such abstract principles as dignity, equality and respect, had been regarded as a key element in the descent into war so shortly after the First World War. Although UNESCO described these as 'democratic principles', they could also be seen as fundamentals of all human rights. However implicit, this recognised that where people were ruled by authoritarian leaders and therefore had not been given the opportunity to voice their opinion and especially their dissent, war could be used as a political tool to conduct politics and settle scores. This in turn presupposed, as the theory of Democratic Peace had stressed, that the people are seen as fundamentally peaceful. Hence, despite its brevity and vagueness, this statement in UNESCO's constitution manifested a causal relationship between peace and democracy (Dutt 1990).

The move in the 1990s to integrate democracy into an already existing peace agenda built on this philosophy. Hence Secretary-General Boutros-Ghali stressed that

> the promotion of democracy is both an end in itself and part of the responsibility of the United Nations to maintain international peace and security. It should be pursued for its own sake, and also because it is one of the pillars on which a more peaceful, more equitable, and more secure world can be built. (Boutros-Ghali 1995: 3)

At times more or less explicit, Boutros-Ghali emphasised that democracies are more peaceful than non-democratic states, stressing either that 'democracies never fight each other' (Boutros-Ghali 1993) or that 'governments which are responsive and accountable are likely to be stable and to promote peace' (Boutros-Ghali 2003a: 540). More than just holding war-prone leaders to account, democracy was intimately linked with the processes and results of development, which in turn ensured peace. Without democracy there could be no development and therefore no peace. More explicitly outlining the potential dangers, Secretary-General Boutros-Ghali further stated that 'unless democracy takes root, violence, coups d'état, wars, and general instability will recur' (Boutros-Ghali 2003f: 386).

Although the Secretary-General had warned in his acceptance speech that despite its obvious benefits for peace, human rights and development, democracy was neither a 'magic potion' which cures all problems, nor would it justify intervention, this voice of caution soon subsided in the light of the challenges confronting the UN to which he sought solutions. Boutros-Ghali soon stressed that democracy was a 'newly recognised imperative' (Boutros-Ghali 1995), following the strong link between democracy and peace. With this he established the authority for the UN to assume an active role in democratisation. This UN authority was based on the assumption that if democratic states do not go to war with each other, the democratisation of states would facilitate international peace. In doing so, the logic of early liberal internationalists was inverted and democracy was no longer seen as an end in itself but as a means to bring about the desired end (Bellamy et al. 2004; Goldmann 1994). Thus, democracy would become the condition for peace, and would no longer be solely the result of it. This then created the possibility, if not the imperative, for the UN to promote democracy as an official UN practice. With this Boutros-Ghali had integrated the idea of democracy into existing practices while legitimising it through new tasks and changes in those practices. Thus, elections and election monitoring increasingly became an integral part of peace-keeping missions and the political settlements underlying them.[7]

In light of this changed understanding and in response to the Managua Declaration of the Second International Conference of New and Restored Democracies in December 1994, the General Assembly encouraged the Secretary-General to evaluate possibilities for the UN to support member states in their democratisation efforts. The Secretary-General's response led to the institutionalisation of the annual report on *Support by the United Nations System of the Efforts of Governments to Promote and Consolidate New and Restored Democracies* providing a vehicle with which to conceptualise democracy. Following the logic of the Democratic Peace Theory, Boutros-Ghali echoed a consensus among Western politicians, in particular in the USA and the UK who had readily adopted the idea that democracy would support or lead peace and had begun to implement policies of conditionality, which tried to force or cajole trading partners and aid recipients to become democratic. Although the Secretary-General's use of Democratic Peace ideas suggested an interaction and movement of ideas between academic and political discourse, Schwartz and Skinner (2002: 172) highlight that both politicians and the UN Secretary-General used the theory of Democratic Peace simplistically, primarily distinguishing between democracy as 'good government' and non-democracies as 'bad government'. In doing so they did not take into account qualifications of the theory, which stated that it was 'liberal', 'mature' or 'established' democracies that were less war prone. However, in the political context and discourse of the early 1990s, enthusiasm for the potential of a tool that not only promised to deal with, if not eliminate conflict, and assist development while ensuring human rights, facilitated such generalisations.

Election assistance in practice

A rise in conflicts between 1988 and 1994 meant that the number of peace-keeping operations jumped from five missions before January 1988 to eleven in January 1992, and seventeen in December 1994 (UNSG 25 January 1995, A/50/60-S/1995/1, para. 4). Elections and election assistance became an increasingly necessary and important part of mission mandates. In a world of sovereign states and within the confines of limited resources, election assistance promised much. In general the missions in Namibia (UNTAG 1989–1990) and El Salvador (ONUSAL 1991–1995) were seen as successes, leading to stable, conflict-free states which were both rated by Freedom

House as 'free' in 2004, with a measure of 2 for political rights and 3 for civil liberties respectively. On the other hand, missions in Haiti (ONUVEH and UNMIH 1990–1996) and Angola (UNAVEM I + II 1988–1991 and 1991–1995) were regarded as failures, and in 2004 Freedom House rated both as 'not free', measuring Haiti 6 on both political rights and civil liberties, and Angola 6 and 5 respectively (Freedom House 2004: 720–721).[8]

Mandated to supervise the transition from South African rule to independence in Namibia and a peace agreement brokered by the UN in El Salvador, the UN was tasked to monitor cease-fire, demilitarisation processes, policing, electoral processes, and human rights. Although in both Namibia and El Salvador peace-keepers had to deal with some violence and logistical problems, local and regional support for the transition and peace processes, as well as the active support of third countries ensured overall success in resolving conflict and holding elections. In Namibia an early breach of the cease-fire by SWAPO was soon controlled by South Africa. In El Salvador, on the other hand, the reluctance of the government to disarm as well as the opposition's apparent breach of the cease-fire was brought to a conclusion through the pressure of Colombia, Mexico, Spain and Venezuela in the shape of the newly established 'Friends of the Secretary-General'. A reduction of US forces further contributed to positive progress. By contrast, missions in Haiti and Angola were deemed failures despite apparent initial success. In Haiti the UN successfully supervised elections on 16 December 1990, verifying the election of Jean-Bertrand Aristide as president. Although previous civilian and military violence as well as political instability could have led to a failure of the elections, at the time no major incidents occurred. Yet, a military coup ousting Aristide in September 1991 demonstrated the lack of experience and ownership of democratic politics in Haiti after 186 years of autocratic rule. Despite near universal condemnation and sanctions, disagreements over appropriate action and the resulting inertia highlighted the inadequacy of existing tools of intervention. Similarly, in Angola the election results were contested by the electoral 'loser' Jonas Savimbi. Despite a successful, quiet and peaceful election event, years of anti-colonial struggle and civil war between the communist government and the independence movement came to the fore, showing that elections had not been able to resolve the conflict (see Beigbeder 1994: 180–184; Paris 2004: 63–69).

According to Richmond (2010a), 13 out of 18 attempts at democratisation had authoritarian regimes within 15 years, clearly demonstrating that merely holding elections was not enough. Commentators suggested that the difference in outcomes – in particular the failures of peace-keeping missions – was due to a lack of coordination between the military and civilian mission components, unclear goals and an inadequate match between a mission's mandate and means, as well as insufficient power to enforce it (Bellamy et al. 2004: 169). Other factors identified were a lack of support by major powers, neighbouring countries or other stakeholders (as the success of Namibia and El Salvador might suggest), as well as the unwillingness of parties to adhere to political settlements (Haiti and Angola). However, many problems were rooted at a deeper level. Problems could be found in the way in which peace-keeping mission functioned and in a failure to understand the nature of conflict and its causes, leading to a failure to adequately facilitate conflict transformation and resolution (see for example, Caplan 2000). Indeed, a key problem was the focus on elections, which led to peace-keeping missions that were modelled on the processes of decolonisation missions in which elections had marked an end-point and thus an exit strategy for UN engagement. Although the *Agenda for Peace* had outlined post-conflict reconstruction as an important new field for peace-keeping activities, an election-as-exit strategy dominated UN missions in the early 1990s. The success of peace-keeping missions became equated with the holding of elections. Elections became an operational milestone that signalled to the observing (Western) public and politicians that the goal of democracy had been achieved. Where this did not lead to the desired results, that is, conflict resolution, the process of supporting post-conflict reconstruction was abandoned early and democracy's failure, or the mission's collapse, declared prematurely.

A focus on elections also led to difficulty in securing the success of peace-keeping missions through democracy where the understanding of the nature of conflicts followed traditional categories. The requirements for UN intervention were based on ideas which saw conflicts as either international in nature or followed traditional ideas of civil war. In both conflict scenarios the parties to the conflict were clearly identifiable as either two states at war or as a conflict between an aggrieved section of the population and its own government. In this traditional view peace-keeping would be used as a tool to oversee the process of implementing a political agreement that had been reached after violence had ceased. The principle of democracy here would serve not only as a tool for negotiation but, in the case of civil war, assure aggrieved minorities a voice that would ensure their human rights. It was assumed that democratic politics would be readily embraced by all parties to the conflict, in particular the victims of war. Conflict parties were assumed to be willing to negotiate and forsake violence. In this situation elections were used as part of a political settlement which peace-keeping forces were sent to enforce and monitor. Elections then signalled the end of both conflict and intervention. However, this understanding of conflict processes proved too simplistic as it ignored the multifaceted origins of 'new' wars (Kaldor 2001) and the role democracy might play in solving such conflicts. In the new wars of the 1990s it was not only the absence of peace and a political agreement which characterised the new peace-keeping strategy – and indeed led to a metamorphosis of peace-keeping into peace-making or peace-enforcement – but an incomplete understanding of conflict causes. Instead of fighting on behalf of minority grievances or in political opposition to the government, conflict parties pursued particularistic goals, often cloaked in ethnic terms. As Kaldor (2001) argued, conflict parties relied on massive human rights violations specifically targeting civilian populations to terrorise and destabilise the enemy. Organised violence, the chaos of a collapsing state and disintegrating governance, as well as new tactics of warfare directed explicitly at civilians, therefore created divisions that increasingly defied easy solutions based on a democratic engagement between conflict parties.

Following this, the UN election-as-exit strategy failed to recognise that elections are by nature antagonistic and competitive, pitting groups against each other. This also means that elections are often accompanied by violence, especially where democracy has not been used and experienced before, let alone consolidated (Mansfield 2005; Rapoport and Weinberg 2001; Snyder 2000), hence Paris (2004) called for institutionalisation before liberalisation. Yet, the repudiation of violence is crucial to consolidating the transformation of relationships at the end of a conflict. As Luckham et al. (2000) note, the logic of peace may therefore run counter to the logic of justice and democracy. To achieve peace, a process of reconciliation between conflict parties is needed, which relies on a transformation of relationships to overcome the boundaries of (ethnic) identity or opposing interests. While democracy requires equal treatment and an opportunity of voice for all groups, conflict resolution and reconciliation may require the provision of additional support for particularly disadvantaged groups (Muslims in Bosnia) or the exclusion of some groups (Nazis in Germany, Taliban in Afghanistan). Moreover, elections may reinforce the divisions that had led to the conflict in the first place.

The volatility of an election-as-exit approach was demonstrated in Cambodia (UNTAC 1991–1993). UNTAC's mandate was broad and focussed on the management of transition with extensive authority over all aspects of the settlement's implementation. Despite the (relative) failure of efforts to demilitarise, enforce security, monitor human rights and control governance, as well as numerous deaths of UN personnel and civilians in political violence, the holding of elections in May 1993 led many commentators to declare UNTAC a success. However, the politically unstable situation allowed former Prime Minister Hun Sen to dispute the election outcomes and to refuse a transfer of power since he seized power in a coup in 1997 (see Paris 2004: 79–90). Although parts of UNTAC's mission had not been achieved, the mission's success was judged on its own terms: the holding of elections. The implementation of an effective and successful settlement and state, on the other hand, was given inadequate consideration. Democratic processes thus remained detached from both the people and the political elites. In other words stakeholders assumed no collective ownership of democracy, which did not allow for a democratic culture to develop and take root.

The focus on an elections-as-exit strategy therefore undermined the significance of democratic institutions and democratic governance that could have promoted peaceful future conflict resolution. In his *Supplement to the Agenda for Peace* issued in January 1995 (UNSG 25 January 1995, A/50/60-S/1995/1), Boutros-Ghali thus emphasised the necessity of supporting and creating democratic structures and institutions, and stated that more attention needed to be given to the institutionalisation of peace. In particular, he highlighted the challenge of failed states in which there was a collapse of government institutions, a breakdown of law and order, and the pervasiveness of 'banditry and chaos'. He stressed that 'international intervention must extend beyond military and humanitarian tasks and must include the promotion of national reconciliation and the re-establishment of effective government' (UNSG 25 January 1995, A/50/60-S/1995/1, para. 13). Thus, post-conflict peace-building needed to be post-conflict state reconstruction, in other words the establishment of effective governance as part of democracy.

In Bosnia first attempts at a broader strategy of democracy support were made; however, a continued focus on elections and the hope that it would alleviate if not solve conflict, did not achieve the desired effects. The electoral system cemented the politics of division and conflict, which presented significant problems for democratisation. With inter-ethnic divisions running deep between ethnic groups, and one group (Muslims) particularly disadvantaged, the international community sought to create a structure in which each group would be represented, while at the same time trying to overcome divisions through these structures. Hopes were pinned on elections as a means to achieve conflict resolution. A considerable number of elections were held, yet within the immediate post-conflict situation satisfactory results were not achieved (Chesterman 2005). On the one hand, this was due to the elaborate nature of the system set up; on the other hand, the international community did not realise, or did not care, that the Dayton agreement emphasised the divisive nature of Bosnian politics by separating ethnic groups within the system (see Chandler 1999). It also falsely implied that if elections gave individuals the opportunity to determine their political choice in a free, secret and universal ballot, they would not necessarily vote along ethnic lines but along political-ideological lines, thereby muting ethnic divisions.

Conclusion: minimal democracy

While the end of the Cold War and with it the predominance of Western power and ideas had not been the only factor in pushing democracy onto the international agenda, the change of global political structures had certainly opened up a space in which democracy could assume a prominent place. This changed the use of democracy from Western rhetoric and ideology to a policy and practice used by the UN as well as member states. With increasing support among its members, and in particular with demand for democracy support from member states outside the West, democracy increasingly gained legitimacy as a UN practice. This legitimacy was essential to address the challenge which a UN democracy practice would pose to state sovereignty. Sovereignty and its corollary, the principle of non-intervention, guaranteed that no qualitative judgement about the nature of a government and its political rule could be made beyond the reciprocal recognition of states and governments. However, supporting or even sponsoring democracy through the UN could be viewed as undermining the freedom from outside interference in a nation's affairs. The first challenge of the democracy agenda was therefore to accommodate these conflicting norms, and it did so by re-interpreting sovereignty as popular sovereignty. This followed a reconstruction of the legal developments of the 1960s, which had deliberately moved international law away from democracy. This reconstruction sought to establish a fit between new and existing ideas and practices, facilitated by an increased emphasis on human rights beyond civil rights to include political rights such as right to freedom of expression, freedom of association and the right of participation. Indeed, the construction of democracy as a right in itself, not just a loosely connected assembly of political rights that more or less vaguely translated into democracy, was part and parcel of this re-interpretation of sovereignty.

The way in which this agenda and organisational practice was developed clearly eased the integration of democracy into the canon of existing norms. Rather than constructing a new practice, which would constitute a break with the old and thus appear to member states as radical change, the new democracy practice was built on existing practices that directly related to UN root ideas. Election support and monitoring had not only been practised successfully as a democratic form, albeit with highly circumscribed time limit, but its use in the process of decolonisation also enjoyed a high status and thus high legitimacy. Thus, the integration with existing practices ensured the legitimacy of the democracy agenda. Utilising existing practices ensured general consent by member states and, as democracy was not adopted as a condition for membership but merely as assistance available on request, opposition to democracy was undermined. Thus, this integration allowed for the democracy agenda to become a normal part of UN activity, no longer in contradiction with core principles such as sovereignty.

Once the veil of ideology over democracy had been lifted, this early practice was a minimal form of democracy. Mirroring the common interpretation of the Schumpeterian definition of democracy, the UN focussed exclusively on the procedural aspects of democracy, namely elections. Although the UN, like Schumpeter, considered or mentioned institutional aspects of democracy, it overemphasised the election event and its results. Elections were seen as a legitimising tool not just for the people of the state in question, but election monitoring was also used as proof of the government's and state's legitimacy. Elected politicians were seen to ensure that the people's will would be carried out, that peace could be facilitated and human rights observed. This focus on elections meant that any attempts to introduce a qualitative dimension of political rule would only affect a single, temporally restricted event. The resulting gap between election events thus left the nature of political rule open to the governments' decision, leading in many cases to what Ottaway had called 'semi-authoritarianism'. Thus, as the experiences of democracy in UN mission showed, a new vision of UN democracy, that is, a new practice that took a broader and increasingly long-term perspective, was needed. This was to be found in governance.

Notes

1   Argentina, Bolivia, Brazil, the Dominican Republic, Ecuador, El Salvador, Greece, Guatemala, Honduras, Nicaragua, Peru, the Philippines, Portugal, Spain and Uruguay.

2   The goals and requests of this declaration as well as the novelty of its content are highlighted by its title, which related the declaration to five different agenda items. Thus, it not only ensured widespread reading but also demonstrated quite early the connection to other issues that would hasten the progress of the concept. Here, the connection to economic issues highlights the tenor of developmental assistance. Thus, the declaration was included under items such as 'Development and International Economic Co-operation', 'External Debt Crisis and Development', 'Importance of the Universal Realization of the Right of Peoples to Self-determination and of the Speedy Granting of

Independence to Colonial Countries and Peoples for the Effective Guarantee and Observance of Human Rights', 'Alternative Approaches and Ways and Means Within the UN System for Improving the Effective Enjoyment of Human Rights and Fundamental Freedoms' and 'Progressive Development of the Principles and Norms of International Law Relating to the New International Economic Order'.

3   Unlike legal scholars who emphasised the aspect of customary practice, political theorists and International Relations scholars talked about 'settled norms' emphasising linguistic aspects. For example, Frost argues that democracy is a 'settled norm' because non-democratic countries have to justify their lack of democracy (Frost 1996).

4   This included the resolution concerning South African apartheid and the subsequent resolutions *Enhancing the Effectiveness of the Principle of Periodic and Genuine Elections*.

5   Votes in favour and against often mirrored the split between developed and developing countries, with Europe almost collectively voting against (UN 1994).

6   Preamble to the Constitution of the United Nations Educational, Scientific and Cultural Organization, as quoted in Dutt (1990: 21).

7   The 1992 *Declaration on the Rights of Persons Belonging to National or Ethnic, Religious or Linguistic Minorities* had similarly expressed this new understanding by stating that 'a democratic framework based on the rule of law would contribute to the strengthening of friendship and cooperation among peoples and States' (Singh 2000). By stressing that the management of different national interests (here group interests primarily along cultural lines, not political lines), was important for international peace, the declaration emphasised that democratisation needed qualitative criteria, which had to exist before real democracy could be achieved.

8   Freedom House ratings are measured 1 to 7, or 'free' to 'not free'.

5

Extending democracy I: governance

The 'internationalisation' of democracy continued apace through the 1990s. Fukuyama's claim that liberalism, and with it democracy, had prevailed over other ideologies appeared to come true as democracy became a major force in the new world order. Now with the support of the UN and UN missions as a broad platform for implementation, democracy became a cornerstone of what the UN did and how it expected to solve the problems it faced. The institutionalisation of an election-focussed democracy practice had been determined not only by existing practices but also by political expediency and the need to accommodate a potentially controversial idea without causing too much disruption or controversy. However, with a second cycle of elections supported by the UN now underway and an election-as-exit strategy not delivering the kind of results the UN had hoped for, a new approach to democracy was needed. This new approach was found in an extension of democracy principles and democracy support practices, rather than a complete overhaul of the democracy agenda.

The third vision of democracy – governance – emerged out of the second vision and became practice in the mid-1990s. This third vision built on both the strengths and weaknesses of elections to create something more comprehensive that would better meet the challenges of an increasing portfolio of demands, in particular in relation to weak and failed states, be that states in post-conflict or developmental situations. It relied on extending democratic principles to other areas, including institutions and processes which support elections, but also more broadly to the functioning of the state in general. To understand the push and the pull of this agenda change, this chapter first analyses the state of democracy and the trajectory of democratisation in the 1990s. A range of drivers, such as both Secretaries-General and changing agendas elsewhere in the UN system, are identified, which contributed to the development of this new, governance-focussed democracy agenda. This chapter shows how this extension of democratic principles was justified and made possible. It demonstrates that as democracy was no longer confined to the constraints of a minimal definition, it assumed a greater degree of substance, thereby moving further to the right of the democratic continuum.

Changing foundations

Since the early 1990s the number of democracies steadily increased, with ever more people living in democracies and therefore enjoying more freedom. From 1987, the year before the First International Conference on Newly Restored Democracies, the number of new, democratically elected governments had increased by 55, an average of nearly four per annum (Karatnycky 2002). In 1988, 60 countries judged as 'free' by Freedom House faced an almost equal number of 'not free' countries and a smaller number of 'partly free' countries. In the 1990s this relationship shifted as the process of democratisation led the number of electoral democracies to increase steadily from 69 to 117 states (see Figure 5.1). At the same time, the number of 'not free' countries decreased accordingly, leading many commentators to herald this change as the 'victory march of democracy', or the 'Democratic Century' (Freedom House 1999). Indeed, by 2003 electoral democracies accounted for 61% of all states, while 46% of states overall were rated as 'free', with 2.78 billion people, or 44% of the world's population, living in freedom. Those living in free countries also enjoyed on average a considerably higher national income than 'partly free' or 'not free' countries, which tended to rank in the lower bracket of national income (Freedom House 2004). Unsurprisingly, regional differences between 'free', 'partly free' and 'not free' countries were great. While the Americas and Western Europe ranked high among the list of free countries, the Middle East with North Africa and Sub-Saharan Africa ranked low on the freedom scale. Freedom House stated that the lack of freedom in the Middle East and North Africa could primarily be related to the presence of Muslim majorities and their practice to merge religion with the state as well as their suppression of women. According to Freedom House, the spread of Islam to less developed countries had further decreased the probability for democracy and freedom to take hold. In contrast to this, and in addition to underdevelopment, the Sub-Saharan story was more closely linked to its multi-ethnic make-up, which diminished the potential for success of democracy and freedom (Karatnycky 2002). By contrast, the region of the Former Soviet Union and Central and Eastern Europe showed a 'deepening chasm' (Karatnycky 2002) as Central and Eastern Europe and the Baltic states moved towards freedom, while the Commonwealth of Independent States regressed on the freedom scale despite maintaining electoral democracies (Freedom House 2004).

The increase of freedom and the growing number of states placing their faith in the democratic process seemed a positive indicator for the spread and deepening of democracy. However, these increases came with two caveats. First, the numbers incorporated not only the spread of the Third Wave, but other developments in the achievement of sovereign statehood in a number of states in the aftermath of the fall of the Berlin Wall. These include not only the re-unification of East and West Germany as well as North and South Yemen, that is, the amalgamation of two non-free states into partly free and free states, but also the increase of numbers through the break-up of the Former Soviet Union and Yugoslavia. Thus, while the absolute number of free countries had risen by nearly a quarter (~21%) between 1990 and 1996, this growth had not been as strong in relative terms. The number of countries classified as 'not free' had risen by three, and those classified as 'partly free' had risen by nine. In relative terms this corresponded to a decrease of the former and a marginal rise of the latter (see Figure 5.2). Secondly, the rise in electoral democracies did not correspond necessarily to a rise in freedom, as a comparison between Figures 5.1 and 5.2 demonstrates. While in 1996 Freedom House counted 118 electoral democracies, it classified only 79 states as free. This gap between freedom and democracy demonstrated a phenomenon which was described as 'illiberal' or 'semi-authoritarian democracy'. As shown in Chapter 2, the democratic method challenges democratic substance, that is, the existence of 'genuine' democracy, where democratic procedures are used to obscure a fundamentally undemocratic exercise of power. Hence, in semi-authoritarian systems elections serve to cement a form of political rule in which, unlike in pure authoritarian systems, some liberties, a free civil society, even multi-party elections and parliaments are allowed while authoritarian control over democratic institutions is generally maintained (Ottaway 2004). Thus, consolidation of democracy was only partially achieved, and in some cases, the regression of states to authoritarianism signalled a small reverse wave.

The number of UN missions peaked in 1992 after the establishment of the UN's election monitoring group in the Department for Political Affairs, only to fall in the next two years and rise slightly again three years later as the second, repeat cycle of elections was underway. This second cycle of elections demonstrated a clear attempt at deepening the democratisation process by offering the possibility for a democratic change of government, a critical test of democratic consolidation according to Huntington (1991). This second cycle of elections was therefore mirrored in a second,

1988	1996	2000	2003	2006	2009
69 (41%)	118 (62%)	120 (63%)	117 (61%)	123 (64%)	119 (62%)

Figure 5.1 *Electoral democracies, 1988–2009*

	Free countries	Partly free countries	Not free countries
1988	60 (36%)	45 (27%)	62 (37%)
1990	65 (40%)	50 (30%)	50 (30%)
1996	79 (41%)	59 (31%)	53 (28%)
2000	86 (45%)	58 (30%)	48 (25%)
2003	88 (46%)	55 (29%)	49 (25%)
2006	89 (46%)	58 (30%)	45 (23%)
2009	89 (46%)	63 (33%)	42 (22%)

Figure 5.2 *Freedom in the world, 1988–2009*

slightly lower peak in requests for UN assistance. Overall, by 1996 the UN had received more than 120 requests for election assistance, of which 99 were accepted, while sixteen states had received UN election assistance twice (UNSG 18 October 1996). All six forms of election assistance were employed with some missions combining several forms of assistance. The largest category of assistance was 'Technical Assistance', employed in nearly half of all missions, followed by 'Coordination and Support', and 'Observation (Follow and Report)' with 25 and 27 missions respectively. In contrast to this, both 'Organisation and Conduct' and 'Training of National Observers' were employed in only three states. Finally, 'Verification' was used in seven states. The regional split in UN election assistance mirrored the findings by Freedom House: until 1996 the only European election receiving assistance took place in a dependent territory, the Netherlands Antilles. At the same time, a single mission in the Middle East, the reunited Yemen, demonstrated the political immobility of the region. Four missions in Asia and the Pacific contrasted with 39 missions in Africa where election assistance also became development assistance. Thirteen missions in the Americas and the Caribbean, and eleven missions in Eastern Europe, accompanied the path of the Third Wave (UNSG 18 October 1996, A/51/512).

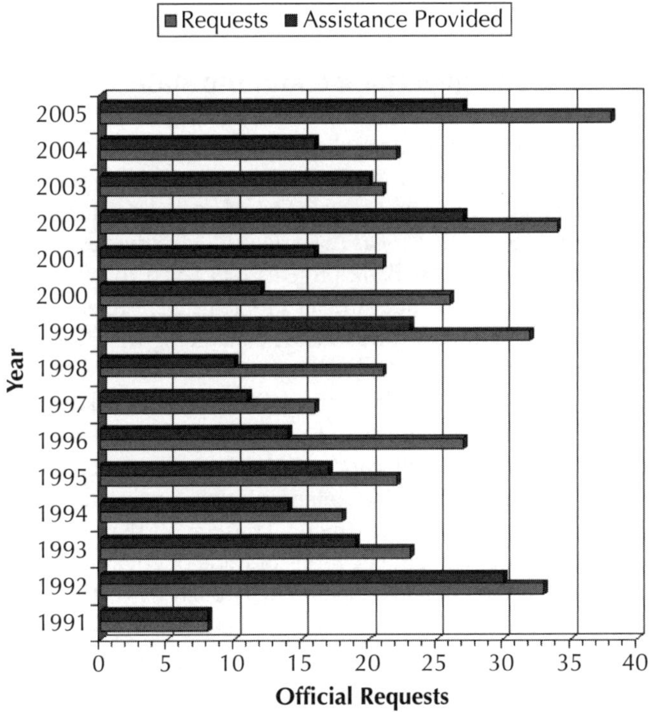

Figure 5.3 *Requests for electoral assistance, 1989–2005*

The resulting challenges for the UN seemed clear: if democratisation was to be sustained and consolidated, and if the idea of popular sovereignty and democratic legitimacy were to take hold, the UN's early focus on elections would not be sufficient. This lesson was further reinforced by experiences of UN peace-keeping missions such as those in Haiti and Angola, where elections did not lead to the envisaged results of peaceful political relations, but instead saw the contestation of election results and renewed political instability. New opportunities to address these issues and to enable a deepening and widening of the democracy agenda could be found in the development community. The new practice of governance support paid closer attention to state structures by addressing the quality of political rule and its execution. Governance, or 'good' governance, aimed at recreating the relationship between those governing and the people by introducing principles such as accountability, transparency and fairness – principles essential to democracies. The ideas and practices of the development community thus connected with those of the Secretariat. Indeed, Secretary-General Boutros-Ghali had highlighted development as one of his key concerns throughout his term, and the call for a reformulation of the ideas and practices of peace, democracy and development, as well as the reconsideration of the foundations of international society, ran through his office as a key thread. These ideas found their clearest expression in his triptych of Agendas, the Agendas for Peace (1992), Development (1994) and Democratization (1996).

Good governance and the state

The concept of good governance and the discourse of the state in development originated in the World Bank in 1989, where it was first mentioned in the Bank's report *Sub-Saharan Africa: From Crisis to Sustainable Growth*, which evaluated the success of Bank projects in Sub-Saharan Africa. Assessing the effectiveness of SAPs in the 1980s, the World Bank noted that Bank projects had failed to achieve the results envisaged. The Bank concluded that Africa's problems were related to its lack of competitiveness and low return on investment, concluding that 'weak capacity in both the public and private sectors is at the very core of Africa's development crisis' (World Bank 1989: 38). A weak public sector had led to loss-making public enterprises, poor investment choices, costly and unreliable infrastructure, price distortions and inefficient resource allocation, while governments endemic with bureaucratic obstruction, pervasive rent-seeking, weak judicial systems and arbitrary decision-making had undermined development. Thus, rather than drawing on external causes such as international markets, terms of trade or environmental disasters, the Bank took the unexpected step in condemning African states, their governments and political elites for obstructing the success of Bank lending projects (Nielinger 1998). The Bank highlighted 'bad governance' as the cause for a lack of lasting project successes. This was due to the appropriation of the government machinery by elites for their own interests, which was seen to reduce trust not only by foreign investors but also by the state's own population (World Bank 1989). Consequently,

Africa needed 'not just less government but better government – government that concentrates its efforts less on direct interventions and more on enabling others to be productive' (World Bank 1989: 5). The Bank therefore reconsidered the goals of its lending policies as well as the strategies with which these could be brought about. By introducing a focus on 'good governance', the Bank aimed at enhancing the recipient states' capability, that is, their 'ability to undertake and promote collective actions efficiently' (World Bank 1989: 3).

In its critique of governance, the 1989 Bank report drew on UNICEF's quest for *Adjustment with a Human Face*, which had strongly criticised the Bank's Structural Adjustment Programmes and their effects on social policies and micro-level poverty. The Bank argued that UNICEF's demand for sustainable and equitable growth would be met by fostering an 'enabling environment' and 'enhanced capacities'. The introduction of the good governance agenda therefore meant 'bringing the state back in[to]' development policy and international discourse (Evans et al. 1985); and the Bank understood that to emphasise the state as an enabling environment by highlighting the need for transparency, accountability and the rule of law was indeed a paradigm shift (World Bank 1994a). Good governance thus extended democracy principles beyond elections, emphasising institutions and processes of the state. The fact that good governance could therefore lead to a broader, more substantive definition of democracy was not lost on commentators who, in the early 1990s, were highly critical of such development. While some regarded the new governance agenda as an opportunity to open up a space for evaluative questions about the 'proper' or best way of governing (Doornbos 2001), critics emphasised that this new Bank policy was too political, too liberal, or just simply too narrowly focussed on economics and hence a simple continuation of previous policies (Abrahamsen 2000; Williams and Young 1994).[1] Critics argued that the Bank had acted in contradiction to its charter, which demanded that the Bank be politically neutral. They claimed that the Bank imposed democracy as a culturally neutral concept through its governance agenda. With this it reconstructed internal politics as international and therefore open to question. This would allow for intervention into and participation in the formulation of national policies (Abrahamsen 2000). Critics argued that good governance and with it democracy were constructed as an 'inevitable trend towards a universal form of government on which all societies will eventually converge' (Smith 2003: 276).

Proponents of the governance agenda countered that 'governance is not equal to democracy [and that] democracy is one institutional set-up that may or may not be the outcome of processes of governance' (Kjaer 2004: 170), and that the good governance agenda had a bureaucratic, not a political origin (Moore 1993). Indeed, the Bank's agenda was perhaps insufficiently political to advance democracy beyond the structural and procedural aspects highlighted by Dahl and Lijphart. The Bank emphasised that while the line between political and economic issues was very thin, its focus was purely technical, concentrating on the economic and social aspects of governance (World Bank 1994a). An early connection made between economic development and human rights was soon retracted and the Bank declared in its 1994 report *Governance – The World Bank Experience* that human rights were not important in themselves but only where they facilitated development (Delevic Djilas 2003). Instead, the Bank stressed that the concept of governance was multidimensional: governance could be understood as either a form of political regime, as the processes by which authority was exercised, or as a government's capacity to develop and implement policies and functions. However, it noted that Bank policy was concerned only with the second and the third dimension, as the first dimension of governance was outside its mission (World Bank 1994a). Indeed, the 1989 definition of governance as 'the exercise of political power to manage a nation's affairs' (World Bank 1989: 60), was subsequently revised and narrowed down to 'the manner in which power is exercised in the management of a country's economic and social resources for development' (World Bank 1992: 1), thereby focussing explicitly on more traditional development sectors.

While in theory the use of UNICEF's 'enabling environment' and 'enhanced capacities' may have been a strategy which integrated the more traditional technical side of assistance with social aspects, in practice the Bank's definition and operationalisation of these terms undermined any social or human rights aspects which good governance could have addressed. It defined 'enabling environment' in technical terms, focussing on economic indicators such as reoriented incentives, active exchange rate policies and reduced costs, the improvement of infrastructures, demand-driven rather than imposed projects, and the utilisation of the private sector. Strategies to build capacities focussed on labour development and human development through the provision of training and education, health care and nutrition, 'good' political leadership and the restructuring of public and private institutions (World Bank 1989). A central aspect of the strategy to achieve better government through better staffing, training and remuneration of the civil service translated into a focus on public sector management, in particular anti-corruption measures. Not only could this be measured more easily but this emphasis on civil service reform, public sector expenditure management and public enterprise reform was 'a reflection that these categories are central to how power is exercised' (World Bank 1989: 55). Therefore efficiency and the effectiveness of systems and structures, which included human *resources*, were conceptualised as the hallmark of good governance and with it good government.

The key objective for the World Bank thus remained its aim to protect and improve the results of its investment. Good governance was the tool through which this could be achieved. The employment of structures and systems was conceptualised as instrumental to the achievement of a goal external to them – macroeconomic growth and development, as well as managerial (project management) and organisational (state) efficiency. Thus, while the World Bank's governance agenda introduced potential opportunities to conceptualise democracy in the context of international democracy assistance, its technical understanding of governance and the Bank's focus on economic efficiency left structures largely devoid of political and social content. Despite its emphasis on structures of liberal democratic societies, the Bank's good governance agenda neutralised state structures by ignoring democratic principles and outcomes. An alternative vision was offered by the UNDP, which had also used the new governance approach in its development policies.

Like the World Bank, UNDP had dealt with projects addressing governance systems and structures, even supporting elections, since the 1970s. Yet it had done so in a much looser and uncoordinated way. It was not until 1995, and after lengthy debate and analysis, that UNDP fully set out its own governance agenda. UNDP's philosophy and therefore its governance approach differed from the World Bank in that it focussed on human development rather than economic development, thereby introducing a qualitative dimension which the Bank had avoided. On the one hand, UNDP followed the Brundlandt Report and the Rio Declaration by introducing a long-term, intergenerational perspective through the idea of sustainability. On the other hand, it built on the work of Mahbub ul Haq and Amartya Sen, which conceptualised development as the widening of choices for people in the context of 'enabling environments'. Translating this philosophy of people-centred development into policy, UNDP formally endorsed the concept of 'sustainable human development' in 1994, which subsequently formed the heart of the organisation's own governance agenda. Following the widespread interest and debate which the World Bank's governance approach had generated since 1989, UNDP published a discussion paper on *Public Sector Management, Governance, and Sustainable Development* in 1995. This then formed the basis for its own governance agenda. The paper defined governance narrowly as 'the exercise of political power to manage a nation's affairs', following the 1989 World Bank definition. Governance, or 'public management', was seen as the 'direct and indirect management of public affairs and regulatory control of private activities that impinge on human affairs' (UNDP 1995: 19).

Like the World Bank, UNDP regarded good governance as key to development, here *sustainable* and *human* development, while public sector management was seen as the key means to its implementation. Like the World Bank, UNDP's first outline of good governance took a strong management-focussed approach and outlined the same key features as the Bank – political legitimacy and accountability, freedom of association and participation, a fair and reliable judicial system, bureaucratic accountability, freedom of information and expression, effective and efficient public sector management, and cooperation with civil society organisations (UNDP 1995: 22). Human resource development played a central part, as this continued an emphasis on efficient management which UNDP had pursued through its Management Development Programme since 1988. In its 1995 report UNDP still regarded democracy as secondary to and instrumental for sustainable human development, emphasising that democratic reforms should not come at the expense of economic progress.[2] However, not bound by the same restrictions as the World Bank, UNDP addressed the issue of democracy more explicitly and first hints of diverging agendas became evident. The difference between governance as economic/market development and governance as sustainable human development implied variances in outcome where governance became part of the democracy agenda. These differences will be explored in greater detail in Chapter 6.

Secretary-General Boutros-Ghali's agenda(s)

The role of the Secretary-General in the development of the UN democracy agenda beyond elections was clearly evident. This was particularly the case for Boutros-Ghali, who was no longer constrained by the same political considerations as his predecessor Javier Perez de Cuellar. Secretary-General Javier Perez de Cuellar saw that democracy could not be equated with elections alone and noted in his first report on *Human Rights Questions, Including Alternative Approaches for Improving the Effective Enjoyment of Human Rights and Fundamental Freedoms: Enhancing the Effectiveness of the Principle of Periodic and Genuine Elections* issued in November 1991, that elections were merely a step on the way to democratisation. He stressed that democracy covered all forms of participation in political life and that 'accelerated economic development is necessary to provide the underpinning required for the consolidation of *genuine* participatory democracy, in which socio-economic as well as political rights are respected' (UNSG 19 November 1991, A/46/609, para 75, emphasis added). However, although this implied a substantive form of democracy and therefore further attention to institutions which facilitate and uphold the electoral process, it was made clear that democracy did not extend beyond the political realm. Instead, Perez de Cuellar emphasised democracy's ideological and procedural dimensions. Consequently, he did not see a role for the UN in the achievement of a democratic *society*. For Perez de Cuellar, to merely envision such an ideal was sufficient and commensurate with the tentative steps taken to develop a democracy agenda by building on existing practices of election monitoring. Thus, UN technical assistance was limited to election monitoring to enable 'genuine' elections, to increase the credibility of the electoral process and thus to enhance the people's trust in the electoral process (UNSG 19 November 1991, A/46/609).

Boutros Boutros-Ghali, who followed Javier Perez de Cuellar into office only weeks after the publication of the above quoted report, had a very different outlook. Boutros-Ghali's key aim was to create a new intellectual framework for the UN to match its new, emerging role in the post-Cold War world (Boutros-Ghali 1999; Lombardo 2001; Rushton 2008). In this, democracy played an important role. In his acceptance speech the Secretary-General declared that he wanted to emphasise the UN's role in 'strengthening fundamental freedoms and democratic institutions which constitute an essential and indispensable stage in the economic and social development of nations' (Boutros-Ghali 2003e: 3). With this, the new Secretary-General demonstrated his departure from his predecessor's understanding of democracy. No longer was democracy an identifier of a particular ideology or political group (i.e. the West), but democracy was seen as a universal concept. More than that, Boutros-Ghali recognised the teleological character of democracy and its nature as 'an essential and indispensable stage' of development. By emphasising this radically different vision of democracy in his acceptance speech, the Secretary-General set the tone for a 'more active and assertive Secretary-General[ship]' (Rivlin 1996: 141). Indeed, Boutros-Ghali assumed more autonomy in his position than most of his predecessors (see Kille 2006), lobbying for his causes and speaking out about conflicts that he thought were neglected by member states. His outspoken style not only led to strained relationships with some member states, in particular the US government, but also led many to conclude that he was 'disdainful, confrontational, too stubbornly independent and bent on self-aggrandizement' (Rivlin 1996: 141). This independence and leadership, however, would have a visible effect on the development of the democracy agenda.

One of Boutros-Ghali's key concerns was the triangulation of peace, democracy and development as the foundation of international society. Accordingly, Boutros-Ghali stated that peace would ensure development, democracy would ensure peace, and to survive long-term, development would need democracy. Although this allowed for a clear connection between development practices and the democracy agenda, Secretary-General Boutros-Ghali at first did not extend democracy beyond this very broad connection, leaving it open as to how this connection could be achieved and where exactly this would happen. As a result, the issue of democratic institutions was rarely mentioned. Where Boutros-Ghali did mention institutions or 'programmes [to create and strengthen] the institutions and processes that are essential for developing the open and pluralistic societies which form the basis for democratic governments' (UNSG 18 November 1993, A/48/590, para 54), these were primarily related to institutions directly managing election processes and events. Consequently, further elaboration of the good governance approach in the context of the development agenda was not forthcoming until his May 1994 *Agenda for Development*. Here the Secretary-General devoted considerable space to the issue, in particular focussing on demonstrating and thereby cementing the connection between development and good governance, democracy and development, and consequently good governance and democracy.

The *Agenda for Development* conceptualised democracy and development as mutually reinforcing processes which also affect peace and security. Although the *Agenda* avoided any questions of causality – whether democracy caused development, or whether development would lead to democracy – it sought to achieve this connection by highlighting that development was not only a fundamental human right but also crucial to the establishment of peace. Development was thus seen as 'the most secure basis for peace' (Boutros-Ghali 1994, para. 3). In locating the reason for conflict both in 'economic despair' and the lack of democratic means, democracy was seen as the only long-term arbiter for tensions within societies, be they political, ethnic, social, or indeed economic (Boutros-Ghali 1994: 122). Although the *Agenda* stressed that democracy was 'the only long-term and sustainable route to successful development' (Boutros-Ghali 1994: 137), it cautioned that democracy was not an instant solution or success. Democracy would bring people closer to their government, especially at the community level, and in so doing allow for input that ensured a better match between development needs, strategies and actual aid. Yet, to achieve people-centred development, each aspect of development – peace, economic growth, sustainable environment, societal justice and political participation – had to be addressed simultaneously (Boutros-Ghali 1994).

In outlining his views of development, Boutros-Ghali borrowed heavily from UNDP's ideas of development and governance. In other words, while he saw economic growth as the motor for progress and its proper functioning as dependent on peace, society, politics and the environment, he claimed that it was not the economy *per se* that was at the heart of development but the fact that development widened choices for people. The Secretary-General therefore claimed that growth should be sustainable, or, in other words, it should 'promote full employment and poverty reduction, and should seek improved patterns of income distribution through greater equality of opportunity' (Boutros-Ghali 1994: 43). It was Boutros-Ghali's conviction that 'the laws of economics cannot be changed, but their social consequences can be eased' (Boutros-Ghali 1994: 110). This very specific definition hinted at particular outcomes which are also attributed to substantive democracy. Thus, the issue of social justice assumed a key part here where 'social development' was made a government responsibility when and if the market could not deliver. What followed was that '[i]mproving and enhancing governance is an essential condition for the success of any agenda or strategy for development [because g]overnance may be the single most important development variable within the control of individual States' (Boutros-Ghali 1994, para 125). Governance was therefore not only an issue of the capability of state institutions, their reliability and accountability, but most importantly an agenda and comprehensive strategy for development. This included a more active dimension of democracy, of which the idea of popular participation beyond the structural support provided by both the World Bank and UNDP was an important element. In this vein, the *Agenda for Development* equated democracy with good governance, presaging changes to the democracy agenda implemented by Boutros-Ghali's successor, Kofi Annan.

In the following months, until the end of this tenure in December 1996, the Secretary-General's annual reports on *Support by the United Nations System of the Efforts of Governments to Promote and Consolidate New or Restored Democracies* reflected this special emphasis on the triangle between peace, democracy and development. In his 1995 report Boutros-Ghali signalled this by dividing the paper into three parts, outlining existing UN activities and potential activities in three areas – democratic culture, electoral assistance and institution-building (UNSG 7 August 1995, A/50/332). He emphasised that for democratisation to take root, institutions were crucial in creating a participatory democracy and democratic culture. Referring back to the governance agenda, he pointed to organisations – such as the World Bank – that had focussed on the administrative aspect of governance and emphasised the public sector, its efficiency and accountability. These organisations, Boutros-Ghali suggested, should in future also consider social and political dimensions of governance (UNSG 7 August 1995A/50/332, para. 126) to achieve democracy, hinting at a governance agenda more in line with UNDP ideas of human development. Moreover, Boutros-Ghali stressed that elections and democratic transitions were only temporary. He noted that as the UN was already undertaking a second round of assistance, there was now a need to move beyond process assistance to capability assistance because 'the purpose of electoral assistance is to assist Governments in achieving their own full capacity as soon as possible' (UNSG 8 November 1995, A/50/736, para 4). In other words, good governance had come to be regarded as a permanent democratic structure while elections were not only limited in their exercise as such but also as a UN practice. Although he recognised that post-election assistance was necessary (but not sufficient) for democracy, this extension was made horizontally across time, not across sectors. Thus, Boutros-Ghali had laid a strong foundation for a substantive democracy agenda by consistently promoting democracy through the triangulation of peace, democracy and development. The latter provided the strongest impact on furthering the understanding of what democracy meant, while the first (peace) provided the political impetus for its acceptance. The expectations for *An Agenda for Democratization*, which Boutros-Ghali had hoped to write for some time, would therefore be to bring together these issues and outline a comprehensive practice and toolkit of democracy assistance, as the *Agenda for Peace* had done for peace-keeping.

The Agenda for Democratization

The development of the UN democracy agenda and UN support for democratisation found its first culmination in the 1996 *Agenda for Democratization*, written as a supplement to the Secretary-General's two previous reports on the *United Nations System's Support of the Efforts of Governments to Promote and Consolidate New or Restored Democracies*, which also served as follow-up documentation for the International Conferences of New and Restored Democracies in Manila and Managua. Boutros-Ghali drafted *An Agenda for Democratization* to summarise UN activities in the area of democratisation, to outline a strategy for further development of UN practice and to sketch his own views on democracy and the process of democratisation in the international system.

According to Hill, Boutros-Ghali was a writer with conviction, who believed that 'policy was made by the written word, that texts make things happen in the realm of high diplomacy and statecraft' (Hill 2003: iii). *An Agenda for Democratization*, like its predecessors *An Agenda for Peace* and *An Agenda for Development*, therefore formed part of Boutros-Ghali's attempt to build an intellectual framework for UN action, an 'holistic vision' of how the UN might contribute to a peaceful and stable international world after the end of the Cold War and meet emerging international challenges. The Agendas were thus 'formed in confrontation of theory with practice' (Russett 2003: 2065) and centred around the three interlocking and mutually reinforcing concepts of peace, development and democracy, which Secretary-General Boutros-Ghali had relentlessly promoted throughout his tenure. As Lombardo (2001), Boutros-Ghali's speech writer, vividly recounts, *An Agenda for Democratization* had long been planned by Boutros-Ghali, who had worked on a draft for four years. However, despite his best efforts, no mandate for this *Agenda* had been forthcoming. Boutros-Ghali considered its publication in mid-1995 as an introduction to a report requested by the General Assembly on *Ways and Mechanism through which the United Nations could support the efforts of government to promote and consolidate new or restored democracies* but ultimately decided against this move as General Assembly staff considered it to be too controversial. Instead, he continued to revise his text (Burgess 2001). In his memoirs he wrote that as the UN bureaucracy got wind of the *Agenda*, 'its counterblast against this was of hurricane force' (Boutros-Ghali 1999: 320). In November 1996 he sought additional feedback from friends and acquaintances who were generally encouraging (see Hill 2003: 1997–1998). Already vetoed out of office by the USA, a move that Boutros-Ghali considered 'a rejection of democracy' (Boutros-Ghali 1999: 318), Boutros-Ghali moved quickly in December 1996 to issue *An Agenda for Democratization* only days before his departure from the UN. To do so he relied on the help of the President of the General Assembly Razali Ismail of Malaysia, to circulate the *Agenda* in the Assembly.

In the *Agenda* Boutros-Ghali outlined both the theoretical-philosophical foundations of UN democracy and the basis for UN involvement in democracy support. Boutros-Ghali found justification for the existence of an internationally recognised norm of democracy in the founding documents of the UN. Based on this, he not only legitimised the claim for democracy but also reached out to groups who regarded different documents of the human rights canon as relevant. Although he admitted that the word democracy did not appear in the Charter, he found it in the spirit of the Charter, the *Universal Declaration of Human Rights*, the *Declaration on the Granting of Independence to Colonial Countries and Peoples* and both human rights covenants. He claimed that the founders of the UN had indeed acknowledged democracy as part of the UN by referring to 'We the peoples' in the opening of the UN Charter, thereby 'rooting the sovereign authority of the Member States – and thus the legitimacy of the Organization ... in the will of their peoples' (Boutros-Ghali 1996, para. 28). From this he followed that democracy was fundamental to the organisation. He concluded that

> the Charter offers a vision of democratic States and democracy among them that both derives from and aims to realize the founders' 'faith in fundamental human rights, in the dignity and worth of the human person ...'. Their commitment to democracy shows in the Purposes of the UN to promote respect for the principle of equal rights and self-determination ... and for human rights and fundamental freedoms. (Boutros-Ghali 1996, para. 28)

Boutros-Ghali thus turned the legalistic interpretation of democracy in the UN Charter on its head, asserting that democracy was indeed written into the founding document of the UN. Like other (legal) commentators such as Franck (1992), he followed the original intention of the American delegation in San Francisco by interpreting 'the peoples' as individuals, not states. At the same time, he drew on other principles and rights – self-determination and human rights – as surrogates to justify democracy as a principle central to the UN. Hence, for Boutros-Ghali this 'new' agenda had in fact no novelty value at all. Instead, he claimed that it was merely the politics of the Cold War that had prevented the 'true and intended' meaning of these documents and the idea of 'we the peoples' to prevail. With the Cold War over, these 'original goals' could now be pursued. Consequently, Boutros-Ghali did not fail to emphasise that the practice of democracy support sat comfortably with existing practices as it was 'essential to progress on a wide range of concerns and the protection of human rights' (Boutros-Ghali 1996, para. 3).

The *Agenda*, however, also reaffirmed the principle of sovereignty as Boutros-Ghali highlighted the UN's impartiality. He stated that the *Agenda* did not offer a particular model of democracy and processes of democratisation but that each society must decide on the nature and pace of the process itself. Democracy must develop freely from within to take hold and to be considered legitimate – no model and no process could be imposed from the outside. The UN's role was thus to facilitate the choice of form and the development of the process of democratisation. The organisation's activities in development support would complement or run parallel to this assistance. However, although the primacy of the state and its freedom to decide the welfare of its people independently and without interference was reiterated, Boutros-Ghali made it clear that recourse to this freedom can only be temporary and short-term. Using this freedom as a pretext to deny and neglect the three key objectives – peace, development and democracy – was seen as incommensurate with the spirit and the 'deeper truth' of democracy.

The Secretary-General stressed that there existed an emerging consensus on democracy and its practical importance, and that while some might still challenge democracy's importance, it was undeniable that there was a 'deeper truth' to democracy. This 'deeper truth' lay in its contribution to the preservation of peace and security, the guarantee of justice and human rights as well as the promotion of economic and social development. Insight into this 'deeper truth' was not based on empirical evidence provided by Boutros Boutros-Ghali. Instead, mirroring arguments brought forward by academics, Boutros-Ghali presented these insights as universals that had to be grasped through an enlightened rationality and logic, thereby leaving challenges to the idea of democracy without foundation. To Boutros-Ghali democracy was an ideal of political power that was based on the will of the people. This ideal did not stop at the boundaries of a particular state or group of states, as many of its opponents might have argued, but was indeed a product of human kind. It crossed cultural, social and economic lines, not only appealing to different groups of people but also inherently belonging to them, no matter what their political-cultural background might be. Indeed, the implication was that there were no political-cultural differences, for democracy was not only rooted in human rights, it had also become a human right. Thus, Boutros-Ghali reached out to both sides of the cosmopolitan and communitarian debate, arguing that democracy did not undermine the collective by endowing the individual alone with rights, as many communitarian critics had feared. Instead, he argued, the rights of individuals and collectives – the rights of persons and the rights of peoples – could best be reconciled through democracy. As democracies are fundamentally open societies, he argued, they would provide the mechanisms for participation and protection for both groups and individuals (Boutros-Ghali 1996). Thus, sovereignty here was ultimately popular sovereignty, as democracy 'fosters the evolution of the *social contract* upon which lasting peace can built' (Boutros-Ghali 1996, para. 17, emphasis added). Elected politicians, he deduced, would be less likely to break this social contract. Instead, elected officials were regarded as better able to cope with social conflict and as more likely to promote and respect the rule of law, human rights and the needs of the marginalised.

Boutros-Ghali saw that the turn to popular sovereignty had important consequences for the achievement of UN goals, namely peace and human rights. Raising the importance of good governance again, he outlined governance support as a new activity offering opportunities for the UN to support the democratisation process. In doing so he focussed on practices already offered by the UN: election monitoring and technical assistance in the development of electoral bodies. Importantly, Boutros-Ghali did not make specific structural prescriptions but emphasised the necessity for the establishment of a democratic culture, as 'a culture of democracy is fundamentally a culture of peace' (Boutros-Ghali 1996, para. 17). For democracy to be successful, a state had to be capable as well as willing to create the conditions for democracy. With this he tapped again into a crucial problem with which the UN had been confronted in the 1990s – failed states and ethnic conflicts – to justify this new extended agenda. In a failed or failing state where authority had ceased to function, the fragile processes of democracy could not be facilitated, leaving them vulnerable to usurpation by authoritarian powers and groups that would pursue their interests violently. A power vacuum resulting from state failure may all too easily allow for authoritarian politics to take over. Instead, it was necessary for the state to 'create the conditions for free and fair elections [and] to support the development and maintenance of the institutions necessary for the ongoing practice of democratic politics' (Boutros-Ghali 1996, para. 21). A general agreement on the idea and rules of democratic politics had to be created, including an understanding that conflicts could be solved peacefully and without violence. This culture would include an acceptance by all parties that there was the possibility of electoral victory and defeat, a culture in which the opposition was recognised as part of the political process and structure. This culture of democracy would be built on a 'societal consensus, *not* … policy' (Boutros-Ghali 1996, para. 21). In contradiction to earlier statements, the Secretary-General merely stated that democracy 'fosters' good governance, a distinction which demonstrated that here democracy was equated with electoral processes alone.

Considering the availability of UN support in institution-building, the Secretary-General did not establish a connection which would infer its necessity. Although he described this 'range of activities' as part of the 'new approach' to peace-building, whose importance had become so obvious in the failures that were Haiti and Angola, he did not follow previous connections made. In these, any attachment to peace had heightened the urgency with which democracy needed to be implemented. One reason for this might be the complexity and number of actors involved in this area. Unlike electoral assistance, this area of activity lacked organisational focus, which meant that so far the UN had only acted as a coordinator to ensure that adequate results were achieved on the ground. The focus of this activity was to keep the needs of states in focus and avoid imbalances, that is, piecemeal solutions in the implementation of other organisation's practices, rather than implement a generic UN practice of institution-building.

Unlike its companion document, *An Agenda for Peace*, which had led to considerable debate in academic and policy-making circles as well as to effective changes in peace-keeping functions, *An Agenda for Democratization* received mixed attention. On the one hand, vociferous criticism was levelled at Boutros-Ghali by a number of member states. Democracy promoters such as the USA did not welcome the independence of his move, while authoritarian states in Asia as well as some of their European allies argued that democracy had no place in the international system because it was a culturally specific (i.e. Western) concept. As such, they even accused Secretary-General Boutros-Ghali of having forgotten his own cultural roots (Russett 2003). On the other hand, there was a considerable lack of discussion outside the event of publication. This lack of attention might be partially attributed to its publication near the end of Boutros-Ghali's term as Secretary-General but also to its rather surprising emphasis on democracy between states and democratisation within the UN organisation.

Boutros-Ghali devoted about half of his *Agenda* to international democracy. According to the Secretary-General, in an era of peace between the main powers and growing globalisation, democratisation at the international level was crucial. Globalisation, Boutros-Ghali claimed, in fact drove the need and demand for democracy, as well as the process of democratisation by enabling people to use technology to communicate, learn and interact with each other. This international democratisation addressed both more democracy and sovereign equality between states irrespective of their relative power, as well as an inclusion of a number of actors in decision-making at the international level, such as NGOs. Interestingly, the Secretary-General claimed that national democracy required global democracy but not vice versa. Following this, Boutros-Ghali saw the main thrust of recent developments as an acknowledgement of the idea of democracy in general, be that as a political system, a decision-making process or as an expression of equality and inclusion. Thus, his own drive to promote democratisation in the reform of the Secretariat found expression in an overall democratisation of the conduct of international relations, for example through the reform of decision-making and membership of bodies such as the Security Council, or the integration of non-state actors in UN affairs. Both enhanced national democracy and international democracy were therefore an essential element in the achievement of global peace (Boutros-Ghali 1996, Chapter V).

Although some argued that *An Agenda for Democratization* was a 'notable statement representing intellectual integrity and courage' (Russett 2003: 2067), the Agenda was generally regarded as a failure due to its lack of mandate. In addition, the lengthy description of international democracy in the *Agenda* presented a missed opportunity for the UN democracy agenda, the elaboration of the UN's role in the process of democratisation and its conceptualisation of democracy and democracy assistance. However, despite these failings, Boutros-Ghali's reflections on the idea of democracy and its place on the wider UN agenda became part of the broader discourse of UN democracy and a developing UN practice as his successor, Kofi Annan, picked up both ideas and practices to develop the UN democracy agenda further.

Governance + elections assistance = democracy assistance

Like Boutros-Ghali, Kofi Annan attached considerable value to democracy. While democracy remained 'dear to [his] heart' (UNSG 19 June 2001, SG/SM/7850),

Annan sought to make development, in particular the reduction if not the elimination of poverty, his central concern. Africa was not only his key target for this developing mission, but also exemplified his thinking on democracy's foundations. On several occasions Annan appealed to his 'fellow Africans' to overcome years of political conflict and poverty, and to 'reap the benefits of globalization and realize its great potential' (UNSG 29 June 1999, SG/SM/7054). He did so by repeatedly emphasising the heritage he shared with Africans, stressing his understanding of Africans' concerns. He often referred back to what he considered his key speech on Africa and democracy, which he gave in June 1997 at the Annual Assembly of Heads of State and Government of the Organisation of African Unity in Harare. Here he called for African states to start new efforts of democratisation and development. Using Huntington's metaphor of a wave, he asked attending heads of state to 'unleash a third wave' to follow the waves of decolonisation and the anti-apartheid struggle, and civil wars, military rule and economic stagnation. This third wave, he stressed, should be one of peace, democracy, human rights and sustainable development. At its heart should be the realisation that the will of the people is the basis of governmental authority. A just society and access to opportunities for development for all, as well as open condemnation of those who undermine democracy at home or in neighbouring countries, would be crucial to this 'new doctrine for African politics'. Annan emphasised that democracy was not a luxury for the rich, but a 'yearning for human dignity [that] resides in every African heart' (UNSG 2 June 1997, SG/SM/6245/Rev. 1*). He stated that democracy is not alien to the African tradition but an element of traditional deliberation in African communities, concluding that Africans have a 'fierce and ever-growing thirst for democracy' (Annan 2000c). Although this may have suggested that Annan may have considered quasi-democratic forms of representation and deliberation (i.e. not involving general elections), he did not elaborate on this relationship between democracy and traditional African politics.

While thus both Boutros Boutros-Ghali and Kofi Annan are commonly associated with the UN democracy agenda, there was considerable difference in style and in the way in which they approached democracy. Annan's calm rhetorical style, careful choice of words and his consideration not to offend governments even when being critical, contrasted with the ambition and sharp tongue of Boutros Boutros-Ghali (Gordenker 2005). This restraint was also evident in his acceptance speech: where Boutros-Ghali had boldly outlined his vision of the triangle of peace, development and democracy, and his intention to support the process of democratisation, Kofi Annan, like Perez de Cuellar before him, emphasised the traditional formula of development, *freedom* and peace. Moreover, when discussing democracy Annan used the concept and idea of democracy in a more nuanced fashion than Boutros-Ghali, avoiding 'sweeping generalizations or confident predictions' (Annan 2002: 135).[3] For example, he eloquently discussed Kant's theory, evaluating issues of weak historical evidence, the question of transparency versus covert policy-making and the assumptions people make about other polities. He interpreted Kant's republics, or liberal democracies, as 'states with open and accountable systems of government', and reiterated that the existence of such states would translate into a more peaceful world. Annan sought to build an *international* democratic peace for which the basis was the restoration, or cultivation, of democracy in places where it had broken down or not yet taken root. With this he clearly derived and justified a UN mandate for peace-keeping missions, including post-conflict state reconstruction. At the same time, he realised that the promise of the democratic peace was not as straightforward as Boutros-Ghali and other politicians had asserted in the early 1990s (see Schwartz and Skinner 2002). He highlighted that it was not democracies *per se* that do not fight each other. Instead of focussing on the presence and use of elections as a sign for democracy, he noted that it was the maturity of democracies that influenced whether their behaviour tended towards the pacifist or the bellicose because 'history shows that young democracies, or ones that are just emerging as great Powers, can behave in quite an aggressive way' (UNSG 19 June 2001, SG/SM/7850). Annan therefore dismissed procedural democracy as too limited and confirmed the UN's experiences that 'what happens between elections is at least as important for democracy as what happens during them' (Annan 2002: 138). Annan addressed this through the development of UN practice.

As the foundations for democracy had been laid by Boutros-Ghali, the democracy agenda no longer needed justification but merely refinement and institutionalisation. While democracy continued to be an important issue during Annan's two terms as Secretary-General, it became a more technical, operational concern. Where Boutros-Ghali had tried and partially succeeded in developing a new intellectual framework for the UN in the post-Cold-War world, Kofi Annan followed a different route. As a career UN bureaucrat, expectations were high for Annan to drive forward and complete issues such as UN reform, and it was Annan's organisational reforms through which the democracy agenda was further developed and institutionalised. Increasing institutionalisation meant that more UN organisations became concerned with democracy while existing programmes extended their reach. This also increased member states' support and acceptance, and the possibility for a deepening of democracy. Annan built on his predecessor's conceptual foundation and referred back to Boutros-Ghali's *Agenda for Democratization* by praising its potential and framing his own first report as a path 'Towards an Agenda for Democratization' (UNSG 21 October 1997, A/52/513, para. 23).[4] Although Annan, like Boutros-Ghali, outlined democracy as a principle that needed to reach from the local to the national and the global, he dropped Boutros-Ghali's focus on international democracy, separating unit-level democracy and international democracy. Instead, he focussed firmly on existing practices concerned with the support and implementation of democracy at the national level.

In his first report Annan then interpreted the results of the now UN sponsored International Conferences of New or Restored Democracies, as well as other developments within the UN system and outlined principles for democracy. Report A/52/513 was far-reaching in the conceptualisation of democracy as the Secretary-General called for a new understanding of democracy, stating that 'democratization and governance [are] two key concepts which I believe should stand together' (UNSG 21 October 1997, A/52/513, para. 6). He called for a joint agenda of democratisation and governance to be created, bringing together the existing practices of electoral assistance and governance support. This would provide substance to the democracy agenda by bridging

> the existing gap between the peace and development agendas of the United Nations. That gap – whether real or imagined – has created tension with the United Nations membership and claims that one or the other agenda has taken over the priorities and the resources of the Organization. Efforts to promote democracy and good governance are fundamental to the consolidation of peace and development, as the Agenda for Development, approved by the General Assembly on 20 June 1997 in resolution 51/240 recognized. (UNSG 21 October 1997, A/52/513, para. 26)

This focus on governance was Annan's 'quiet revolution' of the organisation and UN practice (see Annan 1998). In making the connection between governance and election assistance, the Secretary-General laid the ground for a multi-disciplinary, inter-agency framework of democracy assistance, which joined up the loose ends that remained from Boutros-Ghali's conceptual development. The foundation for this framework was a list of eleven principles of good governance that the Subgroup on Capacity Building for Governance of the UN Administrative Committee on Coordination (ACC) had drawn up in June 1997. These principles were based on the different approaches and experiences of various UN agencies and, as Figure 5.4 shows, circumscribed broadly the structures and processes of democratic societies. Annan stressed that if free and fair elections were added to these fundamental principles of democratic society, 'all essential elements for a solid framework of democratization assistance by the United Nations ... would be in place' (UNSG 21 October 1997, A/52/513, para. 25).

This operational change thus enabled a conceptual move away from procedural democracy in which elections were equated with democracy, and in which institutions

---

1. Effective public sector
2. Accountability/transparency of processes and institutions
3. Effective participation of civil society/political empowerment
4. Effective decentralization of power
5. Access to knowledge, information and education
6. Political pluralism/freedom of association and expression
7. Rule of law/respect for human rights
8. Legitimacy/consensus
9. Attitudes and values fostering responsibility, solidarity and tolerance
10. Equity/voice for the poor
11. Gender equality
   +
12. Free and fair elections.

Figure 5.4 *Principles of democratic governance*

and governance were viewed as separate issues. Now institutions in general and the good governance agenda in particular could be seen as being part and parcel of democracy. Thus, the reconceptualisation of democracy was brought about through the integration of practices, following a technical, not a political route. These principles were officially merged into the concept of *democratic governance* in 2000 (UNSG 13 October 2000, A/55/489). Here, Annan described democratic governance as the framework within which the key concepts and practices of UN assistance, namely election assistance, human rights promotion, good governance support and development assistance, are subsumed. Democracy assistance in various forms, from election assistance to governance support and institution building, subsequently became part of practice at a number of UN agencies and programmes. However, despite the integration of both practices into one democracy support practice, Annan, like others, on occasion continued to refer to democracy along the dividing lines of its individual practices; for example where he stated that 'democratic governance combines the principles and processes of democracy with the institutions and processes of governance' (UNSG 13 October 2000, A/55/489, para. 14).

As democracy became increasingly institutionalised, its adoption as a practice to support member states by the UN system further shaped and refined how democracy should be viewed, and how far and deep it should penetrate a state's system and society. This was supported by member states' increased recognition of democracy as a global principle and by organisational reform measures which offered conceptual 'niches' in which democracy could be embedded without drastic changes from accepted ideas, norms or practices. In 1999, Romania, host of the 1997 Third International Conference on New and Restored Democracies, had proposed to the General Assembly a 'Code of Democratic Conduct' in follow-up to the conference. This Code set out 'a basic set of norms ... for Governments in the exercise of power' (UNGA, letter dated 19 July 1999 from the Permanent Representative of Romania to the UN addressed to the Secretary-General, A/54/178, as quoted in Dumitriu 2003: 21). It went beyond the structural prescriptions implicit in UN practice so far by including not only civil and political rights, institutions of electoral democracy, the rule of law and good governance, but also development issues, which reflected the broader canon of social and economic rights (UNGA 23 November 1999, A/54/L.23). Ideas of equality, inclusion, participation and accountability were extended from the political realm to strengthen not only procedural aspects of democracy but also democratic outcomes, that is, visions of what a democratic society ought to achieve. This included policy prescription to overcome social and economic inequalities and to ensure adequate access to opportunities for all, as well as the provision to meet the social and economic expectations of the people, for example through social protection systems and basic social services for all (UNGA 23 November 1999, A/54/L.23).

Despite initial support from sixty member states, the prospect of codifying democratic behaviour and therefore establishing benchmarks for the assessment of states led to strong opposition and the eventual dismissal of the proposal (Dumitriu 2003: 23). However, in April 2000, only a year after its first proposition, the same proposal was reintroduced to the Commission of Human Rights. Dropping the offensive

'Code' for the title of *Promoting and Consolidating Democracy* (Res. 2000/47) allowed support to be secured, and subsequently enabled the adoption of Resolution A/RES/55/96 by the General Assembly in 2001 (Dumitriu 2003). The new title followed the example of the Commission's 1999 resolution on the *Promotion of the Right to Democracy* (Res. 1999/57) and therefore suggested continuity rather than a drastic break and introduction of new, radical ideas. The proposed Resolution 2000/47 extended the 'right to democracy' outlined in Resolution 1999/57, which was limited to ideas of good governance and civil and political rights, through broader applicability and greater descriptive detail of democracy. The resolution focussed on participation processes, governance and the rule of law, but also emphasised the need 'to strengthen democracy by promoting sustainable development, [and] to enhance social cohesion and solidarity' (UNHCHR 25 April 2000). Resolution 2000/47 introduced a comprehensive list of elements to define democracy that was subsequently matched by the Consultative Committee on Programme and Operational Questions (CCPOQ), which in September 2000 approved on behalf of the Administrative Committee on Coordination (ACC) – the highest internal UN body for the coordination of the UN agencies – a Matrix of Governance. This matrix set out a broad range of policy measures and matched them with relevant elements of democratic societies and governance, which were seen as points of entry and inter-agency collaboration (UN 2000, see Figure 5.5). The scope of the Secretary-General's new practice of democratic governance support was therefore extensive and matched, if not exceeded the list of features outlined by Lijphart (1999) or Luckham et al. (2000). At the same time, recognition by member states enhanced the agenda's legitimacy and its scope. Following this, further entrenchment in the UN system was facilitated through organisational reforms which affected both managerial dimensions and thus the potential to circulate (and perhaps re-interpret) ideas and their connection to different UN practices.

The reform of the Secretariat had been a key task for both Boutros Boutros-Ghali and Kofi Annan. Boutros-Ghali's reform measures, which included the establishment of an Office of Internal Oversight (OIOS), hailed by the USA as 'one of the most significant management reforms adopted by the General Assembly in many years' (Fasulo 2004: 107), a Lessons Learned Unit in the Department for Peacekeeping Operations and of course his three agendas, were at the same time seen as both insufficiently far-reaching enough to address the sclerosis of the organisation, as well as reaching too far in some cases, falling outside the Secretary-General's remit (see Fasulo 2004: 134–138). By contrast, Kofi Annan embarked upon a wide-ranging reform process that Boutros-Ghali had only inadequately attempted, and which had contributed to the failure of his re-election to a second term. On assuming office Kofi Annan addressed the reform of the Secretariat immediately. Thus, a new office of Deputy Secretary-General was established, as well as a Senior Management Group, a Strategy Planning Unit, an Office of Emergency Relief Coordinator, the post of High Commissioner for Human Rights and a UN Development Group that brought together UNICEF, UNDP and the United Nations Population Fund (UNPF). While the role of the Deputy-General was to improve day-to-day management and oversee all cross-departmental work, the Senior

Management Group, composed of the coordinators of the sectoral groups, heads of the regional commissions and other Under-Secretaries-General, functioned like a cabinet (Beigbeder 2000). This meeting of senior managers supported and enhanced the flow of ideas through the organisation and UN system.

In the context of these structural changes and new management culture, the reconceptualisation of human rights as an organisational principle and practice was a key factor in bringing about significant changes for the democracy agenda. The Secretary-General's reforms made the Office of the High Commissioner of Human Rights (OHCHR) into a system-wide focal point for human rights, democracy and the rule of law, and charged it with the task of facilitating the mainstreaming of human rights into development programming. Following this, in a 1998 report to the Economic and Social Council (ECOSOC) the Secretary-General called for a human-rights-based approach (HRBA) to be adopted as a fundamental part for the execution of all activities carried out by all UN agencies, in particular development aid. UNDP was a 'notable intellectual leader' in conceptualising this human-rights-based approach, focussing on institutions of governance, even if others (such as UNICEF) were ahead in translating theory into practice (Cornwall and Nyamu-Musembi 2004: 1426). Key to UNDP's strategy was its 1998 policy document on *Integrating Human Rights with Sustainable Human Development* and the 2000 Human Development Report *Human Rights and Human Development*. Following the new, streamlined management culture, interagency workshops in 2001 and 2003 under the auspices of the UN Development Group further sought to develop the HRBA, resulting in a *Common Understanding Among UN Agencies* (UNSG 26 September 2003).

The HRBA not only aimed at the development of projects and programmes specifically targeting human rights but also sought to re-orientate existing programmes towards human rights aspects (UNSG 26 September 2003, A/58/392). With democracy increasingly recognised as a human right, the HRBA allowed democracy to be used in a much broader context and with greater legitimacy. Thus the restructuring of human rights as a cross-sectoral goal and principle brought about a period in which conceptual linkages between the root ideas of development and human rights were reasserted and strengthened. In the process of organisational restructuring the human rights agenda not only received new impetus but also became functionally more deeply integrated with the development agenda, which in turn had also seen the integration of democracy.

These organisational reforms forced a rethinking of how practices were implemented throughout the organisation and further innovations, such as the establishment of a UNDP Democratic Trust Fund in 2001 sought to focus and streamline assistance, and to enable the dispensation of aid more rapidly and more closely to the local or national level. As Mark Malloch Brown, UNDP Administrator, observed: 'One of the most important lessons of the last two decades is that democratic governance is the glue that holds all other development priorities set out across the Millennium Development Goals together' (UNSG 11 September 2003, SG/SM/8860, para. 4). Hence, the Democratic Trust Fund was intended to serve a critical function in enhancing effectiveness by focussing on the importance of democracy as an axis

Policy measures	Core elements	Areas of programmatic collaboration
1. Democracy and participation	1.1 Electoral processes	1.1.1 Promote constitutional and electoral law reform; provide expertise in revision of voter rolls and defining voter districts so as to ensure greater participation, particularly among the poor
		1.1.2 Promote independent election commissions before and during elections and in inter-election periods: major focus on capacity for election management, training of poll workers and training materials
		1.1.3 Promote the publication and dissemination of election results through print and broadcast media
	1.2 Legislative reform	1.2.1 Provide support to legislatures in law-making, establishing effective oversight and improving representation (particularly so as to give the poor a voice): including a focus on newly elected legislators in roles and responsibilities and constituent relations, committee system, role of political parties in legislature, legislature's relationship with other branches
		1.2.2 Provide support to legislators to build competence in economic and governance issues
	1.3 Decentralisation and local governance	1.3.1 Promote policies to bring government closer to the people and strengthening local and regional governance systems for service delivery, policy formulation and resource management, and local and regional development
		1.3.2 Promote the participation of all social groups in economic, social and political decisions at the local and regional level
		1.3.3 Strengthen the ability of cities and towns in developing countries to deliver services to their populations and to increase their potential for tackling the problems of urban growth and poverty
		1.3.4 Involve local governments, the private sector, NGOs and community members who collaborate as partners in identifying problems and seeking solutions to development issues (particularly urban issues)
	1.4 Civil society empowerment	1.4.1 Promote CSOs and NGOs as advocates and interlocutors and as actors in social, economic, political, cultural and environmental fields

		1.4.2 Promote legislative and tax frameworks for CSOs improving their ability to fill their roles in advocacy and development
2. Equity	2.1 Socio-economic equity	2.1.1 Promote poverty eradication efforts via credit, training, markets and basic services
	2.2 Gender equality	2.2.1 Promote the inclusion of women in all aspects of the electoral process; enhancing women's access to decision-making and support to their inclusion as candidates on party lists; strengthening local and regional governance systems for pro-poor and women-inclusive policies and programmes
		2.2.2 Promote CSOs and NGOs that, as advocates, interlocutors and actors, advance women's issues in social, economic and cultural fields
		2.2.3 Promote reforms of economic and financial management systems focusing particularly on gender-sensitive budget planning and management and national account gender disaggregated statistics. Support to provide more reliable gender disaggregated economic and social statistics for long-term gender-sensitive development planning
3. Environment protection and management	3.1 Environment protection and management (commons)	3.1.1 Promote initiatives that conduct environmental impact assessment and enforcement of environmental laws and regulations
		3.1.2 Promote activities of environmental sensitisation and rejuvenation (e.g., reforestation)
		3.1.3 Support community-based capacity to manage resources
4. Human rights	4.1 Human rights conventions and norms, including the right to development	4.1.1 Promote political, civil, economic, social and cultural rights including the integration of human rights principles and norms with all aspects of development
	4.2 Human rights standards	4.2.1 Promote labour reforms and basic standards; Geneva convention and other protocols
		4.2.2 Promote national conformity with international human rights standards
	4.3 Human rights implementation	4.3.1 Promote the implementation of human rights conventions and standards in domestic and international law; strengthen human rights institutions

Policy measures	Core elements	Areas of programmatic collaboration
5. Rule of law	5.1 Constitutional reform	5.1.1 Promote the drafting of new constitutions or constitutional amendments that promote the rule of law, human rights and representational government
	5.2 Legal reform	5.2.1 Programmes to improve the legal analysis and drafting capabilities of government and legislature
	5.3 Judicial reform and access to justice	5.3.1 Programmes to reform the judicial system and to train the staff of this system
		5.3.2 Promote universal access to justice and reduce court delays
		5.3.3 Support in areas like training of police and prosecutors, legal aid, integrity of judges
	5.4 Penal reform	5.4.1 Programmes with national institutions to reform prison systems and prison management, review penal codes and apply international human rights standards in the treatment of prisoners (special focus on HIV/AIDS)
	5.5 Civil police	5.5.1 Promote training and institutional reforms, with stress on awareness of human rights standards, community responsibility and community participation
6. Public administration and service delivery	6.1 Globalisation, liberalisation and trade	6.1.1 Promote measures to strengthen both the negotiating capacity of developing countries, in particular LDCs, in global trade and investment and the capacity to adjust to new terms of international competitiveness, particularly emphasising the need to protect vulnerable groups of the population
	6.2 Civil service reform	6.2.1 Promote civil service reform, management development institutions and comprehensive programmes aimed at improved performance of the public sector (recruitment, training, promotion, etc.)
		6.2.2 Programmes to enhance the role, prestige, professionalism, ethical values and standards in the public service
		6.2.3 Programmes highlighting the value and virtue of 'public service' as service to the community at the national, sub-national and international levels
		6.2.4 Programmes intended to enhance critical skills in key priority areas, including policy advice, resource management, performance measurement, and gender mainstreaming

	6.3 Macroeconomic management	6.3.1 Promote reforms of economic and financial management systems focusing particularly on (i) tax and customs administration; (ii) budget management, accounting and bank supervision, and national account statistics; (iii) strengthening public finances; (iv) enhancing confidence in the banking system; and (v) more reliable economic and social statistics for long-term development planning
	6.4 Private sector development	6.4.1 Facilitate interaction between the state and the private sector and promotion of a socially responsible involvement by private business in public affairs
		6.4.2 Promote formal consultative mechanisms to facilitate information exchanges between business associations and the state
		6.4.3 Promote community-based capacity to manage resources
		6.4.4 Promote employment-generating investments
	6.5 External debt management	6.5.1 Promote national debt management programmes, including capacity for debt negotiation, donor coordination and efforts to link debt relief resources to human development objectives
	6.6 Aid coordination and management	6.6.1 Programmes to strengthen national capacity for aid coordination and to integrate external resources with national development efforts and in this context to promote close cooperation between recipient governments, civil society, the private sector and the donor community
7. Transparency and accountability	7.1 Strengthen institutions of control	7.1.1 Promote rule of law as a precursor of anti-corruption initiatives in the state
		7.1.2 Support CSOs that monitor and combat corruption
		7.1.3 Support independent ombudsman institutions, auditors, Ministries of Finance, including support for agencies of horizontal accountability
	7.2 Information systems	7.2.1 Strengthen information systems for budgetary management, monitoring and expenditure control
	7.3 Strengthen capacity of investigative journalism and media	7.3.1 Promote training institutions for journalists; support programmes to strengthen print and electronic media

Policy measures	Core elements	Areas of programmatic collaboration
8. Security, peace-building and conflict	8.1 Security of person and property	8.1.1 Promote the improvement of security from crime for all citizens as a public good that all citizens have the right to enjoy
		8.1.2 Promote the protection and security of humanitarian workers and beneficiaries
	8.2 Civil-military relations	8.2.1 Support for programmes highlighting civic and democratic values and the responsibilities of the military in the context of national security
	8.3 Conflict management and peace-building	8.3.1 Promote the compilation of indicators to assess conflict and post-conflict situations
		8.3.2 Undertake programmes with an emphasis on conflict prevention and conflict resolution; programmes of national dialogue and reconciliation; programmes to address root causes of conflict; emphasis on women's participation in peace-building processes
		8.3.3 Undertake programmes for resettlement and reintegration of affected populations; promote the development of local, community-based capacity to manage resources; promote micro-credit and area development schemes that serve the needs of disadvantaged, reintegrated or war-affected populations
		8.3.4 Programmes that promote rule of law, stability, security and public order within the context of disarmament and demobilisation of ex-combatants and reintegration of war-affected populations
		8.3.5 Programmes celebrating diversity in public life; programmes combating stereotypes; encouraging respect for ethnic, religious, political and cultural diversity; building tolerance
		8.3.6 Empowerment of citizens in rural, distant and/or isolated areas through poverty reduction programmes; better public service delivery systems and public information
		8.3.7 Promote reconstitution of civil registries

9. Informed citizenry	9.1 Eradicating illiteracy	9.1.1 Support literacy programmes
	9.2 Universal access to education	9.2.1 Support policies and programmes aimed at increasing universal access to quality education
	9.3 Public information systems	9.3.1 Support programmes and actions for improving public information and for making the actions of officials come before public scrutiny
		9.3.2 Promote civic education and voter education of men and women, boys and girls
10. E-governance	10.1 Use of IT in governance	10.1.1 Promote use of information technology to strengthen relationship between the governing and the governed; to educate citizens; and to encourage greater involvement by citizens and civil society in governance
		10.1.2 Promote the technological innovation of voter registries, election procedures, accountability and transparency mechanisms and other measures to improve the effectiveness of good governance and the voice of the poor in it
		10.1.3 Promote electronic networks, partnerships and communication systems that encourage greater participation in and education about governance between North and South, and between South and South.

Figure 5.5 *ACC Matrix of Governance*

around which other practices converged. Organised in six service lines – parliamentary development, electoral systems and processes, access to justice and human rights, access to information and e-governance, decentralisation and local governance, and public administration and civil service reform – the Trust Fund offered a number of services from advice to capacity-building (UNSG 11 September 2003, SG/SM/8860).

Governance and democracy assistance in practice

Opportunities to develop the democracy agenda towards greater democratic substance emerged through both ideas and practices. Throughout the UN system ideas and practices served as vehicle for this broader democracy practice, while greater recognition for the establishment of a culture of democracy (and with it a longer-term perspective) gained hold. In practice, that is, in the field, failed states, 'new' wars and 'complex political emergencies' (see Cliffe and Luckham 1999; Goodhand and Hulme 1999; Kaldor 2001) all required new thinking and imposed increasing demands on the international community to respond with a myriad of support activities to achieve peaceful solutions. With an election-as-exit strategy no longer considered appropriate, elections now increasingly served as an *entry point* for assistance (Ponzio 2004: 218). Thus, while mission mandates before 1989 primarily focussed on observing cease-fires and separating conflict parties, mandates now increasingly included a broad range of activities, such as election observation, civil society support and police training (Durch 2001). Governance dimensions as part of democracy support were used in missions such as those in East Timor where the introduction of transitional administrations led to new tasks in governing (see Chesterman 2005; Paris 2004).

In East Timor, following the rejection of a vote for 'special autonomy' within Indonesia, anti-independence militias sought to prevent separation from the archipelago by terrorising the population and destroying most of the country's physical and political-administrative infrastructure. While in East Timor the security dimension was less problematic than in other post-conflict situations as violence had been topical, that is, related only to the referendum, the need to restore the capacity of East Timor to govern itself was far more demanding (Chesterman 2005).[5] Hence, after a successful intervention to restore order and peace, the Security Council established UNTAET and gave it the power to assume overall responsibility for the administration of East Timor and 'to exercise all legislative and executive authority, including the administration of justice'. According to Paris, the extraordinary powers given to UNTAET, including the 'robust' rules of engagement for military contingents and permission to react to fire by militias, showed that 'the success of the East Timor mission to date is a testament to the willingness of peacebuilders to assume full responsibility for the reconstruction of a functioning state apparatus' (Paris 2004: 220). The 'success' of the East Timor mission was, however, relative to its own terms: while independence had been established and both electoral process and democratic governance appeared to be functioning, that is, allowing for the turnover of power, the political culture of East Timor continued to include violence as events in 2006 and 2008, and the intervention of foreign troops, showed.

The reconstruction of institutions, in particular in failed states, required large-scale and long-term commitment by the UN and aid donors as not only the physical environment of institutions needed to be reconstituted but also a system's human resources, regulations and customs. As Chesterman (2005: 128) rightly points out, politics do not cease to exist in failed states. Instead, spontaneous and unregulated relationships develop in the political-bureaucratic vacuum of conflict states. Returning these relationships to a public forum regulated by law, in a transparent and accountable fashion, proves difficult as individual profits may be lost in the process. Thus, the sustainability of a newly created society is dependent on how well an intervention interacts with local circumstances and the degree to which the people have been able to form a democratic culture or 'culture of peace', which both Secretaries-General Boutros-Ghali and Annan had repeatedly highlighted. These requirements then create a paradox for UN assistance in which the quality of the desired end contrasts with the ability (and willingness) of the UN to provide this end. The 2000 Brahimi Report, commissioned by Annan in response to his call for new thinking on peace-keeping, questioned whether the UN should engage in such missions at all, and if so, how many missions would be feasible at any given point in time. Following the principles of organisational and operational streamlining implemented elsewhere, the Brahimi Report sought to balance the tension between expansive goals and needs, and efforts for efficiency and cost-effectiveness (Peou 2002). Brahimi concluded that peace operations should not be commissioned in too many places and that they should be robust, ensuring a match between capabilities and mandates, while reducing UN commitment through increased engagement of regional organisations or lead states. Controversially, the report called for mandates to be finalised *after* resources had been pledged by member states (UN 21 August 2000, A/55/305-S/2000/809).

An alternative to the means–end dilemma and the ambitious goals of establishing a culture of democracy through institution-building and elections, was the UN mission in Afghanistan, which was based on a 'light footprint' and intended, among other aspects, to show the potential benefits of using local quasi-democratic processes as both a democratic means, that is, an expression of self-determination, as well as an efficiency measure.[6] In Afghanistan a comprehensive approach for an almost complete state reconstruction was chosen which built on and utilised indigenous political structures and processes to complement – not replace – the implementation of liberal democratic structures. Embedded in a larger process to establish a democratic society, the use of local traditions was thought to enhance the legitimacy and 'ownership' of the new system. Thus, conflicts could be resolved and a democratic culture could be 'learned'. To enable a cooperative reconstruction of the now defunct Afghan state and society, as well as to enable warlords to take part in this process and not work counter to it, the traditional *loya jirga* (Great Council) provided a vehicle through which a form of democracy could be practised.[7] Although in large parts unelected, this *loya jirga* represented different clans and sections of Afghan society. Furthermore, it was envisaged as part of a multi-stage process with elections, a new constitution and parliament as endpoint (Schneider 2005: 186). In contrast to Cambodia, for example, this was intended to allow for an 'enculturation' of Afghans into a new, Western political system while maintaining at least the appearance of a self-determined solution.

The utilisation of indigenous practices remains an exception, despite hints that at least Kofi Annan would have considered these practices feasible to some extent. For example, in Somaliland the use of indigenous quasi-democratic practices and liberal democracy were ignored by the UN. While the negative reaction to Somaliland's efforts was conditioned by broader concerns of secession[8], the lack of support by the UN for Somaliland in the early 1990s also showed that democracy and self-determination are not the same. Similarly, while the international community may choose to support 'undemocratic' solutions as it did in Kosovo, the utilisation of indigenous practices to achieve the democratisation goals of UN missions also raises the question of what should be done when local populations chose undemocratic solution (Fukuyama 2005: 86). Can the goals of democracy (and conflict resolution) be pursued in a framework of efficiency, cost-effectiveness and limited engagement? In this vein the conflict and state failure in Somalia in the 1990s was a hard case for the UN. While the south of Somalia remained chaotic and conflict-prone, the northern region of Somaliland achieved peace by drawing on traditional methods of conflict resolution and democratic consultation.[9] Today Somaliland is a peaceful, stable, constitutional state with unique democratic features,[10] yet its democratic achievements, as well as its status, remain unrecognised by the international community.[11] As Afghanistan continues to struggle towards democracy in an unstable security situation in 2010, it becomes increasingly evident that to judge the democracy agenda on its record in peace-keeping missions is misguided. The saying that East Timor had the mission that Kosovo should have had, while Kosovo had the mission that Bosnia should have had (Chesterman 2005: 256), highlights the complexity of each conflict situation and the difficulty in creating appropriate missions for individual circumstances. Instead, UN development practice offers a multitude of opportunities to envision, structure and implement democracy in a longer term perspective.

Conclusion: MiniMax democracy

At the end of Boutros Boutros-Ghali's term as UN Secretary-General in December 1996, democracy had long ceased to be hidden under the veil of ideology. Using democratic tools for peace-building and post-conflict state reconstruction, or indeed as a way to facilitate economic and social development, the idea and practice of democracy had become more or less normalised. The persistent rhetoric of Secretary-General Boutros-Ghali, and his promotion of peace, democracy and development as a triangle of 'indissolubly linked' ideas and practices that form the foundation of international society, ensured that the democracy agenda could develop and remain central to UN activity despite tensions with the principles of sovereignty and non-intervention. The governance agenda of the development community allowed for an extension of democracy beyond elections. After the introduction of elections primarily through peace-related practices, the development of the democracy agenda was thus facilitated by the parallel development of a new governance approach in the development community.

The good governance agenda's mantra to 'bring the state back in' redressed neoliberalism's tendency to overemphasise the market and its regulating forces in bringing about economic growth and socio-economic development. This practice, conditioned accordingly by key development organisations such as the World Bank, highlighted the importance of qualitative aspects in governing. This move mirrored the goals that proponents of universal human rights aimed to achieve, such as the understanding that statehood, political rule and governance were not, and should not be seen to be, independent of the quality of their performance, in particular in relationship to their people. Yet, the criticism levelled at the World Bank's conditionalities demonstrated ultimately the limits of its practice. While many regarded the Bank's governance agenda as too political, for the purposes of the democracy agenda and the human development approach the Bank's agenda remained too technical and too focussed on economic growth, leaving aside questions of social and economic democracy. In the Bank's governance approach democracy only referred to the shape of governance structures in democratic states, even if it included principles such as accountability, fairness and transparency. UNDP's human development agenda, on the other hand, addressed these principles by focussing on outcomes. In this sense the goal of the good governance agenda was to shape outcomes; first, in order to ameliorate the potential effects of liberal market strategies and private enterprise, and second, to achieve a translation of economic growth into individual human development. While input from member states and the lessons learned in reviewing peace-keeping activities provided the impetus for the merging of the development and security agendas, the Secretaries-General contributed to connecting the practice of election monitoring and the practice of good governance as a comprehensive package of democracy assistance, thereby cementing a 'new' practice of democracy assistance. Thus, at the end of Boutros-Ghali's term the foundations for a more substantive UN concept of democracy had been laid conceptually, while Kofi Annan ensured its institutionalisation.

How substantive was this form of democracy? The governance agenda provided the democracy agenda with the potential to move away from a purely procedural notion of democracy by emphasising not only the necessity of elements such as the judiciary, bureaucracy, parliament and civil society for a working democracy, but also stressing the importance of principles such as accountability, fairness, openness and transparency. However, characteristic of this early merging of the security and development agendas into a new concept of UN democracy was the consistent push and pull between form and substance. On the one hand, these democratic principles offered the opportunity to allow structures and actors to be judged by a measure of democratic quality. This provided a yardstick to distinguish them from quasi-democratic, semi-authoritarian regimes in which the quality of democratic institutions and actors was obscured by centralised, authoritarian power distribution and diffuse application of these principles. Goals such as participation and ownership stressed the importance of the individual, therefore aiming to democratise UN programmes and programme outcomes. On the other hand, the structures promoted through the governance agenda often remained instrumental to other goals, be that economic development or simply the long-term ability to hold elections independently and without UN support.

This tension between instrumentalism and the introduction of democratic structures and principles for their own sake was clearly demonstrated where peace-keeping and development were concerned. The philosophy of people-centred development provided the ethos for a substantive definition of governance and democracy. Yet, like the World Bank, UNDP's concept of democracy remained ultimately process-oriented, focussing on technical aspects of practice albeit to a lesser degree. The peace-keeping discourse and practice showed that attention afforded to the quality of institutions and processes was only crucial where this promised to yield positive results for peace-keeping missions. In this sense they served the purpose of enabling a mission to be declared successful, which also aimed at precluding any need for further financial and practical investment in a future UN mission. Thus, democracy here was what could be described as a form of MiniMax democracy. It was minimal in that it stressed the importance of elections around which the democratic state was built. The expansion of democratic principles to institutions, structures and systems which are essential for the functioning of an effective democratic state extended this minimal definition. It was maximal insofar as the philosophy of 'good' rule, participation and people-centred politics played a part in the discourse of democracy. However, in large parts this philosophy remained as yet detached from the forms that it was to inhabit. Attention remained firmly on quality for efficiency's and effectiveness' sakes. Quality and substance were merely a means to an end, not an end in themselves. They were not given independent justification. As such the democracy agenda stopped short of being a maximal, substantive framework. Instead, MiniMax democracy was located towards the middle of the democratic continuum.

Notes

1   This criticism included not only the political aspect of good governance but also economic issues. For example, critics argued that good governance merely represented a continuation of previous neo-liberal economics. According to Williams and Young, the concept of the economic rational actor model inherent in the concept of good governance was the idea of a liberal self that actively posed demands on its government instead of remaining a quiet recipient. This underpinned the Bank's economic model, which meant that so-called 'technical' reforms were not neutral but based on a particular idea of the 'good', which was here specified as a market economy and a 'neutral' state that ensured the economy's proper functioning. Thus, the Bank found itself trapped in a cultural paradox. While it did emphasise that indigenous cultures should be the starting point from which to build indigenous structures, claiming that Western models cannot be imposed, the Bank in effect concluded that only indigenous cultures compatible with the

goals of modernisation were worthwhile investing in (Williams and Young 1994: 94–97). Similarly, Abrahamsen argued that the good governance agenda did not break with the ideals of neo-liberal SAPs but continued to support the minimal state. Abrahamsen criticised the failure to achieve a people-centred approach. As the state was not the main provider of public goods, but primarily the facilitator for private activity and investment – merely administrating not executing adjustment programmes – good governance remained instrumental to achieving economic growth (Abrahamsen 2000).

2   Similarly, although the Human Development Report emphasised the importance of political issues for human development, such as the ability to participate, measures of political participation were not included in the Human Development Index as they were regarded too subjective to operationalise (UNDP 2002). Hence, the HDI subjugated the importance of political issues under a more neutral development governance concept.

3   Unsurprisingly perhaps, Michael Doyle (author of the Democratic Peace Theory) was Kofi Annan's Assistant Secretary-General and Special Adviser to the Secretary-General with responsibility for strategic planning, outreach to the international corporate sector (the 'Global Compact') and relations with Washington, 2001–2003. Doyle was a member and Chair of the Advisory Board of the UN Democracy Fund from 2006 to 2010.

4   Further references to the *Agenda* were made in the 1999 report on *Support by the United Nations...* but subsequently dropped (UNSG, 22 October 1999, A/54/492).

5   According to Chesterman (2005) only ten lawyers remained in the country after the violence.

6   Only 75% of the money pledged for 2002 ($2 billion) had been paid in that year, while in 2003 only $200 million were given. Similarly in Cambodia in the early 1990s about 55% of the amount pledged in 1992 had been paid out until 1995 (Chesterman 2005: 190).

7   A *loya jirga* was suggested by the former King Zahir Shah, a suggestion readily taken on by Secretary-General Kofi Annan who stated that Afghans needed to feel that they have the opportunity to decide their country's future. Crucially, Annan stated that it was the UN's task to help Afghans to realise that they could benefit from 'politics of compromise and power-sharing that will address the needs of the people' (UNSG, 29 November 200, SG/SM/8049- AFG/171). However, while the process of peace-making was intricately bound up in the idea of a power-sharing and representation, the idea of democracy was not central. Instead, the idea of a 'truly representative, broad-based, multi-ethnic government' became the formula around which the UN's efforts and understanding revolved. By contrast, the Afghan commitment to democracy appeared to be much clearer. At a press conference at Petersberg, Germany, in December 2002, Afghan President Hamid Karzai, when asked which form of compromise he would make in favour of either security and a concentration of power, or democracy and the delegation of power, replied 'Definitely, a country where people will have the right to vote, where people chose [sic] their government. Now whether that government should be presidential or parliamentary, or some other form of government, it is up to the Constitution to determine ... Whatever form of government, whatever structure of administration Afghanistan will chose [sic], has to [be] democratic, has to be chosen by the people of Afghanistan.' (United Nations Information Centre 2002: 8). Despite this, elections were regarded as a 'linchpin of the [political transformation] process and an essential element of UNAMA's mandate' (UNSC, 27 March 2003, SC/7708).

8   Somaliland's claim to sovereignty rests on its status as independent state for a few days in 1960 after gaining independence from Britain, before joining another former colony to form the state of Somalia. The international community favours a solution within Somalia as a whole. When a new government in Somalia, a Transitional National Assembly, was created and a president elected as part of an attempt by the president of Djibouti to bring about a political solution in Somalia, the new government was recognised as the legitimate government for the entire state of Somalia. It subsequently resumed membership in several international organisations on behalf of the country (Anonymous 2002).

9   The peace process relied on the traditional conflict resolution system of *xir*, which had survived through British colonial rule. Traditional methods are based on the assembly of village elders chosen on the basis of personal attributes, not tribal chiefs. Democratic participation is encouraged and all meetings are public, with women assuming a central role in the mediation of disputes (Ahmed and Green 1999: 123). Although conflict ensued in 1993–1995, this system was able to reintroduce peace with the support of expatriate Somalis. According to Prunier (1997) the increasing process of democratisation was 'not, as elsewhere in Africa, to satisfy foreign donors (the country does not have any) but to meet a real practical need. The choice is between true democratisation and civil war.'

10   Somaliland is a republic with a mixture of a modern elected house of parliament and a traditional unelected, representative council of elders. The judiciary is independent and press freedom guaranteed (Somaliland Forum 2001).

11   The Somaliland Forum (2001) indeed criticises the UN as one of the most critical opponents to Somaliland as it continues to pursue the goal of a unified Somalia. In 1993 a UN representative who presented President Egal with a plan by the UN to divide the country and assign regions to different clans, was 'politely sent away to exercise his diplomatic skills elsewhere' (Prunier 1997). This disregard for indigenous structures over Western democratic methods, even where they are successful in achieving and maintaining peace, is highlighted by Bryden of the UN Emergencies Unit for Ethiopia. At the end of the second conflict, Bryden wrote, 'the best hopes … may … lie outside the 'traditional' sphere' (Bryden 1995), claiming that the best solution would be the framework of a liberal democracy.

6

Extending democracy II: developmental democracy

The idea that democracy encompasses more than processes and structures has been expressed by the UN and its Secretaries-General on several occasions. However, while the three visions of democracy explored thus far – civilisation, elections, governance – have all found expression at the UN in both ideational and practice form, democracy as governance did mark a conceptual and practical endpoint for the UN democracy agenda. This chapter then takes a different turn and looks towards the future, analysing the shape a UN democracy agenda could assume if it developed a substantive vision of democracy. The construction of this new vision of democracy is driven by an exploration of the full range of the democratic continuum. If 'civilisation' was outside the continuum, 'elections' covered the left-hand side of the continuum and 'governance' the middle, then 'developmental democracy' seeks to move further to the right of the democratic continuum. Building on the ideas of a 'citizen's democracy' set out by a UNDP report on the state of democracy in Latin America, this chapter develops a framework for 'developmental democracy'. To understand the potential for the extension of the democracy agenda towards a substantive vision of democracy, the five dimensions of developmental democracy outlined here – market development, human development, democratisation, participation and citizenship – will be analysed in turn to show how the UN has already addressed these dimensions and where further development is needed. The question then is whether the individual parts of developmental democracy have become a greater whole or whether they remain fragmented in both theory and practice.

Towards a definition of substantive UN democracy

The 2004 UNDP report *Democracy in Latin America: Toward a Citizen's Democracy* (hereafter: Latin America report) marked a potential turning point in thinking about democracy at the UN. Although not an official document and solely focussed on Latin America, its in-depth engagement with the application and meaning of democracy provided an opportunity to envision a new form of UN democracy support. Like the 2002 Human Development Report *Deepening Democracy in a Fragmented World* (hereafter: HDR), the Latin America report analysed the development of democracy, battling in particular with the phenomenon of 'limited' or 'low-intensity' democracy, that is, the lack of substance sufficient enough to infuse democratic institutions and processes to achieve sustainability, in many cases even legitimacy. Both reports found common ground in the idea that more democracy meant better democracy, stating that a deepening and widening of democratisation was necessary. However, their attempts to justify and enable such increased democratisation had markedly different outcomes. The HDR thus serves as a contrapoint to illustrate the potential of a developmental democracy as outlined by the Latin America report.

'Deepening democracy' and the Human Development Report 2002

The HDR, which analysed the relationship between human development and democracy, called for a third pillar to be added to the practice of human development. In addition to investment in education and health, and the promotion of equitable growth, the report added participation through democratic governance to human development. The HDR recognised that while democracy was important in its own right, it was also 'the only political regime compatible with human development in its deepest sense, because in democracy political power is authorized and controlled by the people over whom it is exercised' (UNDP 2002: 55). Thus, the popular foundation of democracy resonated fully with human development's mantra of 'development *of* the people, *for* the people and *by* the people' (UNDP 1993: 8). The HDR repeated that democracy is important in advancing human development not just because political freedoms and participation were fundamental human rights, but also because democracy was better able to deal with a number of challenges such as famine, chaos, and the management of conflict. Moreover, democracy triggered a virtuous cycle of development by providing the freedoms that empower people to 'press for policies that expand social and economic opportunities, and [through] open debates help communities shape their priorities' (UNDP 2002: 3). Governance for human development was consequently a qualitative development from other concepts of governance: 'governance for human development must be democratic in substance and in form – by the people and for the people', hence 'from the human development perspective, good governance is democratic governance' (UNDP 2002: 51–52).

Despite apparent complementarities between the principles of democracy and the foundations of human development, the HDR found that the ethos and goals of human development had failed to connect and infuse democratic institutions and processes. Without an automatic link between democracy and human development in either direction, the report found that the goals of democracy and equity should be considered separately, as 'social injustices are widespread in democratic and authoritarian regimes alike' (UNDP 2002: 59–60). Thus, the HDR (and UNDP) were not prepared to push the boundaries of established conceptions of democracy, but instead saw existing practices as a limit for understanding democracy. Although the HDR regarded all three elements – elections, (good) governance and human development – as important, it conceptualised democracy in procedural or structural terms, as either elections or democratic governance, and excluded the substantive goals of human development as intrinsic to democratic society. Instead, human development remained conceptually separate. While the Human Development Report struggled to integrate the different elements of electoral democracy, good governance and human development into one coherent vision of democracy, the Latin America report attempted and succeeded at closing this gap by setting out a clear and cohesive agenda for a reconceptualisation of the processes and goals of a functioning sustainable democracy. It did so by stating *why* the goals of human development needed to be achieved within the context of a democratic society.

The UNDP 'Democracy in Latin America' report

The Latin America report analysed the state of the region's democracy and how it was viewed by its citizens. It drew on two methodological innovations to support its analysis: an Electoral Democracy Index and a Democracy Support Index. The Electoral Democracy Index measured the openness of the electoral process and the translation of voters' preferences by the process. The Democracy Support Index registered the intensity of citizenship, that is, the degree of activism and the orientation of people towards democracy. It categorised people as democratic, ambivalent and non-democratic, and analysed how these groups were linked to each other.[1] Using a variety of methods such as questionnaires and workshops with the general public, academic experts, politicians and business leaders, as well as data from 18 countries[2], the report concluded that the greatest tension in Latin America was a – real or perceived – choice between economic development and democracy (UNDP 2004a: 137). Pronounced inequality and poverty potentially endangered democracy's stability. While electoral democracy had successfully spread throughout the region and democracy had become accepted as a viable political system, many people found themselves dissatisfied with their government's ability to deal with social and economic issues and acknowledged that they would choose a non-democratic system if this solved their economic problems. More positively, Latin Americans had learned to distinguish between those elected into office, their policies and actions, and the system of government offered by democracy.

As UNDP Administrator Mark Malloch Brown likened Latin Americans to 'dissatisfied democrats' rather than 'closet autocrats' (UNDP 2004b: 10), the Latin America report faced the same 'cruel dilemma' that democratisation scholars had debated before: Was development more important than democracy, or could both coexist? The Latin America report followed in the intellectual footsteps of those optimistic about the relationship between democracy and development and concluded that 'problems with democracy need to be solved through more democracy' (UNDP 2004b: 68). Based on the conviction that 'democracy implies a way of envisaging the human being and guaranteeing individual rights' (UNDP 2004a: 55), the report sought to develop a theory of democracy to address these challenges.

Following the works of T.H. Marshall and Guillermo O'Donnell, the authors of the Latin America report re-stated the foundations of democracy as a 'citizen's democracy' and extended democracy beyond the political. Building on Sen's (1999b) capability approach the authors of the Latin America report went beyond political processes and conceptualised democracy as a means of guaranteeing and broadening freedom, justice and progress. They rejected the notion of a separation of political democracy (elections) from other elements of society and the state, such as the social and economic agenda, stressing that '[an] important consequence stemming from an understanding of democracy as only a system of government is a segmentary view of public policies' (UNDP 2004a: 44). Instead, the state needed to integrate the needs of society into politics. Integration was necessary because democracy's 'civilising promise' inextricably linked the social and economic agendas to democracy as citizens have specific expectations about economic performance. In other words, people expect the 'egalitarian promise' that underlies the idea of democracy also to be realised in areas other than the political. Secondly, because both market and economy could critically affect democracy – for example, as unemployment creates a disconnect between economic and social development, between basic equalities and the capability to participate in public life (UNDP 2004a: 122) – the integration of societal needs into politics required debate about the nature of the market and the organisation of the economy.

Unlike previous reports, the Latin America report rejected the idea of the market and market forces as natural and therefore outside political debate (UNDP 2004a: 186). Instead, it argued that the market was not independent of the state. The market contextualised the organisation of the state, bestowing on the state a necessary role in guiding the market. Hence economic policies were just another democratic tool to enable the widening of freedom and equality. While the report, like previous UNDP and World Bank reports, concluded that enhancing 'stateness' was central to development, it stated, unlike previous reports, that what was needed most of all is an 'all-encompassing, inclusive and *compassionate* state' (UNDP 2004a: 183, emphasis added). As democracy should be measured by its capacity to guarantee and expand all dimensions of life, a citizen's democracy would follow a different approach, implementing a hierarchy and *subordinating* the market to democracy. In this framework society *chooses* the market rather than adjusts itself to market forces. Convinced that 'capitalism has survived as the dominant form of economic organization not in spite of democracy but because of it' (UNDP 2004a: 189), the report argued that the legitimacy of the economic system would be enhanced through a citizenship focus because democracy curtails the exclusion brought about by the market.

The Latin America report stressed that the individual was the source of the state's and the government's mandate and authority, claiming that as 'democracy deals with life … its principal figure is the citizen rather than the voter' (UNDP 2004a: 36). Despite the individualism inherent in this model, the individual's context was seen as being by nature collective. As such, the idea of citizen's democracy bridged the individual and the collective by recognising that a basic equalisation emanating from social welfare was a 'primary aspect of fairness' intrinsic to a universal right of rights and capabilities. As individuals are endowed with innate rights, citizenship is a basic equality for members of community. Thus, 'by virtue of simply being citizens, people have the right to have their dignity respected, and they also have the right to be granted the social conditions necessary to engage freely in all activities related to their social existence' (UNDP 2004a: 68). Consequently, the report argued, democracy ought to be measured by its capacity to guarantee and expand the role of citizens in the civil, social and political sphere.

In order to demonstrate how social and economic rights had to be seen in conjunction with civil and political rights, and how the contradiction between the market's individualism and inequality, and democracy's basis of collectivism and equality could be reconciled, the authors of the Latin America report drew on T.H. Marshall's work on citizenship. While the concept of development as part of the democratic relationship recognises the need for social cohesion and social justice to be realised, this only gains full force through the notion of citizenship which circumscribes the relationship between rights and duties for both individuals and the state. Using education as an example, Marshall showed how the individual and the state are connected. According to Marshall, the 'duty to improve and civilise oneself is … a social duty, and not merely a personal one, because the social health of a society depends upon the civilisation of its members' (Marshall 1992: 16). Education includes not only an individual right to a public service for the purpose of intellectual (and professional) development with the aim to gain future material opportunities, it is also a public duty owed by the individual to society as a whole: 'education is a necessary prerequisite of civil freedom' (Marshall 1992: 16). In other words, society and the individual are connected, mutually constituting each other. While individuals have an obligation towards each other as part of the community, the state equally has an obligation towards society as a whole since 'what matters is that there is a general enrichment of the concrete substance of civilised life, a general reduction of risk and insecurity, an equalisation between the more and the less fortunate at all levels' (Marshall 1992: 33). Education, a 'genuine' right, shapes future citizens and therefore contributes to the development of both individual and society as a whole. Following this, democracy has a developmental role in the facilitation of individual and collective rights. These rights include a basic level of economic welfare and security, as well as the right to share one's social heritage and live life as a 'civilised being'. Social services and education are necessary to achieve this.

Citizenship and a citizen's democracy was thus UNDP's solution to resolve the contradiction between market and democracy. The introduction of a citizenship democracy in the Latin America report was critical for the profiling of a potentially new form of UN democracy. Where the HDR 2002 had separated the state and the citizen from each other, the Latin America report provided a clear justification for why people should participate in society and development and why they should benefit from development: individual development depends on macro-economic development and vice versa. In a developmental democracy the individual, society and the state cannot be seen as separate. Citizenship is therefore both individual and social. It circumscribes the relationship between rights and duties for both individuals and the state. Thus, in a citizen's democracy people are moved to the centre of politics.

Developmental democracy defined: a summary

As Chapter 2 showed, a substantive democracy is essentially a developmental one as it emphasises both the conditions for and the processes of developing individuals, markets and the state. As discussed in Chapter 2, the ideas of developmental democracy have been in use since the nineteenth century although the concept has found more explicit usage in recent democratisation studies. According to Held (1996), developmental democracy and the developmental state were first expressed by John Stuart Mill and may therefore be one of the earliest concepts of the democratic welfare interventionist state and the mixed economy. By contrast, democratisation studies debated the question of the developmental democracy, or developmental state, in the context of stalling transition processes of the Third Wave, also with historical reference to successful development in non-democratic states such as Singapore.

Political theorists regard substantive democracy as developmental in that it considers participation as an end in itself and believes in a 'democratic humanism' that needs to be spread throughout society. In this view democracy is 'a way of life: it "cannot … depend upon or be expressed in political institutions alone"' (Dewey 1939: 130). Developmental democracy combines the protection and regulation of the market by the state with a free market and the right to property. Yet, developmental democracy is also a state that aims to foster both economic development and societal well-being. Despite an apparent collectivist focus, political theorists see the development of the individual as taking centre stage. Democracy is the framework and vehicle through which individual development is facilitated. Discursive action and a variety of participatory mechanisms enable citizens to transform themselves (Pateman 1970) as they gain an enlightened understanding through critique and self-critique (Stokes 2002: 38–39). Therefore democracy has an educative and moral function:

> the exercise of citizenship is crucial for the development of the individual's moral maturity. The person grows as a social being: judgement requires thought; participation dispels inertia; and consideration of the common good nurtures altruism … A citizen is a different kind of person from the vassal of a feudal lord, a landowner's serf or the subject of a divine-right monarch. The distinction lies primarily in the moral autonomy and high level of moral behaviour which characterises at least the 'good citizen' in his ideal form. (Heater 2004: 188)

Material aspects of individual development are equally important in this developmental democracy insofar as the individual is not just a consumer and appropriator but 'an exerter, developer, and enjoyer of his capacities' (Macpherson 1977: 48). The individual's worth depends on the extent to which such developmental potential is realised. Following this, a 'good' society protects a system in which people are able to develop their human capacities. This task of development falls to democracy as Macpherson concludes that 'a democratic society is seen as both a result of that improvement and a means to further improvement' (Macpherson 1977: 47).

In contrast to political theory, scholars studying democratisation processes define 'development' primarily in economic, not moral terms, as the Latin America report showed. Hence the debate about developmental democracy is related to the question of how (economic) development is facilitated, the relative strength of the state and the level of freedom, rights and liberties guaranteed by the state. Central to this is the question of democracy's place in the development process, be that at the end of development, as modernisation theory had posited, or as an integral part or facilitator of the process regardless of the level of development (Diamond 1992; Leftwich 2000; Lipset 1959; Sirowy and Inkeles 1991). The arguments for democracy versus the 'strong' state or the (quasi-) authoritarian state as development agent were rehearsed in Chapter 4. Chapter 5 showed how the introduction of the human development agenda may have led to further recognition of individual development over macro-economic development to this discussion, mirroring Macpherson's call for material development to support individual development. Thus, while political theory and democratisation studies have different foci, that is, either the individual or the collective, they highlight the interdependence between them and emphasise the process of democracy beyond election day and the importance of 'development' in everyday life.

Taking into account both strands of analysis, it follows that a substantive or developmental democracy has at its heart the imperative to provide and maintain development. This development ought to focus on the individual as well as the state (i.e. macroeconomic factors), as they are interdependent and mutually constituting: 'a developmental democracy would combine a reasonable measure of social justice, defined as fairness in the distribution of wealth, with economic and political freedom' (Sklar 1996: 37). Following this, 'democracy implies the public management and nurture of markets so that they will flourish with affordable fairness in the distribution of opportunities and wealth' (Sklar 1996: 39). Figure 6.1 outlines the dimensions of a developmental democracy emerging from both political theory and democratisation studies: the development of the economy as a whole irrespective of distribution issues across groups and individuals, the economic development of the individual taking into account distribution across society (equality), the political development of the state (democratisation) and the political development of the individual (enlightenment/participation).

It is important to note that despite a focus on the state's responsibility to provide and ensure development, the state in a developmental democracy does not necessarily

	Political	**Socio-economic**	
State	Democratisation	Market development	**+** **Citizenship**
Individual	Participation and enlightenment	Human development	

Figure 6.1 *Dimensions of developmental democracy*

replace the market as it does in a social democracy (Delanty 2000). Following Giddens (1996), the introduction of welfare rights, as in Marshall's democracy, does not imply the establishment of an economic democracy in the Marxist tradition. Instead, the broad institutional-bureaucratic commitment of the welfare state may be just one expression of the state's responsibility towards citizens but not the only one. Marshall's theory, for example, is one of a process of democratisation to develop and deepen democracy between citizens, mirrored by Secretary-General Boutros-Ghali's views in *An Agenda for Democratization*. In this, the market complements rather than creates or sustains democracy, by aiding the self-development of individuals and thus society as a whole. With this and the Latin America report's concept of citizenship, Evans et al.'s notion of 'bringing the state back in', which had underlined the change from neo-liberal minimal government to good governance in the 1990s, takes on a new meaning. It describes a form of society in which some degree of communitarian responsibility leads to policies, institutions and structures that try to ameliorate the effects of market activity and other social dynamics. Substantive democracy thus contains a number of ideas and goals which the UN seeks to promote in various areas of its work, which have not been associated or combined with democracy thus far. The following sections investigate to what extent the UN has met or addressed the goals of developmental democracy.

Markets, states and people: whose development?

The first contribution to the concept of developmental democracy was made through the good governance agenda. Despite the qualitative dimensions introduced by good governance (such as transparency, accountability and the functional strength of institutions), the practice of good governance was initially conceived as apolitical. However, out of this new practice and the discourse surrounding it emerged something more important: a statement by the UN on its relationship to markets and capitalism, and the role of development practice in relation to this. While this has been largely taken for granted, in the context of conceptualising democracy such statement plays a central role. The UN is committed to the market model insofar as the goals of progress, development and modernisation are enshrined in the UN Charter: 'to promote social progress and better standards of life in larger freedom' (UN Charter, preamble). As UNDP had highlighted in its Human Development Reports, the idea of modernisation and its macroeconomic focus are in conflict with the demands of people-centred development that achieves the kind of equality envisaged by models of substantive democracy, or at a minimum prevents socio-economic deprivation and poverty. Following the provisions of the UN Charter, a substantive vision of democracy would have to be located within a market-based framework. Developmental democracy, with its focus on both markets and people, could be the middle way between the competing demands of both.

The vision of democracy that emerged through the introduction of the good governance agenda is one of a substantive liberal democracy. This is neither a contradiction nor a surprise, despite the battle played out in democracy theory between substantive democracy and liberalism where the individualism inherent in capitalism is seen as running counter to the communitarian dimension of substantive theories of democracy. As Gould (1988) argues, liberalism fails to take sufficient account of social cooperation and social equality, while socialism subordinates individual rights to the community and the welfare society. Liberalism thus stresses individual liberties and it is in capitalism that this liberty expresses itself. For example, the right to property is an individual liberty and central aspect of equality and freedom. With this right to property, capitalist market economies function effectively. Yet, the imperative of political equality to provide individuals with the same rights, here the right to property, may indeed lead to larger economic inequality. Because of this, political equality is distorted and cannot be fully exercised. Not only does greater economic power lead to greater possibilities to participate in the political process, be that physically or intellectually (e.g. access to health care and education), it may also lead to an effective distortion of the political process as economic interests are combined with political power. This distortion and political-economic inequality is at the heart of the communitarian dimension of substantive/developmental democracy. While Marxism saw this equalisation imperative as universal, others, such as theorists of social democracy, recognised a general guiding role of the state in tempering rather than eliminating market forces as sufficient. In a developmental democracy, the communitarian dimension centres on the goal to achieve more social and economic equality through the reduction of the most excessive results of market forces. Developmental democracy seeks to develop markets, states *and* people, recognising the connection between them.

As organisations dedicated to supporting and implementing development goals, the World Bank and UNDP form the 'international machinery' for the promotion of the economic and social progress. Their policies and practices affect the processes and outcomes of development and could therefore determine whether the developmental dimension of democracy could be realised. The good governance agendas of the World Bank and UNDP had suggested different approaches to development in which different emphases were placed on economic and individual development. The World Bank made clear that it pursued a pro-capitalist agenda in which good governance was merely a means to an end. Its mandate, which stresses economic assistance and prohibits political activity in any form, reinforced this. Whereas at the World Bank development, and with it good governance, was directed towards the efficiency and effectiveness of institutions and processes to ensure economic development, UNDP claimed that this approach was insufficiently focussed on macro-economic criteria such as GDP, ignoring people's lived experiences in this developmental process of the state and the economy. These differences, as well as any similarities between the World Bank and UNDP, were most obvious in their 1997 reports on governance and the state. The World Bank's World Development Report *The State in a Changing World* sought to redefine the state, emphasising state effectiveness as key to the Bank's strategy. This included a redefinition of the state's responsibility to be more selective in its activity, as well as the increase of state capability to 'undertake and promote collective actions efficiently' (World Bank 1997: 3). The resulting strategy was to match the state's role to its capability and to raise capability through the reinvigoration of public institutions. This included a better provision of public services and increased state responsiveness to the needs and wishes of citizens, which could be achieved through greater decentralisation but also through increased participation. One way to achieve this was elections, as the Bank claimed that 'the best-established mechanism for giving citizens voice is the ballot box' (World Bank 1997: 10). Despite acknowledging the merits of elections for the first time, the Bank continued to reject substantive democratic practices and instead focussed on effectiveness.

By contrast, in its discussion paper *Reconceptualising Governance* and its policy paper *Governance for Sustainable Human Development* UNDP embraced democracy more openly and sought to include substance through human development criteria. UNDP claimed that governance had to go beyond public management and even participatory decision-making processes, to include democracy and the question of legitimate authority (UNDP 1997: 86). Governance was seen as relating to all areas of state and society, encompassing economic, political, administrative and systemic governance. Hence, a sound governance system would be able to produce the goals of sustainable human development (including poverty reduction, job creation and sustainable livelihoods, environmental protection and the regeneration and advancement of women) (UNDP 1997: 11, 13). UNDP, like the World Bank, emphasised state effectiveness as crucial to the achievement of these objectives. However, unlike the Bank, UNDP saw it necessary 'to create an efficient and effective system of social benefits' including systems of social insurance and social assistance for the protection of the vulnerable and the achievement of social integration to narrow the gaps between rich and poor. Thus, 'governments should … work to ensure the satisfaction of basic needs in ways that are human. In many circumstances this can best be done by increasing *economic democracy*' (UNDP 1997: 30, emphasis added).

UNDP allowed for a broader, more political governance agenda and thus highlighted the potential for a vision of democracy that moved beyond the procedural and institutional aspects of democracy towards more substantive forms of democratic societies. Although these democratic structures which UNDP supported did not differ significantly from those addressed by the World Bank's good governance approach, it was UNDP's philosophical approach, summarised in the concept of 'sustainable human development', which extended the concept of governance. Building on Sen's capability approach and measuring development as an improvement of people's life rather than macroeconomic progress, UNDP took up the UN Charter's ideas to promote social progress and better standards of living, that is, to enable 'life in larger freedom'. By focussing on outputs beneficial to people rather than effectiveness and efficiency, UNDP's governance agenda offered the possibility to embed governance structures with substance and meaning. Here, social issues were not subservient to wider economic goals but an end in themselves. Political and economic structures, processes and policies were mutually constitutive. This emphasised that democratisation was a never-ending process, not an historical endpoint. As such, the development of democratic structures was supposed to propel the process of political and economic development forward in a concerted effort to achieve *human* development, that is, the development of both individual and society. While UNDP's focus on human development may appear to be in tension with a pro-market agenda, the introduction of human development made a significant contribution to the concept of developmental democracy by highlighting the importance of individuals in relation to the state as collective, therefore providing a (new) foundation for the relationship between the people and the state.

The development of markets and the fight against poverty have of course been part of the UN's agenda since its inception. However, establishing a relationship between them beyond the idea that the former (development of markets) inevitably leads to the latter (relief from poverty) had not been made by policy or statements before. Secretary-General Boutros-Ghali hinted that the World Bank approach was too market-focussed, yet he did not make any particular statement in support of either the World Bank's or UNDP's approach. Instead, he referred to both as examples for the efficacy of the governance agenda. The introduction of anti-poverty policies by the new Bank president James D. Wolfensohn in 1998 somewhat narrowed the gap between the two governance approaches, providing a foundation for Kofi Annan to embrace and institutionalise the human development approach as the key guiding UN principle through the introduction of the Millennium Development Goals (MDGs).

The Millennium agenda served as a framework of *humane* governance as Secretary-General Annan emphasised that 'no shift in the way we think or act can be more critical than this: we must put people at the centre of everything we do' (UNGA 18 September 2000, A/RES/55/2, para. 7). This then established a type of people-centred politics that at its heart expressed the same foundations as democracy. Annan expressed the MDGs in detailed operational targets which mirrored the indices set out by the HDI and emphasised the impact of development (or underdevelopment) on people's life, be that life expectancy, health or education. Thus, by adopting a focus on humane governance and people-centred politics, Kofi Annan in effect denounced the World Bank's original governance approach as insufficiently focussed on systems and structures. Accordingly, speaking about globalisation, Secretary-General Annan emphasised that globalisation must mean more than just bigger markets. Instead, 'to survive and thrive, a global economy must have a more solid foundation in shared values and institutional practices – it must advance broader, and *more inclusive, social purposes*' (Annan 2000a: 10, emphasis added). With this in mind Annan followed Sen's philosophy that had formed the basis for UNDP's human development agenda and claimed that extreme poverty was an affront to the world's common humanity. While the MDGs relied on translating substantive goals into technical-operational strategies, they also signified a shift in the understanding of the relationship between individuals, states and international society, a shift that was mirrored by developments in security concepts (see below). People were increasingly seen as being at the centre of UN goals, be that in development or security. Together with the recognition of democracy as a human right, the opportunity for a further entrenchment of the democracy agenda was given. Despite this, the MDGs relegated democracy to second place, relying on democracy as a supporting mechanism, not as an end in itself.

Although Annan had initiated the Millennium Assembly, he did not use this as a platform for democracy promotion. Annan stated that democracy played a central role in ensuring freedom, development, and human rights. Yet, the Millennium Report did not express this. The Roadmap for the Implementation of the Millennium Declaration, which the Secretary-General subsequently devised to operationalise the Millennium Goals, indeed no longer featured democracy at all. Instead, its eight goals, eighteen targets and forty indicators, focussed on quantifiable development factors such as the eradication of extreme poverty and hunger, and the achievement of universal primary education by 2015. Although the importance of other goals, such as democracy, was emphasised, this focus relegated democracy to the background, making it into a means through which the Millennium Goals could be achieved, rather than a goal itself. Making an explicit connection between democracy and the elimination of social inequalities and poverty through 'equal access to economic opportunities and equal pay and other rewards for work of equal value ... [and] ... social protection systems and working towards ensuring basic social services for all' was left to other agencies, as outlined here by Resolution 2000/47, UNHCHR, which established the right to democracy (UNHCHR 25 April 2000).

Democratisation: deepening democracy?

Among the five criteria outlined in the matrix of developmental democracy, democratisation is perhaps the most visible. Without a doubt, the UN has continued its support of and involvement in democratisation over the last twenty years. Indeed a clear trajectory of broadening and deepening the scope of involvement is evident. Democratisation is supported not only by an increase in volume of UN support as well as the institutional integration of democracy into the UN system, but also through greater recognition of democracy by member states. This recognition lends credibility to the UN agenda and creates a parallel network of democracy support activity that gives further impetus to democracy and the process of democratisation. In this process, the UN became a member, if not the hub, of a global network of international and transnational democracy support activities.

Secretary-General Annan's first democracy support report may have suggested that after the decided yet controversial lobbying by Boutros Boutros-Ghali the democracy agenda would operate more quietly and perhaps falter. Annan suggested that a great deal of paperwork in compiling an annual inventory of democracy support activities was unnecessary and he therefore proposed to reduce the number of reports relating to democracy. Until then the Secretary-General had compiled an annual report, providing an inventory of assistance given by the UN system to governments to strengthen new and restored democracies. Now, in line with his organisational reform efforts, a publication was to be compiled only in preparation for the International Conferences of New and Restored Democracies, which were held irregularly every few years (UNSG 26 September 2003, A/58/392). This change in publication practice hinted at reduced opportunities for the Secretary-General to effect substantive change by moving this discourse outside the organisation into a broad, but not universal, conference. A potential result could have been the decline of the democracy agenda due to a lack of attention by member states. Yet by emphasising the operational dimension of democracy, in which democracy support practices served as vehicle to distribute or promote democracy throughout the UN system, democracy remained very much in view of UN member states.

Following increasing institutionalisation of the democracy agenda and a greater emphasis on the philosophy of people-centred politics, Kofi Annan's proposals in the Millennium Report to strengthen democracy found broad support among member states. Indeed, in some aspects member states went beyond the Secretary-General's proposals. As world leaders gathered in New York for the Millennium Summit in September 2000, they agreed to 'spare no effort to promote democracy and strengthen the rule of law, as well as respect for all internationally recognised human rights and fundamental freedoms, including the right to development', and promised to 'work collectively for more inclusive political processes, allowing genuine participation by all citizens' and to 'strengthen the capacity of all our countries to implement the principles and practices of democracy and respect for human rights' (UNGA 18 September 2000, A/RES/55/2, para. 24–25). Moreover, an increasing number of member states showed interest in and participated in pro-democracy conferences such as the International Conference of New or Restored Democracies, which was now organised in close cooperation with the UN and which had opened up participation to all interested governments. Other organisations such as the International Organisation of the Francophonie and African Unity adopted declarations which emphasised the importance of democracy, good governance and human rights, and developed strategies for their achievement. In June 2000 the first meeting of the Community of Democracies, initiated by Polish Foreign Minister Bronislaw Geremek and US Secretary of State Madeleine Albright, led to a pledge of 106 states to work together to uphold and promote democratic principles and values. In his closing speech to the Warsaw Ministerial Conference, Secretary-General Annan praised the Community's efforts and remarked that the idea of *Towards a Community of Democracies* 'represents my own most profound aspiration for the United Nations as a whole' and that 'when the United Nations can truly call itself a community of democracies, the Charter's noble ideals of protecting human rights and promoting "social progress in larger freedoms" will have been brought much closer' (Annan 2000b). The Community of Democracies movement (and its parallel democracy-promoting NGO movement) then fed back into the UN by organising a UN Democracy Caucus in September 2004 where member states sought to collaborate on democracy and democracy-related issues to advance the global democracy agenda. In 2005 the follow-up meeting to the Millennium Summit further supported and legitimised the democracy agenda, leading member states to confirm democracy as one of the 'universal and indivisible core values and principles of the United Nations' and to agree 'to resolve to create a more … democratic world' (UNGA 24 October 2005, A/RES/60/1, para. 16).

Operationally the democracy agenda continued to develop apace, even if in 2003 Kofi Annan stressed that the organisation was still in the process of determining how best to support democratisation processes. He highlighted that he needed to continue to emphasise the need for good governance, that is, 'legitimate, democratic governance that allows each individual to flourish and each State to thrive' as the promotion of democracy was 'one of the main goals of the Organization for the twenty-first century' (UNSG 26 September 2003, A/58/392, para. 12). In his 2005 report *In Larger Freedom*, Annan proposed the establishment of a Democracy Fund, following a previous proposal at the 2000 Community of Democracies meeting. Stating that it was 'time to join up the dots' as there were still significant gaps in UN capacity in several areas, the fund was envisaged to facilitate closer cooperation between the Electoral Assistance Division of the DPA and the democratic governance work of UNDP. Not only should there be better coordination and resource mobilisation, but Annan stressed that 'the United Nations should not restrict its role to norm-setting but should expand its help to its members to further broaden and deepen democratic trends throughout the world' (UNSG 21 March 2005, A/59/2005, para. 151). Established in 2006, the UN Democracy Fund (UNDEF) is a trust fund by Secretary-General which works with a number of UN bodies to coordinate democracy support activities. Addressing democracy support from the supply side, it offers states, NGOs and civil society financial support for the implementation and development of democracy support projects. The Fund has proven popular as almost 6000 applications have been received and to 600 projects have been funded in the first three years (see http://www.un.org/democracyfund/).

Does this continued engagement in democratisation indicate a move towards substantive democracy? Is this democratisation support a sign that developmental democracy can be achieved? While the resolution of the 2005 Summit showed that the idea of democracy may have been accepted by member states, it did not resolve or indeed address the dilemmas and tensions built into the agenda. Not only did member states focus on the rule of law and human rights as the main theme defining democracy, and placed good governance and democracy in the context of *economic* development, they separated democracy from UN root ideas ('our common values'). Member states thus reinforced existing dilemmas and the concept's position on the borderline between procedural-systemic and substantive democracy. Morevover, both *A More Secure World: Our Shared Responsibility* by the Secretary-General's High-level Panel on Threats, Challenges and Change and the Secretary-General's own subsequent report *In Larger Freedom: Towards Development, Security and Human Rights For All*, written in preparation for the summit, emphasised the importance of sovereignty and state capacity, and framed UN activity in the context of its obligation to support weak states, helping states to perform the tasks of sovereignty effectively (see UN 2004; UNSG 21 March 2005, A/59/2005). A wider definition of democracy, that is, popular sovereignty, might have been hinted at but a traditional interpretation of sovereignty could not be overcome. Democracy was therefore understood as limited technical support, primarily aimed at a certain group of states.

Operationally, the scope of the Democracy Fund raises questions about the breadth and depth of democratisation (processes) supported by the UN. Considering that the majority of its funding is allocated to projects in partly free states and in the lower end of the category of 'free states', with very few projects funded in non-free states (Freedom House 2006), the question begs whether UNDEF may be preaching to the converted. Moreover, the promise of the Democracy Fund may be limited by its strong emphasis on supporting 'the voice of civil society', that is, select groups, and its narrow focus on political democracy, especially elections (e.g. electoral support, strengthening political parties). This shows that an integrated practice and substantive democracy is not part of the Fund's approach, even where the concept of citizenship has entered its discourse. On its webpage UNDEF asks its Advisory Board to consider whether the Fund should indeed address all three dimension of citizenship highlighted by the 2004 Latin America Report as it recognises that 'the process of democratisation identified inter alia in the Millennium Declaration cannot be truly disentangled from poverty reduction and the achievement of the Millennium Development Goals themselves' (http://www.un.org/democracyfund/XSituatingDemocracy.htm). Unfortunately, an answer is not discernable to date. In summary, the UN's engagement in democratisation therefore appears to focus on *spreading* and *continuing* democracy where it already exists, rather than *deepening* democracy.

Participation and democracy: two false friends?

The good governance agenda not only extended democratic principles such as accountability and transparency towards state structures, but also extended the principle of participation beyond elections. Although this demonstrated the attractiveness and pervasiveness of the idea of democracy, the practice of participatory development, a form of 'micro' or grass-root level democracy (Weiss et al. 1994), did not necessarily prove to be a democratic one.

In line with UNDP's people-centred approach, the 1993 Human Development Report had introduced a focus on participation to the human development agenda, claiming that previous reports had focussed on 'development *of* the people and *for* the people' only. This focus on participation, however, added the notion of 'development *by* the people'. Placing people at the centre of political and economic developments, the report called for a 'revolution in our thinking … a profound human revolution that makes people's participation the central objective in all parts of life. Every institution – and every policy action – should be judged by one critical test: how does it meet the genuine aspirations of the people?' (UNDP 1993: 8). Participation was seen as an essential element in human development, being both means and end, an investment in and achievement of human capabilities. People should be involved in the cultural, political, economic and social processes that affect their lives. They might do so individually, for example through the ballot box, or in groups as part of civil society.

In this participatory framework democracy was not regarded as limited to elections, neither was it seen as the only arena of participation. Instead, it was regarded as a way of life. Accordingly, democracy was a general means for interaction in a number of arenas, connecting the individual with society in more meaningful ways. Thus, democracy was both a means to achieve participation and an end, a condition, system or state in which the individual was given the opportunity to flourish and take charge of their own development. Hence, the 1993 HDR stated that democracy would be crucial even in the workplace as only within a democratic environment would people achieve satisfaction from work and a sense of contribution to the development of society (UNDP 1993: 21–23). UNDP's very broad understanding of participation clearly focussed on the *principle* of participation, rather than its form. This emphasis mirrored the value placed on participation in democracy theory as discussed in Chapter 2. Here it was demonstrated that participation, together with equality, was seen as the key to *demos kratein*, the people's rule. While elections were a central feature of participation for minimal democracy, a broadened scope of participation beyond elections was the key aim of proponents of substantive democracy. Most importantly, in the substantive vision of democracy, the process of participation had value in itself, as it was the means to empower and enlighten people, creating an 'informed citizen'.

Critics, however, pointed out that the application of a practice of participation in development assistance had in fact de-politicised participation and instead formalised a form of aid delivery in which blame for failure could easily be shifted away from the aid organisation to the 'participants' (Henkel and Stirrat 2001: 183). As Cleaver (2001) states, by moving away from a focus on *democratic* participation and empowerment, participatory development practice had become formalised, focussing on formal organisations and problem-solving rather than institutions of informal interaction, problematising and critical engagement. Further criticism was directed at the agencies' misunderstanding and inadequate conceptualisation of local power. By viewing the community as a singular entity, while emphasising community as the sole source of knowledge, power and interests, agencies ignored local power differentials and questions of community membership. Critically, however, by using the language of emancipation, people were incorporated into capitalism and existing power structures. This was made possible by using participation and 'agreement' of previously marginalised groups as a justification for the existence of an 'authentic' process and product (Williams 2004: 558). Thus, as Parfitt stressed, participatory development was inherently contradictory and ambiguous, shifting between a focus on either means or ends, between project efficiency and output, and empowerment (Parfitt 2004: 554). Again, this was emphasised by the World Bank's narrow approach to participatory development, which stood in opposition to the broader, political approach adopted by UNDP.

Participatory mechanisms had been used by the World Bank since the 1960s and 1970s, primarily in agricultural and rural development (World Bank 1994b). In the 1990s the Bank further developed these early experiences of quasi-democratic processes parallel to its governance agenda, as its 1994 report *The World Bank and Participation* showed. However, the Bank's position on participation mirrored its position on governance – both were instrumental to the achievement of economic outcomes by improving the utilisation of human and physical resources. Even where direct links to the poor were sought, this was done through the market. The World Bank justified this approach by stressing that although stakeholders ought to be involved in the development process in order to increase the effectiveness and ownership of the project, the main stakeholder remained the government not the people (World Bank 1994b)

The Bank's disconnect from the people (i.e. project recipients) was evident where it outlined the different levels of participation and participatory mechanism it employed. According to the Bank, participation could take place in four ways. First, participation could involve information-sharing in which knowledge was simply made available to recipients. Secondly, participation could be based on consultation, that is, a two-way communication in which recipients were given the opportunity to feed back into the project process. Thirdly, it could take the shape of collaboration where control over decisions and resources was shared. Fourth, the World Bank's final stage of participation was defined as empowerment, in which resources and decisions were transferred to the recipients and the Bank's main role was to enable recipients to make use of these powers (World Bank 2001: 2). While this last stage was most obviously in harmony with the principles of substantive democracy, it was also the least used mechanism. The Bank was clearly aware that by using 'instrumental approaches [such as information-sharing and consultation], the Bank is basically engaged in social marketing of its operational plans' (World Bank 1994b, annex 6, p. 6), which meant that a move towards empowerment had not taken place in most development projects. Similarly, UNDP did not facilitate a transformative process of development and change, despite its recent focus on creating more participatory structures through decentralisation, local governance and civil society programmes (UNDP Management and Governance Division undated).

However limited those participation mechanisms utilised by either UNDP or the World Bank were, their use certainly facilitated a discourse of democracy. Both Secretaries-General Javier Perez de Cuellar and Boutros Boutros-Ghali had emphasised the participatory element of democracy, thereby drawing attention to the importance of individual empowerment, which was conceptualised in stark contrast to authoritarian, non-democratic regimes. Indeed, participation often served as the key differential between two endpoints of the democratisation process (UNSG 7 August 1995, A/50/332; 19 November 1991, A/46/609). Their hope thus mirrored Williams' claim that transparency and openness might serve as pressure points at which political capabilities could be used and subsequently further developed, potentially leading to a wider debate of political rights:

> actually existing participation, for all its shortcomings, provides a range of opportunities through which state power can be actively called to account. These opportunities will not be isolated moments of liberation or professional 'reversals', nor do they require a post-developmental retreat to idealised 'local' spaces to escape participation's totalising power. Rather, they will be found within longer-term political struggles and reshaped political networks that link themselves to a discourse of rights and a fuller sense of citizenship. (Williams 2004: 573)

Following his general approach to conceptualise democracy through practice, Secretary-General Annan highlighted the importance of institutions such as the rule of law and most importantly, the general acceptance of the mechanics of the system by everyone so that 'all citizens ... feel that their rights and views are respected and that they have some say in decisionmaking' (Annan 2002: 138). He therefore justified not only participation as an important democratic principle but also the particular choice of democracy support through institution-building, claiming that these were important channels to achieve the participatory goals of democracy. Moreover, the democratic process was conceptualised as central to the achievement of the human-rights-based approach, which was introduced as part of the mainstreaming of human rights and organisational reforms. Participation was regarded not only as a right in itself but also an important procedural goal as 'rights should not only be *promoted* and *protected* by duty-bearers, but *practised* and *experienced* by rights-holders' (Ljungman 2004: 13). With this, the HRBA introduced a move towards more inclusive and democratic processes in which people were involved in decisions over resources and institutions (Cornwall and Nyamu-Musembi 2004: 1424) as 'in a dynamic world, democratic processes and poverty reduction would continuously feed into strengthening the rights-based effort' (Ljungman 2004: 8).

Citizenship or people-centred politics?

The most controversial criterion of those outlined in the developmental democracy matrix is without a doubt citizenship. More than anything else citizenship here highlights the relationship between the people and the state. It defines how the state and the people should relate to each other. Democracy may have raised the importance of the people, yet it is citizenship which adds a formal and foundational dimension to the idea of 'people's rule'. Yet, despite the (renewed) importance afforded to the people as part of the democracy agenda, neither a discourse nor an agenda of citizenship have emerged. Where the idea of citizenship has gained some traction, for example in the context of the UN Democracy Fund, this has centred on participation. Reminiscent of the transformative ideal of participation outlined by democracy theorists such as Macpherson (1977) or Pateman (1970), citizenship as participation seeks to offer more opportunities for involvement and ownership. However, citizenship as participation is only relatively more substantive than other procedural forms of democracy, such as elections. While it offers multiple opportunities to engage in the democratic process and therefore educate the 'democratic citizen', its procedural focus does not meet the expectations set out by the concept of a citizen's democracy and its foundational perspective. It does not fundamentally change or address the relationship between citizens, the state and the market.

The lack of a substantive engagement with citizenship, however, does not undermine the significant effects of a move towards people-centred politics. People-centred politics refocussed ideas and practices onto people, their experience of development, human rights and security. In theory, people-centred politics raised associations with democracy, for if politics were centred on people then this implied the people's participation in or even control over politics. To be sure, as the analysis of participatory development showed, very different forms of participation existed, including several that were pseudo-democratic. These pretended to involve stakeholders while retaining power with development organisations. At the same time, people-centred politics could be seen as a call for benevolent rule and the observance of human rights. The fact that member states had recognised a right to democracy certainly gave the UN democracy agenda an important impetus and, most of all, legitimacy. The increased emphasis on and recognition of human rights indeed highlighted the value of the individual in a system of states and therefore raised the question of what to do when these rights were violated. Similarly, by placing positive development outcomes for people at the centre, human development was a key element in creating people-centred politics. In other words, people-centred politics could be conceptualised through frameworks such as human development, human security or the 'Responsibility to Protect'. These served as 'conceptual niches' in which democracy could nestle. By coupling democracy with these new, people-centred frameworks, the democracy agenda not only gained broader application and greater legitimacy, it in turn validated some of the more 'radical' ideas, especially those relating to peace and security.

The focus on the relationship between state and people, and the language of rights and duties, as implied by the idea of citizenship here, was expressed in the human-rights-based approach (HRBA) to development, which Secretary-General Annan had called for in 1998 as part of his organisational restructuring efforts. The HRBA reconceptualised the relationship between actors in the development process by stating that governments, states or international society had duties to facilitate. Rather than conceive of development as a relationship of dependence and hierarchy, the HRBA dismissed the notion of 'charity' as an inadequate motivation for development assistance. Instead, following international human rights law which defined states as duty-bearers with obligations to respect, to protect and to fulfil the human rights commitments for all citizens, development was seen as an entitlement or right. Consequently, the HRBA not only aimed at better understanding the context which contributed to deprivation, addressing structural and procedural problem causes, but sought to identify all duty-bearers and rights-holders (Ljungman 2004). The anchor for the operationalisation of development programmes under the HRBA was therefore the principles underlying human rights: universality and inalienability, indivisibility, interdependence and interrelatedness, equality and non-discrimination, participation and inclusion, and accountability and the rule of law. To achieve its goals, the HRBA was centred on a strategy of empowering and enabling rights-holders to claim their rights, and to strengthen the capacity of duty-bearers to meet their obligations (UNSG 26 September 2003, A/58/392).

The similarities between human rights and human development were thus more than superficial as both shared the goal of human freedom and the values of human well-being and dignity (Manzo 2003: 447). In this sense, the HRBA would help to support the human development aspect of developmental democracy, while its focus on rights mirrored the relationship between citizens and the state described by citizenship. However, while the introduction of the HRBA opened up new opportunities to institutionalise the democracy agenda, supported by the growing acceptance of a right to democracy[3], it remained fundamentally an operational principle for UN development practice. With its two-pronged strategy of empowerment and capacity-building reminiscent of existing governance and human development programmes, the HRBA was another form of advocacy for human development[4] rather than an advance towards the democratic principle of citizenship.

Just as Ljungman (2004) noted that a move to talk about rights would not necessarily guarantee the end of poverty and underdevelopment because states could legitimately violate the right to development if poverty persisted, the Responsibility to Protect similarly raised the promise of citizenship but fell short of even institutionalising a general strategy of people-centred politics. Following Secretaries-General Javier Perez de Cuellar and Boutros Boutros-Ghali, who both had emphasised that sovereignty was no longer absolute, Kofi Annan supported the idea of popular sovereignty and people-centred politics in its security dimension. Annan went further than both Perez de Cuellar and Boutros-Ghali to demonstrate that sovereignty had two dimensions and that the international community could no longer ignore the individual for the state. Following the ideas of Francis Deng, UN Special Representative on Internally Displaced Persons, and Roberta Cohen, Senior Fellow at the Brookings Institution, Kofi Annan used the changing political atmosphere in the wake of the 1998 waves of ethnic cleansing by Serbian forces in Kosovo to change the topic of his Ditchley Foundation lecture to speak about intervention, sovereignty and responsibility (Bellamy 2009). Following this, in his 1999 *Economist* article Annan underlined that states were now widely understood as 'instruments at the service of their peoples, and not vice versa' (Annan 1999), thus redefining traditional state sovereignty. Inherent in this new understanding was the recognition of a new individual sovereignty, which was an expression of the world's 'indivisible humanity' that ultimately demanded a new approach to the question of intervention. Annan claimed that 'just as we have learnt that the world cannot stand aside when gross and systematic violations of human rights are taking place, we have also learnt that, if it is to enjoy the sustained support of the world's peoples, intervention must be based on legitimate and universal principles' (Annan 1999). The collective interest of people thus had to become national interest in order to uphold individual sovereignty. In 2000, the Secretary-General then challenged the international community to find answers to the question of how intervention should be addressed. The International Commission on Intervention and State Sovereignty took on this challenge and outlined a people-centred framework which advanced a strategy of 'proactive cosmopolitanism' (Taylor 1999), promoting 'liberal peace' (Chandler 2004; Newman, Richmond and Paris 2009).

The concept of a Responsibility to Protect, which the Commission outlined, sought to redefine and rephrase the question of humanitarian intervention, not just through different language but also by reconceptualising sovereignty. At the heart of this was a move from 'sovereignty as control' to 'sovereignty as responsibility', shifting the point of view from the interveners to those who were in need. In the Responsibility to Protect framework governments were seen as responsible for maintaining the functioning of safety and welfare institutions. If and when states would no longer be able or willing to maintain this function, the international community should step in to assist the population of the state. However, it was stressed that prime responsibility lay with the state – governments were accountable to their citizens and ultimately to the international community (ICISS 2001; see also Bellamy 2009 and Thakur 2005a). The Responsibility to Protect therefore allowed individual rights to trump state rights as the state was conceptualised as a moral agent by matching the state's legal and political legitimacy with how well it upheld human rights and citizen welfare (Chandler 2004: 62). However, neither the violation of human rights nor the overthrow of democratic governments were included among potential intervention causes. Instead, stimuli for intervention included the collapse of states, mass starvation, civil war and natural or environmental disasters (ICISS 2001: 32–33). Accordingly, intervention was described broadly as a 'continuum of intervention', including a responsibility to prevent and to re-build (ICISS 2001: 67).

Although the idea of the Responsibility received mixed responses from member states (see Macfarlane et al. 2004), the Secretary-General was highly satisfied with the report and considered it meeting his challenge. Annan embraced the idea and supported an extension of the military dimension to human security (Thakur 2005b). For Annan the connection between intervention and democracy tightened. Although Annan, like his two predecessors, took great care to emphasise that 'democracy cannot be imposed from outside' (UNSG 11 September 2003, SG/SM/8860), he praised the Cotonou Declaration, which stated that 'the growing international trend to condemn unconstitutional removals of Governments or attempts at outright subversion of democracy is a welcome development' (Annan 1999). Moreover, in a 2001 report reviewing the Cotonou Declaration, the Secretary-General boldly stated that

> In my view, the benchmark for a sustainable democracy is the extent to which a State acts in accordance with universal and indivisible human rights: the civil and political rights, as well as the economic, social and cultural rights defined in international human rights law. I therefore consider the status of human rights to be an important barometer of a healthy democracy. The current state of international human rights law clearly shows that democracy is not only a universally recognized ideal and a goal, but also a fundamental right of citizens. (UNSG 23 October 2001, A/56/499, para. 27)

The 2005 Summit then provided Secretary-General Annan further opportunity to emphasise the importance of the principles underlying the Responsibility to Protect and its relationship to ideas and practices used in the areas of human rights and development. Both *A More Secure World: Our Shared Responsibility* by the Secretary-General's High-level Panel on Threats, Challenges and Change and the Secretary-General's own subsequent report *In Larger Freedom: Towards Development, Security and Human Rights For All* therefore emphasised the importance of state capacity, sovereignty and the UN's obligation to support weak states, helping them to perform the tasks of sovereignty effectively (UN 2004; UNSG 21 March 2005, A/59/2005). While the Secretary-General emphasised that sovereign states remain the building blocks of the international system, he also stated that they needed to 'serve' their people (UNSG 21 March 2005, A/59/2005, para. 19). Hence, sovereignty was defined in terms of the ability to meet new challenges and guarantee rights and freedoms. Strong states would thus be able to ensure freedom from want, freedom from fear and the freedom to live in dignity. Development could only take root where governments were representative and responsive to people's needs, where strong institutions enable peaceful conflict management, where the rule of law prevails and governments could be held accountable (UNSG 21 March 2005, A/59/2005).

At the Summit member states recognised only genocide, war crimes, ethnic cleansing and crimes against humanity as falling under the list of potential triggers for action under the Responsibility to Protect. Thus, while many regarded the 2005 World Summit as a failure because agreement on a number of issues could not be reached, Secretary-General Kofi Annan emphasised that 'historic gains' had been made. The recognition of the Responsibility to Protect and the importance of the rule of law and human rights signified for Annan an 'intellectual breakthrough'. He stressed that 'any human rights agenda worth the name must have the promotion of democracy as a cornerstone of its endeavours' (UNSG 12 October 2005, SG/SM/10161); and it was in his view the achievements in the area of human rights that had prevented the Summit from being a disappointment as 'human life, human dignity [and] human rights [were] raised above even the entrenched concept of State sovereignty' (UNSG 12 October 2005, SG/SM/10161). Thus, while the Responsibility to Protect might have galvanised the concept of the 'new' relationship between state and individuals in theory, in practice it would prove to be too radical to be accepted by member states. Irrespective of this, the Secretary-General continued to uphold a discourse centred on popular sovereignty and the Responsibility to Protect, while emphasising as more practical a broader notion of human security.

The concept of human security mirrored that of human development, promising an extension of the principles of people-centred politics into the third area of UN goals: peace. Overall, people-centred politics in the context of peace and security proved to be conceptually richer but also politically more divisive, as the Responsibility to Protect had shown. Thus, their promise could only be fulfilled in the abstract, that is, by promoting the general idea of democracy, citizenship and the people at the heart of politics. The concept of human security blended ideas of human development and peace to achieve a new focus on international and national security, enhancing further the importance of individual life. The concept of human security was described by the Charter's ideas 'freedom from fear' and 'freedom from want'. Rather than view security purely in terms of state security, the concept of human security focussed on the individual as referent and allowed for a number of actors, state and non-state, to contribute to the achievement of security (McDonald 2002: 277–295, 279; Newman 2001). Defined as the absence of both direct and structural violence (Cockell 2001: 17), human security not only involved military and arms security issues but extended the sphere of security to governance and the political process, to societal and communal stability, as well as to human rights and questions of personal, economic and resource security.

According to Newman (2004), this high number of variables, that is, factors which could pose as a security threat, meant that the concept's potential for application remained ambiguous. Thus, while normatively attractive, human security was analytically weak. The sources of this analytical weakness were differences in approach and subject focus. Competing ideas of human security had emerged which pointed in different directions, referring to different UN practices, therefore undermining the meaningfulness of the concept of human security. These included a focus on basic human needs and development, an 'assertive/interventionist' aspect focussed on the redefinition of sovereignty and collective action, a 'new security' approach which highlighted non-conventional security issues such as drugs, terrorism and cyber war, and a 'social welfare/developmentalist' focus which, although mirroring the basic needs focus, extended this to a form of human welfare that was equitable, participatory and distributive (Newman 2001). These differences in approach then were associated with different strategies of implementation. While the social welfare/developmentalist focus most closely resembled the framework of developmental democracy, it and the Basic Human Needs perspective expressed human security in terms of human development and good governance, and could be implemented by either development or post-conflict peace-building in practice. In this scenario, human security was 'an active and substantive notion of democracy, one that ensures the opportunity for all to participate in the decisions that affect their lives. Therefore it is engaged directly with discussion of democracy at all levels, from the local to the global' (Thomas 2001: 162). This positive security dimension obviously stood in contrast to negative security aspects, which are primarily expressed through the absence of war and conflict.[5] In the assertive/interventionist and 'new security' approach, human security overlapped with a more traditional conflict prevention strategy in that development and democracy would help to overcome conflict.

In summary, the principles of democracy and democratic citizenship may have been recognised as an element in the achievement of the UN's key values of peace, development and human rights, yet reconceptualising the relationship between the people and the state in this vein was too big a step at this time. Despite this, recognising a (however limited) Responsibility to Protect and therefore the inherent value of citizens was an important first step. Further engagement with the human rights canon in all its dimensions would be needed to fully understand the opportunities and limitations of democratic citizenship as a concept to define UN practice (and the foundation of the state).

Coherent and connected or disjointed and accidental?

In the months following the publication of the *Democracy in Latin America* report UNDP held a number of workshops and seminars in Latin America and Europe where the report generally received positive responses. In an EU co-sponsored seminar in Brussels Elena Martinez, UNDP's Assistant Administrator and Regional Director for Latin America and the Caribbean, noted that 'we have a great deal to learn from Europe in the quest for a citizens' democracy. Learn from its commitment to the Rule of Law, from its *social market economy*, from its achievements in *social cohesion* and from its exemplary process of *integration*' (Martinez 2005: 5, emphasis added). Thus, unwittingly perhaps, Martinez reintroduced ideas of an earlier World Bank document which had made similar references to the European model of substantive democracy. In its 1989 report on Sub-Saharan Africa and governance, the World Bank had outlined in a small illustration box the 'Nordic model' as an example of successful governance (World Bank 1989). This idea had received little attention and was not referred to again in Bank publications. Although the World Bank presented this Nordic model in terms of market and labour regulation, excluding the social democratic provisions of the state, the idea of the European social model versus the Anglo-American market model of the Washington consensus did indeed embody distinct images.

Irrespective of its geographic or ideological association, the 2004 UNDP report on democracy in Latin America presented a new and different approach, providing a theoretical foundation for democracy and with it an explanation, or justification, as to why certain outcomes needed to be achieved. This vision of democracy was a substantive one that provided the rationale for a democratic *society*, a democracy that reached beyond the structures and processes of a particular kind of state to include a description of how the interaction between states and citizens was to be shaped. In fact, more than previous documents and reports, which merely *insisted* that the citizens were the source of authority, it drew attention to the fact that the state and citizens were not distinct. Previous reports did not deny this, yet never justified this connection between state and citizens. More importantly, they conceptualised the market as an overwhelming structural force (almost) beyond the reach of the state, a force to which people had to mould themselves, rather than the other way round. The Latin America report did away with this separation of the state, market and citizen by conceptualising the state and the market as subservient to the needs of citizens. Here then, democracy had substance – the foundations for a democratic society were provided.

The idea of a guiding state that is pro-active, regulating the market and providing for people to overcome the market's shortcomings, can be summarised as the 'responsibility to care and protect'. Unsurprisingly, the semantic similarities to the ICISS' Responsibility to Protect are not coincidental. Both place the individual and the people at the heart of their concern and redefine the national and international response to the needs and well-being of the people. Here, the 'responsibility to care' stresses the state's obligation to ensure development for the state as a whole and to consider the benefits for all citizens, especially for the disadvantaged. It does so without necessarily aiming at a process that seeks to equalise society economically, as Marx stressed. Instead, it recognises any type of social and political arrangement, policy approach or governance model so long as the extremes of social and market arrangements can be avoided and opportunities for all provided.

The idea of citizenship thus made explicit the special role that democracy plays in enhancing people's lives and the place it affords them in the state. Democracy may have raised the importance of the people, yet it is citizenship which adds a formal and foundational dimension to the idea of 'people's rule'. Citizens are the state and by their very nature as citizens they have the right to participate in the affairs of the state through democratic processes. Democracy is thus an inalienable human right. In a foundational perspective of citizenship, the state is responsible to – and for – the people, a relationship that is best highlighted by international law. In international law both state and government are objects of separate forms of recognition. Whereas the state refers to a self-governing (independent) political community, government is defined as the political apparatus that upholds this status of independence externally while exercising a monopoly of force and control internally.[6] The classic definition of statehood (a permanent population, a defined territory, a government, and the capacity to enter into relations with other states) shows that government is part of the state yet conceptually distinct: 'although a state is a *political* community whose existence is tied to existing, remembered, or foreseen patterns of governance within it, its existence is conceptually independent of and precedent to that of the particular government that purports to rule it. The government does not define the state any more than the tail wags the dog' (Roth 2000: 132, emphasis as in original). Consequently, reinstating the people as the state, reconceptualising it as a collective of citizens and redefining government as the group of people authorised to exercise political control on behalf of citizens, creates more than a semantic change. It means that society (i.e. the collective of citizens) equals the state. This highlights the role of government as the 'caretaker' of the physical reality of the state, including its territory and its citizens. In turn, it adds a qualitative aspect of rule that may question the performance of government.

To what extent has the UN conceptualised, promoted or supported this type of democracy? Developmental democracy exists in pockets of UN ideas and practice as the UN has clearly addressed the five criteria of developmental democracy in its activities and thinking. The UN has sought to develop both markets and people, increasingly recognising that an overemphasis of the former over the latter does not lead to best results. Following a general emphasis on the people as both an expression of the fundamental principle of democracy and people-centred politics, the UN continued to promote and support democratisation processes in all areas and all levels of state activity, including the support of non-state actors. It also promoted and supported the ideals, structures and processes of participation on various levels. The UN may have recognised the idea of citizenship, yet focussed on its procedural expression as participation, not on its foundational dimension, which the Latin America report highlighted. While this fifth criterion remained a particular weakness in the achievement of developmental democracy, the lack of an overall theory, or vision of developmental democracy (or other forms of substantive democracy) meant that the different pockets of developmental democracy remained just that: disjointed ideas and practices, related more by accident than intent. This disjointed nature of the idea (and practice) of developmental democracy was further highlighted and reinforced by operational limitations.

The democracy agenda had been driven thus far successfully by operational objectives, allowing Secretary-General Annan to complete the triangle of the 'inextricably linked' concepts of peace, democracy and development by bringing together what had been previously connected only in logic but disjointed in practice. Yet Kofi Annan highlighted in his report *In Larger Freedom* that although the UN does more than any other international organisation in the field of democracy assistance, 'the impact of [its] work is reduced by the way we disperse it among different parts of the bureaucracy' (UNSG 21 March 2005, A/59/2005, para. 151). Indeed, as missions or projects are prepared and deployed, organisational boundaries that may have become blurred in the development of ideas sharpen again in practice. Each organisational unit remains concerned with projects relating to its respective organisational focus and role. Despite attempts to reduce overlaps or contradictory policy orientation through programmes rather than projects, and despite increased interorganisational cooperation[7], UN agencies remain decentralised and independent. This means that not only are UN staff often reluctant to cooperate across organisational boundaries, different understandings of a situation and different task management styles influence the general approach to and success of a mission or project[8], which has been repeatedly stressed as a factor for diminished mission or project success. The process of joining up ideas and practices thus may have helped to create a democracy agenda, increasingly moving it towards the middle of the democratic continuum, yet the same operational (i.e. practice) dimension also limited the democracy agenda conceptually and with it practically. As a result substantive UN democracy remains an idea, its potential obvious but its actualisation set well into a more distant future.

Notes

1   For example, the report found that although Democrats constituted the largest group of respondents, they did not form a majority. Democrats agreed with Ambivalents on the importance and value of democratic institutions, yet those ambivalent about democracy shared the Non-democrats' view on delegative practices. Both Ambivalents and Non-Democrats believed that in times of crisis presidential powers may be appropriated to solve problems more effectively. The distance in orientation between these three groups was roughly similar, leading the researchers to conclude that Ambivalents had to be further convinced of the value of the democratic system in order to increase the stability of democracy in Latin America (UNDP 2004a: 131–148).

2   Argentina, Bolivia, Brazil, Chile, Colombia, Costa Rica, Dominican Republic, Ecuador, El Salvador, Guatemala, Honduras, Mexico, Nicaragua, Panama, Paraguay, Peru, Uruguay, Venezuela.

3   Since the 1993 Vienna World Conference on Human Rights, democracy had been subsumed by the human rights community under the right to development. Now, with the human-rights-based approach to be applied in development practice, the reinforcement of the 'right to democracy' by member states brought about a further justification for democracy support by UN agencies, adding a new normative perspective to the democracy agenda (Dumitriu 2003). As the Commission on Human Rights confirmed the existence of a right to democracy and outlined correlating aspects of the right to democratic governance (UNHCHR, 27 April 1999, Res. 1999/57), it firmly entrenched democracy in the human rights canon and UN practice.

4   The question of whether this was the case was raised by the Overseas Development Institute (Manzo 2003: 447). Martinussen (1996) indeed identified this two-pronged approach as a central strategy of the human development approach, using the idea of 'reaching up' and 'reaching down' to emphasise the literal meeting of the state and its citizens.

5   Unsurprisingly, the roots of the concept were found in very different documents and events. Focussing on the positive security aspect of human security, the 1994 Human Development Report, which was written in preparation for the 1995 World Summit for Social Development, was often seen as the source of the concept of human security. Yet, McCormack argued that a shift towards human security had been evident as early as 1991 when the Security Council passed Resolution 688 on Iraq stating that the treatment of the Iraqi population by its government constituted a threat to international peace and security. With this resolution the Security Council suggested that internal instability was an international concern and that state sovereignty was not absolute but dependent on the state's performance in ensuring human security (McCormack 2005: 4).

6   Thus, while the state of Afghanistan may be regarded as legitimate, the Taliban government may not be. The result may be an uncontested territory, but also an empty seat in the UN or attempts to discredit (or remove) the government regarded as illegitimate. As Griffin emphasised, unlike in Haiti, Sierra Leone and Cambodia, it was not the Taliban's overthrow of a democratically elected government that led them to be denied UN accreditation, but 'the unwillingness of the UN to reward seizures of power through civil wars, the attempt to use the credentials process as means to promote democratic resolutions to domestic conflicts, and the condemnation of systematic violations of human rights' (Griffin 2000: 758).

7   For example, to increase interorganisational cooperation and to better utilise knowledge and resources the UNDP resident coordinator was appointed directly to the Special Representative of the Secretary-General in post-conflict situations such as Haiti, Tajikistan and Sierra Leone (Griffin 2003).

8   Mohan Das (2005) describes problems involved in interdepartmental communication and difference in work styles. Contrary to established practice, the Department of Peacekeeping Operations (DPKO) instead of the Department of Political Affairs (DPA) assumed prime responsibility in East Timor. Unfamiliar with the task of governance and more attuned to short-term, military-style missions, DPKO was less able to connect with the local population and tried to impose solutions. Moreover, DPKO rejected an offer by DPA for joint mission planning, ignoring the suggestion. 'Rivalries' such as these may undermine the flow of ideas and practices such as the democracy agenda. Similarly, Chesterman criticises the UN's lack of a central institutional capacity for transitional administration, noting, for example, that each operation had developed idiosyncratic mission structures (Chesterman 2005). As transfer of capacities does not happen, experience, knowledge and with it an understanding of a vision or goal gets lost, potentially undermining the vision of democracy.

7

The future of UN democracy

The idea of democracy clearly has been an integral part of the UN since its inception. Yet the meaning of democracy has evolved over time through its development and application as a UN practice. Definitions of democracy have been shaped in reaction to the organisation's changing environment, be that in the context of decolonisation, ethnic wars or the process of democratisation (the Third Wave). In this sense, democracy, or the practice of democracy assistance, was part of an attempt at problem-solving. Because democracy served a purpose, its meaning (and the shape of the associated practices) would change according to the needs of the situation. Moreover, democracy would mirror the organisational context within which it was conceived and applied, with an increasing number of agencies and programmes adopting democracy as a practice that would link or anchor other practices. Democracy practice thus captured contemporary developments in associated areas such as peace, development and human rights.

Broadly speaking, four conceptualisations of democracy could be identified, which stood in different relationship to the democratic continuum. Democracy as civilisation described a concept that was based not only on the notion of difference but also hierarchy, that is, a degree of superiority for those who were democratic as opposed to those who were undemocratic, uncivilised and 'barbarian'. In this view, the lack of democracy also implied a lack of independence or self-determination. As questions of scope did not arise in this ideologically defined vision of democracy, democracy as civilisation was not represented on the democratic continuum. By contrast, democracy as elections marked the starting point of the democratic continuum by describing the minimum criteria for democracy in both theory and practice. Democracy as elections described the most commonly held vision of democracy – a procedural definition focussed on the casting of the ballot. A third vision of democracy was defined through the practice of (good) governance support. Democracy as governance moved further along the democratic continuum to describe a broader, systemic-procedural view of democracy that takes into account not only those structures and procedures which support elections but also those institutions which sustain political life and society between elections. While broadening the conceptualisation of democracy, this vision also introduced a range of qualitative principles which raised questions about how deep, or qualitative, UN democracy really had become. This point was further developed under the label of 'developmental democracy'. Developmental democracy looked towards a (potential) future to understand whether and to what extent UN democracy already supported a substantive form of democracy. Developmental democracy was conceptualised as an all-encompassing, holistic and deep vision of democracy – a democratic *society*. While a number of UN practices as well as agencies and programmes addressed aspects of developmental democracy, the existence of a single practice or idea of developmental democracy at the UN was put into question by the challenges of operationalisation as well as the recognition by the UN and member states.

Following this, it became clear that the three vehicles of definition – ideology, practice and vision – created very different realities for UN democracy. They not only described what democracy was, but also what it could be. They showed that democracy had broadened over time, yet put into question whether it had really deepened. The vision of developmental democracy then highlighted that today democracy is in a somewhat ambiguous place as it appeared to have a reached a conceptual endpoint towards the middle of the democratic continuum. Developmental democracy and the distinction of the three vehicles of definition raised a number of questions: Where next for UN democracy? Can there be a practice of developmental democracy? What would the conditions be for the UN democracy agenda to develop beyond governance?

Ideology

The definition of democracy and therefore the process of defining democracy is without a doubt bound up with ideology, be that to justify 'civilisation' or to distinguish Western democracy from its Eastern European counterpart in the twentieth century. While liberal democracy and the idea of 'people's democracy' represent particular forms of democracy, not only building on differently constructed conceptual clusters but also radically different (historic) experiences of them, ideology rarely marks a conscious effort at defining democracy. Instead, its primary association has been one of politicisation. Indeed, ideologically defined democracy is not represented on the democratic continuum as the question of scope is secondary if not irrelevant compared to questions of authoritarianism versus freedom and liberty. However, ideology as a vehicle for conceptualisation raises questions about the boundary between real and façade democracy.

Where democracy has been defined through ideology, the UN as an organisation played no role in supporting or even promoting democracy. While the UN had been engaged in election and plebiscite monitoring, this did not constitute or account for democracy in the same way democracy support did since the 1990s. While here the goal was to establish a system of democracy in the long run, earlier plebiscite and election monitoring merely confirmed that the people had not been arbitrarily moved from one regime to another. This was a one-off measure based on short-term

UN involvement. Questions of how the regime was constituted before or after the plebiscite or election were irrelevant. Thus, with the UN taking a back seat, ideology as a vehicle for conceptualisation focussed on states as the creators of legitimate definitions of democracy. Questions of whether democracy served a wider purpose for the UN and its member states, that is, addressing issues of peace, human rights and development, did not feature. Instead, the main question was which type of democracy one would support – liberal or otherwise – and therefore how one (state) would distinguish itself from another (state). Thus, focussing on ideology as the main identifier of democracy means little engagement with the concept beyond surface level, leading to 'common sense' definitions of democracy to prevail, as Schwartz and Skinner (2002) showed. These definitions are based on binary categories such as democratic/not democratic, Western (liberal)/non-Western (non-liberal) and, most significantly, bad/good. The subtle differences highlighted by the 'democracy with adjectives' debate or the democratic continuum are ignored for the simplicity of political argument. Hence, Justice Stewart's statement, 'I know it when I see it', is all too common and indeed reinforces the Schumpeterian approach which defined the smallest common denominator of existing democracies as the essence of democracy.

Given these conditions, ideology as a vehicle for conceptualisation may not be the means of choice. However, it raises important questions of what democracy ought to achieve. The insistence on liberal democracy places certain demands on the UN and its missions. Where goals such as peace, human rights and development remain as relevant as democracy (if they are indeed not primary to it), the form of democracy may have to be adjusted accordingly, as the case of Afghanistan showed. For example, ideology as a vehicle for conceptualisation raises the question whether representative, that is, quasi-democratic, forms of politics are sufficient to meet democratic requirements, in particular where the achievement of peace and (rectificatory) justice (see Mani 2002) is paramount. Alternatively, is liberalisation enough where societies are well-ordered, that is, stable and peaceful?

The question of what needs to be achieved by democracy thus highlights the elements of the conceptual cluster which are considered as merely sufficient or indeed necessary. An important dimension here is the question of legitimacy. As Franck (1992; 1995) showed, the question of legitimacy through the democratic process was raised both nationally and internationally, putting into question the legitimacy not only of governments and states but also of the international community. In this sense, democracy could be defined negatively as the freedom from authoritarianism and the violation of human rights. In other words, an elected government would be *assumed* to refrain from human rights violations or aggressive foreign policy. On the other hand, democracy could be defined positively as a means to achieve a degree of participation and accountability, or, more broadly, institutions to support participation, be that rules and regulations, legal frameworks, affirmative action or resources through welfare. While ideology does not provide answers to these questions, UN practice offered a very different opportunity in defining these criteria.

Practice

Practice proved to be a powerful vehicle for the development of ideas. Practice not only influenced the meaning of democracy, describing its conceptual cluster, it also created facts. Practice was a tool to solve problems, which the UN faced in meeting the new demands of the post-Cold-War world. The bureaucratic nature of practice depoliticised this controversial idea and thus largely avoided potentially unproductive negotiations by member states on defining democracy. Indeed, member states may have been less willing to agree to a right to democracy in 2005 had there not been already an extensive UN practice in place to suggest that democracy is a desirable, appropriate and effective solution to the problems which the UN faced. The focus on results helped move the idea of democracy along the democratic continuum. Practice therefore justified and legitimised an ever deeper and broader meaning of democracy and democracy assistance, as was expressed by the ACC Matrix of Governance.

Using practice as a tool to conceptualise ideas, organisational actors such as the Secretary-General relied on strategies and organisational processes that would make sense of this 'new' idea and justify it to member states by creating effective 'frames'. Framing transcends the boundaries of agenda-setting as it is associated with relatively stable ideological repertoires (Béland 2005), while 'an effective frame is one which makes favoured ideas seems [sic] like common sense, and unfavoured ideas as unthinkable' (Bøås and McNeill 2004: 2). The compatibility of ideas with dominant values is therefore a key factor in the survival of ideas and policy proposals, with recombination (the coupling of ideas with existing and familiar elements) more important than 'mutation' (the development of completely new elements) (Kingdon 2003). Establishing congruence with existing ideas is therefore an important element of the 'framing' of ideas by policy. Secondly, an idea has a greater chance of rising on the agenda if connected to an important problem (Kingdon 2003: 198), presenting a solution. These problems could be a crisis or a prominent event, a change in a widely respected indicator, a process of gradual accumulation of knowledge among specialists or changes in the political process. Frames and windows of change can be created or manipulated by policy entrepreneurs like the Secretary-General, in particular where these have been preceded by a process of 'softening up' the system through the consistent promotion of their ideas.

The role of the Secretary-General

Both Boutros Boutros-Ghali and Kofi Annan used the authority of their role to develop and promote the UN democracy agenda. They did so differently but largely followed the same ideas and conceptualisations of democracy. From the outset Boutros-Ghali stressed that democracy had a place in the canon of UN ideas, goals and practices, thereby shaping member-states' understanding of democracy in a specific way. With this he followed a leadership style, which Kille (2006) described as 'visionary'. Visionary leaders challenge the boundaries of their roles, following their own ideals and goals. By contrast 'managers' are constraint respecters, retreating to a bureaucratic style. Although Annan followed a less visionary leadership strategy than Boutros Boutros-Ghali, his impact on the democracy agenda was equally significant. Annan's leadership style was 'strategic', a style that lies between the pro-active visionary style of Boutros-Ghali and the reserved style of 'managers' such as Kurt Waldheim (Kille 2006). In other words, as strategist Annan was a constraint accommodator who sought to balance the demands of the office by neither unduly challenging set boundaries nor retreating within these boundaries. Thus, the development of practice in shaping the UN democracy agenda was a tool well used by Kofi Annan.

Throughout his term Boutros-Ghali continued to advance the democracy agenda. By maintaining a discourse of democracy situated between the UN root ideas of peace, development and human rights, and their related practices, the Secretary-General facilitated a cognitive change among member states. Member states thus recognised that democracy would help to address the problems of the post-Cold-War world, leading to the acceptance of democracy as a UN agenda. Thus, when problems in peace-keeping led to the realisation that an election-as-exit strategy was not a panacea for conflict resolution, a window opened through which the Secretary-General promoted a more expanded vision of democracy assistance, taking into account broader institutional aspects of democracy and democratic societies. These suggestions were not new but had been already outlined by Boutros Boutros-Ghali in his *Agenda for Peace*. In other words, they had contributed to the 'softening up' process and had served as a ready-made solution to a now imminent problem.

By contrast, the Secretary-General's attempt to advance the democracy agenda through the *Agenda for Democratization* appeared to fail to achieve its intended aims. As Rushton (2008) notes, the promotion of norms does not take place in a political vacuum, and thus the Secretary-General failed to achieve his potential as 'an agent of democracy promotion' due to his inept use of leadership instruments and by ignoring his political environment. Indeed, visionary leaders like Boutros-Ghali are less responsive to their environment as they try, more than any other type of leader, to lead and influence an organization's agenda according to their own views and intentions. In other words, visionary leaders challenge constraints, they 'bend' the leadership tools available to them and do so 'to the extreme in order to gain as much influence as possible without recognizing the danger of "breaking" the tool' (Kille 2006: 59) or considering their audience. However, the fact that Kofi Annan continued Boutros-Ghali's ideas and plans through the operationalisation and streamlining of practice showed not only that practice is a powerful vehicle for conceptualisation beyond political deliberation, but that ideas remain within the (bureaucratic) system and may be picked up and developed across time and place.

Following a strategic leadership style, Annan developed the democracy agenda through the means of organisational reform and the integration of practices from different UN agencies, while diffusing the idea of democracy throughout the UN system. His goal to bring about a 'quiet revolution' (Annan 1998) of good governance and cooperation shaped his first contribution to the democracy agenda and member-states' understanding of democracy. By integrating the practices of election assistance and governance support into one practice of democracy assistance, Annan influenced the understanding of what democracy entailed for both member states and those agencies now tasked to cooperate in its implementation. While this move pointed to the possibilities for the Secretaryship-General to influence UN activities by 'stealth', the limitations of this strategy are obvious where existing practices do not easily fit conceptually. In other words, the integration of ideas and practices relied on the existence of practices similar to each other, and it further depended on a conceptual fit to be established between these practices in order to be seen as legitimate. Considering this, less strident pro-democratic rhetoric could be compensated for partially by the use of conceptual niches and by organisational diffusion that facilitated further conceptualisation and broader application.

Linking concepts

The UN democracy agenda changed at critical moments, for example at the end of the Cold War with the increase of ethnic conflicts and the first evaluation of UN missions in ethnic conflicts, as well as in the process of organisational reconstruction, and again in the learning process of transitional administration. These moments opened windows of opportunity for conceptualisation. By connecting democracy not only to problems but to UN root ideas, it became unnecessary to create a paradigm shift and with it political controversy. Instead, a UN democracy agenda could develop 'by stealth', promoted by the Secretaries-General and supported by organisational dynamics, which circulated the idea and practice of democracy through the UN system. This circulation consisted of a number of movements towards the centre (the Secretariat) and outwards into the UN system.

First, there was a linear movement of conceptualisation in which the UN democracy agenda was developed out of existing practices: plebiscite and election monitoring in the context of decolonisation. This was followed by a process of embedment in and connection to existing practices where democracy would enhance the outcomes of these practices, namely peace-keeping and development. Secondly, this linear development was accompanied by a circular movement of ideas. In a centripetal motion practices were drawn on from across the UN system and incorporated into democracy to form a practice that became increasingly substantive in character – a change indicated by a change of name from *election assistance* to *democracy assistance*. The centripetal character of this process was also highlighted by its focus on and location in the UN Secretariat. This process was paralleled by a centrifugal motion in which ideas were directly fed back into practices of other UN agencies and programmes, leading to further reconceptualisation, or refinement, of ideas and practices to accommodate democracy. Particularly distinctive in this movement was the spread of democracy to the Human Rights Commission. While the Human Rights Commission had picked up the idea of democracy already at the 1993 Vienna Conference, it did not start a process of conceptualisation until 1999. Fed back to the centre, this enriched the overall concept of democracy by adding to the notion that democracy was beneficial for human rights the idea that democracy itself had a rights-based dimension. The combination of human rights, democracy and development then challenged existing practices of development further, creating a human-rights-based approach to development.

This process of conceptual circulation was achieved through conceptual linking and syllogistic conclusions. While democracy might have been central to the philosophy of international organisations, the idea was left implicit in the Charter, opening possible avenues for later interpretation. Developed out of self-determination, a practice supported by the root idea of independence, democracy was triangulated by the other three root ideas – peace, development and human rights. While democracy could be seen as independent of either, the overlap between its values, goals and processes with those of the Charter's root ideas ensured a convergence in idea and practice, and, most of all, a degree of legitimacy. This overlap led to the conclusion that if democracy was part of peace, development or human rights, and that if these were central UN ideas, then democracy could be part of the UN agenda, too. Moreover, conceptual niches provided opportunities to further develop democracy without addressing democracy itself. Indeed, in some cases democracy became a by-product of a general move towards people-centred politics. For example, Kofi Annan's promotion and mainstreaming of human rights, the practice of human development and the idea of human security, further highlighted the core principles by encouraging a new understanding of the people in international relations and the relationship between states and their people. It did so without explicitly referencing the idea of democracy.

Overall, there has been a considerable merging between the ideas and practices relating to democracy within the UN. These practices have increasingly incorporated elements of the other. Hence election assistance now includes institution-building to support electoral systems, while development aid has embraced institution-building from the perspective of development delivery, sustainability of state structures and good governance. Agreement on a procedural definition of democracy, expressed through election assistance, was relatively easily found. A focus on elections could enable even sceptics to accept this practice as elections had been utilised in many states without reference to the wider nature of the political system. At the same time, the short-term involvement of the UN in monitoring elections would not substantially undermine the sovereignty of the state but merely support a state's electoral undertaking. Election assistance was thus conceived as technical, short-term and based on request only. As such, it could be regarded as another form of development assistance. Secondly, the UN's continued insistence that the democratisation process was more important than a particular form of democracy, that states were free to choose their own pace and form of democratisation (Boutros-Ghali 1996, para. 11), and that states could be 'differently democratic' (UNDP 2002: 4) meant that UN democracy support would accommodate a variety of political systems. In other words, a procedural definition of democracy along Schumpeterian lines retained an acknowledgement of self-determination and self-government as external sovereignty, which served the political purposes of many states. By contrast, the good governance agenda enabled the conceptualisation – and institutionalisation – of a wider definition and practice of democracy beyond elections to include structural features that support the stability of a democratic state and enable more qualitative electoral results. This democracy could be located on the democratic continuum further to the middle, yet short of fully substantive democracy.

Vision

Envisioning democracy means more than joining up existing practices, it means *constructing* a theory of democracy. In this process of envisioning democracy a number of questions need to be addressed, most importantly: What purpose would this construct of democracy serve? Which problems would it solve? Does this construct, or theory, of democracy achieve a level of purity, or coherence, which a practice-based joined-up construct could not achieve? Would a coherent concept or theory of democracy necessarily lead to coherent practice? If so, would this result in optimised outcomes? Most importantly, is the achievement of a construct realistic or does the involvement of a great number of actors, both organisational actors and states, mean that this 'purity' is fiction? Secondly, the question of what issues a substantive democracy would solve is raised: Would it necessarily lead to better outcomes, such as more peace, more sustainable and equitable development, greater opportunity for participation, and genuine fairness, justice, accountability and transparency? A substantive democracy could indeed achieve a variety of things, as the open-endedness of the democratic continuum suggests.

The purpose of substantive democracy from the UN's perspective could be extrinsic, primarily located in the broader goals which the UN tries to achieve: peace, development and human rights. This has been without a doubt an essential dimension in constructing the democracy agenda in the first instance. However, substantive democracy could reach much farther than this by emphasising the intrinsic value of developmental democracy, that is, by defining the principles of developmental democracy as a human right. Developmental democracy as outlined here (and especially the 2004 UNDP report) highlighted the inherent value of the individual, their rights and entitlements as part of being citizens who *constitute* society. According to developmental democracy, entitlements are not conferred but can be claimed *qua* membership of society. Government and the state are then the caretakers who facilitate the provision of these entitlements. How these entitlements are provided is not specified, yet a variety of formats can be envisaged, from welfare to the facilitation of provision by third parties, or the steering and regulating of the economy towards a developmental end. This then leads to another important question which developmental democracy needs to address: Is democracy to empower or to legitimise, or both?

The difference between empowerment and legitimisation may set different thresholds for its relationship to security. As research has shown (Mansfield 2005; Rapoport and Weinberg 2001: Snyder 2000), democracy is inherently conflictual. Indeed, democracy theory expects 'conflict' in order to balance divergent interests. The democratic political process then forms the rules of the game in which conflict is channelled peacefully. Where cultures of democracy have become established, this political conflict is non-violent. However, in unstable, failing or post-conflict situations democracy may bring violence and entrench social and political divisions. As the UN tends to operate in the latter situations, developmental democracy highlights the evolutionary process of 'growing into' the democratic game, emphasising in fact the long-term need for democracy support. Where democracy merely legitimises, the UN need only be involved for the purpose of certifying legitimate outcomes – as it has done with early election monitoring practices. However, where democracy seeks to empower, the process of democratisation is an ongoing one. This process does not stop with the first set of elections, or indeed the second, but moves towards an enculturation into cultures of democracy, including peace. On the other hand, becoming democratic can also mean using democratic principles outside conventional arenas and accepting (at least temporarily) representative, yet quasi-democratic processes such as those used in Afghanistan.

Substantive democracy in the form of developmental democracy here served as a potential vision to show the practical and theoretical advantages and disadvantages of creating a UN-specific concept of democracy. Developmental democracy integrated existing ideas of substantive democracy to develop a holistic view of a democratic society in which political democracy is complemented by social democracy and, at least partly, by economic democracy. Analysing the ideas and practices of the UN, it is clear that many aspects of a substantive UN democracy exist. However, a 'vision' of a substantive UN democracy does not exist, either in theory or in practice, because of the existing focus on practice and the practice's institutional fragmentation. This means that if practice has been an important vehicle for the development of the UN democracy agenda thus far, its potential to move beyond a place towards the middle of the democratic continuum is limited. UN democracy successfully emerged out of the joining up of practices to address certain issues and problems, not out of an attempt to develop a cohesive theory, strategy or agenda. An exception to this would be Secretary-General Boutros-Ghali's Agenda for Democratization, which made some effort at explicating the scope and foundations of UN democracy. Unfortunately, the circumstances of its publication, and perhaps the association with the then already failed tenure of Boutros-Ghali, undermined both the Agenda and any further attempt at a similar process of envisioning democracy. Instead, it reinforced the importance of practice as a vehicle for conceptualisation. While this may have been important for political expediency, this practice focus may have been counterproductive for the envisioning of democracy. The joining up of practices from a number of agencies and programmes of the UN system, as well as the translation of democracy into other practices similar or related to democracy, highlighted a process of institutional spread. While this institutional spread supported the development of the democracy agenda, it also translates into institutional fragmentation.

Despite a widespread concern with elections and electoral institutions by several agencies and programmes, election assistance remains the task of the Department for Peacekeeping Operations (DPKO). This means not only that the focus remains on peace-keeping and elections as an exit for UN missions, but that it remains too easy for actors such as the Secretary-General to describe democracy as elections and label other aspects of (the much broader) democracy assistance as something else. Indeed, as UN documents show, there is a tendency to talk about 'democracy and governance' even where *democracy assistance* identifies elections and governance as part of one comprehensive assistance package. This reinforces the question of what is political about democracy, as was highlighted by Carothers' analysis of US and European approaches to democracy support. Carothers claimed that the US follows an approach narrowly focussed on election and liberties. By defining democratisation as a 'process of political struggle in which democrats work to gain the upper hand in society over nondemocrats' (Carothers 2009: 5), the US directs aid towards institutions that support the political 'struggle'. This stands in contrast to European democracy assistance, which sees democratisation as 'a slow, iterative process of change involving an interrelated set of political and socioeconomic developments … emphasizing governance and the building of a well-functioning state' (ibid). While Carothers notes the inclusion of concerns of equality and justice in the European approach, he also criticises this approach as too development-oriented, allowing for the possibility of semi-authoritarianism. According to Carothers, the political obviously does not include the developmental.

Finally, the institutional fragmentation of practice also raises the question whether there is sufficient communication between different departments, agencies and programmes to potentially enable the delivery of a coherent vision of democracy should there be one. Is there a duplication or complementarity of efforts? Do different organisational approaches, opinions and views ultimately lead to a disintegration of the agenda or the frustration of each other's efforts? Similarly, the supply–demand split instituted by the UN Democracy Fund potentially disconnects the goals of the UN with those of local or national groups supporting democracy. Organisationally speaking, the call to 'deliver as one' is put under pressure by a framework of developmental democracy.

In summary, re-envisioning democracy and its implications for policy should serve the dual purpose of re-invigorating democracy where it already exists and forcing the UN and donors to match the desired ends with adequate means so that a viable democracy can be created. Moreover, envisioning a substantive democracy, here developmental democracy, aimed at highlighting the potential of human development and at reconceptualising the relationship between state, government and the people in which the achievement of human development becomes a duty for government. By highlighting a 'responsibility to protect *and* care' towards citizens, developmental democracy marked a deeper, more substantive version of democracy. Enabling participation in society on several levels, developmental democracy therefore questions the definition of 'inalienable rights' – political, social and economic.

Conclusion

Where does the future for UN democracy lie? Is substantive democracy possible, or indeed desirable? Is it necessary or indeed important to reconsider ideological aspects? Is practice able to provide further avenues for the development of the UN democracy agenda or for democratisation in general? In view of the history of UN democracy thus far, it is clear that the next step towards substantive democracy would be a large step. To make this step by continuing to use or develop institutional practice appears difficult if not unlikely. Existing practices are limited in their reach and are institutionally disjointed. A vehicle for practice development beyond good governance does not exist. Thus, instead of utilising institutional channels and institutional practices to promote the idea of developmental democracy, a 'softening up' of the system appears once more necessary. This softening up could be achieved in two ways. First, by familiarising member states with the idea and concept of developmental democracy through active promotion in general and by highlighting the need for states to adhere to their responsibility to protect and serve citizens in all areas: security, human rights *and* development. This would create a new frame of reference for existing ideas and practices relating to developmental democracy. Moreover, by focussing on further democratisation as a management issue and developmental democracy as a potential solution, depoliticisation would allow for greater acceptance and subsequent adoption as part of the UN democracy agenda. Again, 'stealth' then signifies incremental change through the connection of new, even radical ideas with existing ones. Secondly, norm entrepreneurs are needed to promote a different vision of democracy. The challenge they face is enormous – only by building on existing achievements and coupling developmental democracy with UN root ideas can norm entrepreneurs be successful in achieving member states' support for a broad, substantive democracy agenda. Organisationally, attention needs to be paid to the management of communication at the organisational interface. This applies not only to the process of agenda development and idea conceptualisation within the UN system, but also to the translation of ideas into policy, that is, between Secretariat and member states. Experience suggests that the success of ideas, practices and policies depends on the establishment and communication of a coherent vision and agenda. Norm entrepreneurs therefore need to continue to support democracy as a global value, be that to solve specific (UN) problems or, more radically, as a human good. Finally, the question of what kind of democracy a UN democracy is, or ought to be, should take account of Gaventa's argument:

> If we understand democracy not as a set of institutional designs, but as a concept constantly under construction through contestation among actors in different settings, then to support the process of democracy building we must also find and support emerging visions and imaginations of what democracy might become. (Gaventa 2006: 27)

While the question of the threshold between democratic and non-democratic regimes remains as relevant as, for example, criteria of human rights observant or non-observant, discussion about these thresholds as well as the meaning of democracy should be clearer than the response 'I know it when I see it'. In furthering the goals of the UN, the discussion about democracy must be an integral part of its future.

References

Abrahamsen, Rita (2000) *Disciplining Democracy: Development Discourse and Good Governance in Africa*, London, New York: ZED Books.

Ahmed, Ismail I. and Regionald Herbold Green (1999) 'The heritage of war and state collapse in Somali and Somaliland: local-level effects, external interventions and reconstruction', *Third World Quarterly* 20 (1): 113–127.

Alston, Phillip (2001) 'Peoples' rights – their rise and fall', in ibid. (ed.), *People's Rights*, Oxford: Oxford University Press.

Annan, Kofi (1998) 'The quiet revolution', *Global Governance* 4 (2): 123–138.

Annan, Kofi (1999) 'Two concepts of sovereignty', *Economist* 352 (8137): 49–50.

Annan, Kofi (2000a) *'We the Peoples': The Role of the United Nations in the 21st Century*, New York: UN Department of Public Information.

Annan, Kofi (2000b) 'UN Secretary General Kofi Annan's Closing Remarks', Warsaw, Poland, 27 June, http://ccd21.org/articles/annanwarsaw.htm, accessed December 2009.

Annan, Kofi (2000c) 'Africa's thirst for democracy', *International Herald Tribune*, 5 December.

Annan, Kofi (2002) 'Democracy as an international issue', *Global Governance* 8 (2): 135–142.

Anonymous (2002) 'Government recognition in Somalia and regional political stability in the Horn of Africa', *Journal of Modern African Studies* 40 (2): 247–272.

Barry, Norman (2000) *An Introduction to Modern Political Theory*, fourth edition, Basingstoke: Macmillan.

Beetham, David (ed.) (1994) *Defining and Measuring Democracy*, London: Sage Publications.

Beetham, David (1997) 'Linking democracy and human rights', *Peace Review*, 9 (3): 351–356.

Beetham, David (1999) *Democracy and Human Rights*, Cambridge: Polity Press.

Beigbeder, Yves (1994) *International Monitoring of Plebiscites, Referenda and National Elections*, Dordrecht: Martinus Nijhoff Publishers.

Beigbeder, Yves (1997) *The Internal Management of United Nations Organizations*, Basingstoke: Macmillan.

Beigbeder, Yves (2000) 'The United Nations Secretariat: reform in progress', in Paul Taylor and A.J.R. Groom (eds.) *The United Nations at the Millennium: The Principal Organs*, London: Continuum.

Béland, Daniel (2005) 'Ideas and social policy: an institutionalist perspective', *Social Policy & Administration* 39 (1): 1–18.

Bellamy, Alex J. (2009) *The Responsibility to Protect: The Global Effort to End Mass Atrocities*, Cambridge: Polity Press.

Bellamy, Alex J., Paul Williams, and Stuart Griffin (2004) *Understanding Peacekeeping*, Cambridge: Polity Press.

Bhagwati, Jagdish (1995) 'The new thinking on development', *Journal of Democracy* 6 (4): 50–64.

Bøås, Morten and Desmond McNeill (2004) 'Introduction. Power and ideas in multilateral institutions: towards an interpretative framework', in ibid. (eds.) *Global Institutions and Development. Framing the World?*, London: Routledge.

Bollen, Kenneth (1991) 'Political democracy: conceptual and measurement traps', in Alex Inkeles (ed.) *On Measuring Democracy: Its Consequences and Concomitants*, New Brunswick: Transaction Publishers.

Bosco, Andrea (1995) 'Lord Lothian and the federalist critique of national sovereignty', in David Long and Peter Wilson (eds.) *Thinkers of the Twenty Years' Crisis: Inter-War Idealism Reassessed*, Oxford: Clarendon Press.

Boudreau, Thomas E. (1991) *Sheathing the Sword: The UN Secretary-General and the Prevention of International Conflict*, New York, NY: Greenwood Press.

Boutros-Ghali, Boutros (1992) *An Agenda for Peace*, New York: UN.

Boutros-Ghali, Boutros (1993) 'An Agenda for Peace, one year later', *Orbis* 37 (3).

Boutros-Ghali, Boutros (1994) *Agenda for Development*, New York, NY: UN Department of Public Information.

Boutros-Ghali, Boutros (1995) 'Democracy: a newly recognized imperative', *Global Governance* 1 (1): 3–11.

Boutros-Ghali, Boutros (1996) *An Agenda for Democratization*, New York, NY: UN Department of Public Information.

Boutros-Ghali, Boutros (1999) *Unvanquished: A U.S.-U.N. Saga*, New York: Random House.

Boutros-Ghali, Boutros (2003a) 'Address to the American Publishers Association, Washington DC, 1993', in Charles Hill (ed.) *The Papers of UN Secretary-General Boutros Boutros-Ghali, Volumes 1–3*, New Haven, CT: Yale University Press.

Boutros-Ghali, Boutros (2003b) 'The Kreisky Lecture, Vienna, 11 June 1993', in Charles Hill (ed.) *The Papers of United Nations Secretary-General Boutros Boutros-Ghali, Volumes 1–3*, New Haven, CT: Yale University Press.

Boutros-Ghali, Boutros (2003c) 'The 1994 Gauer Distinguished Lecture in Law and Public Policy, National Center for the Public Interest, New York, 18 October 1994', in Charles Hill (ed.) *The Papers of United Nations Secretary-General Boutros Boutros-Ghali, Volumes 1–3*, New Haven, CT: Yale University Press.

Boutros-Ghali, Boutros (2003d) 'Statement at the Opening of the World Conference on Human Rights, Vienna, 14 June 1993', in Charles Hill (ed.) *The Papers of UN Secretary-General Boutros Boutros-Ghali, Volumes 1–3*, New Haven, CT: Yale University Press.

Boutros-Ghali, Boutros (2003e) 'Oath of Office taken by Boutros-Ghali [in Arabic], 3 December 1991', in Charles Hill (ed.) *The Papers of UN Secretary-General Boutros Boutros-Ghali, Volumes 1–3*, New Haven, CT: Yale University Press.

Boutros-Ghali, Boutros (2003f) 'Address to the conference on Global Development Cooperation, The Carter Center, Atlanta, Georgia, 4 December 1992', in Charles Hill (ed.) *The Papers of UN Secretary-General Boutros Boutros-Ghali, Volumes 1–3*, New Haven, CT: Yale University Press.

Boutros-Ghali, Boutros (2003g) 'Statement at the Opening of the World Conference on Human Rights, Vienna, 14 June 1993', in Charles Hill (ed.) *The Papers of United Nations Secretary-General Boutros Boutros-Ghali, Volumes 1–3*, New Haven, CT: Yale University Press.

Box, Richard C., et al. (2001) 'New Public Management and substantive democracy', *Public Administration Review* 61 (5): 608–619.

Brooker, Paul (2000) *Non-democratic Regimes: Theory, Government & Politics*, Basingstoke: Macmillan.

Bryden, M. (1995) 'Somaliland and peace in the Horn of Africa: a situation report and analysis', Addis Abba: UN Emergencies Unit for Ethiopia, www.h-net.org/~africa/sources/somalirpt.html, accessed 23 December 2005.

Burgess, Stephen F. (2001) *The United Nations Under Boutros Boutros-Ghali, 1992–1997*, Lanham, London: Scarecrow Press.

Byers, Michael and Simon Chesterman (2000) '"You, the people': pro-democratic intervention in international law', in Gregory H. Fox and Brad R. Roth (eds.) *Democratic Governance and International Law*, Cambridge: Cambridge University Press.

Caplan, Richard (2002) *A New Trusteeship? The International Administration of War-torn Territories*, Adelphi Papers 341, London: Routledge.

Carothers, Thomas (2009) 'Democracy assistance: political vs. developmental?', *Journal of Democracy* 20 (1): 5–19.

Cassese, Antonio (1995) *Self-determinaton of Peoples: A Legal Reappraisal*, Cambridge: Cambridge University Press.

Chandler, David (1999) *Bosnia. Faking Democracy after Dayton*, London: Pluto Press.

Chandler, David (2004) 'The Responsibility to Protect? Imposing the "Liberal Peace"', *International Peacekeeping* 11 (1): 59–81.

Checkel, Jeffrey T. (1998) 'The constructivist turn in International Relations theory', *World Politics* 50 (2): 324–348.

Chesterman, Simon (2005) *You, The People: The United Nations, Transitional Administration, and State-building*, Oxford: Oxford Scholarship Online (www.oxfordscholarship.com).

Cleaver, Frances (2001) 'Institutions, agency and the limitations of participatory approaches to development', in Bill Cooke and Uma Kothari (eds.) *Participation: The New Tyranny?*, London: ZED Books.

Cliffe, Lionel and Robin Luckham (1999) 'Complex political emergencies and the state: failure and the fate of the state', *Third World Quarterly* 20 (1): 27–50.

Cockell, John G. (2001) 'Human security and preventive action strategies', in Edward Newman and Oliver P. Richmond (eds.) *The United Nations and Human Security*, Basingstoke: Palgrave.

Collier, David and Steven Levitsky (1997) 'Democracy with adjectives: conceptual innovation in comparative research', *World Politic*, 49 (3): 430–451.

Connolly, William E. (1993) *The Terms of Political Discourse*, third edition, Oxford: Blackwell.

Conze, Werner (1972) 'Demokratie', in Otto Brunner, Werner Conze, and Reinhart Koselleck (eds.) *Geschichtliche Grundbegriffe. Historisches Lexikon zur Politisch-sozialen Sprache in Deutschland*, Stuttgart: Klett-Cotta.

Cornia, A. Giovanni, Richard Jolly, and Frances Stewart (eds.) (1987) *Adjustment with a Human Face*, Oxford: Clarendon Press.

Cornwall, Andrea and Celestine Nyamu-Musembi (2004) 'Putting the "rights-based approach" to development into perspective', *Third World Quarterly* 25 (8): 1415–1437.

Crawford, James (2000a) 'Democracy and the body of international law', in Gregory H. Fox and Brad R. Roth (eds.) *Democratic Governance and International Law*, Cambridge: Cambridge University Press.

Crawford, James (2000b) 'The right to self-determination in international law: its development and future', in Phillip Alston (ed.) *People' Rights*, Oxford: Oxford University Press.

Dahl, Robert A. (1956) *A Preface to Democratic Theory*, Chicago, IL: University of Chicago Press.

Dahl, Robert A. (1979) 'Procedural democracy', in Peter Laslett and James Fishkin (eds.) *Philosophy, Politics and Society*, fifth series, Oxford: Basil Blackwell.

Dahl, Robert A. (1985) *A Preface to Economic Democracy*, Cambridge: Polity Press.

Dahl, Robert A. (1989) *Democracy and its Critics*, New Haven, CT: Yale University Press.

Davenport, Christian (1999) 'Human rights and the democratic proposition' *Journal of Conflict Resolution*, 43 (1): 92–116.

Delanty, Gerard (2000) *Citizenship in a Global Age: Society, Culture, Politics*, Buckingham: Open University Press.

Delevic Djilas, Milica (2003) End, Not Means: Democracy and Human Rights in Conditioned Development Finance, PhD thesis, University of Kent.

Dewey, John (1939) *Freedom and Culture*, New York: Putnam.

Diamond, Larry (1992) 'Economic development and democracy reconsidered', in Gary Marks and Larry Diamond (eds.) *Reexamining Democracy*, Newbury Park, CA: Sage Publications.

Diamond, Larry (1999) *Developing Democracy: Toward Consolidation*, Baltimore: Johns Hopkins University Press.

Diamond, Larry, Juan J. Linz, and Seymour Martin Lipset (1989) 'Preface', in ibid. (ed.) *Democracy in Developing Countries*, Boulder, CO: Lynne Rienner.

Doornbos, Martin (2001) '"Good Governance": the rise and decline of a policy metaphor?', *Journal of Development Studies* 37 (6): 93–108.

Doyle, Michael W. (1996) 'Kant, liberal legacies, and foreign affairs', in Michael E. Brown (ed.) *Debating the Democratic Peace*, Cambridge, MA: MIT Press.

Doyle, Michael W. (1997) *Ways of War and Peace*, New York, NY: W.W. Norton.

Dumitriu, Petru (2003) 'The history and evolution of the New or Restored Democracies movement', *The Fifth International Conference of New or Restored Democracies* (Ulaanbataar, Mongolia: www.icnrd5-mongolia.mn/papers/paper11.pdf).

Durch, William J. (2001) *UN Peace Operations and the 'Brahimi Report'*, The Henry L. Stimson Center, http://www.stimson.org/fopo/pdf/peaceopsbr1001.pdf, accessed 19 August 2010.

Dutt, Sagarika (1990) The Politicization of the United Nations Specialized Agencies – A Case Study of UNESCO, PhD thesis, University of Kent.

Emmerij, Louis, Richard Jolly, and Thomas G. Weiss (2003) *Ahead of the Curve? UN Ideas and Global Challenges*, Bloomington, IN: Indiana University Press.

Emmerij, Louis, Richard Jolly, and Thomas G. Weiss (2005) 'Economic and social thinking at the UN in historical perspective', *Development and Change* 36 (2): 211–235.

Evans, Peter B., Dieter Rueschemeyer, and Theda Skocpol (eds.) (1985) *Bringing the State Back In*, Cambridge: Cambridge University Press.

Fasulo, Linda (2004) *An Insider's Guide to the UN*, New Haven, CT: Yale University Press.

Femia, Joseph V. (1993) *Marxism and Democracy*, Oxford: Clarendon Press.

Finnemore, Martha and Kathryn Sikkink (1998) 'International norm dynamics and political change' *International Organization* 52 (4): 887–917.

Fox, Gregory H. (2000) 'The right to political participation in international law', in Gregory H. Fox and Brad R. Roth (eds.) *Democratic Governance and International Law*, Cambridge: Cambridge University Press.

Franck, Thomas M. (1992) 'The emerging right to democratic governance', *Journal of International Law* 86 (1): 46–91.

Franck, Thomas M. (1995) *Fairness in International Law*, Oxford: Clarendon Press.

Freedom House (1999) *Democracy's Century. A Survey of Global Political Change*, http://www.freedom-house.org/reports/century.pdf, accessed 26 October 2004.

Freedom House (2004) *Freedom in the World 2004*, http://www.freedomhouse.org/template.cfm?page=363 &year=2004, accessed 17 September 2009.

Freedom House (2006) *UN Democracy Fund: A First Year Analysis*, http://www.freedomhouse.org/uploads /press_release/UNDEF_analysis_19dec06.pdf, accessed 28 August 2009.

Frost, Mervyn (1996) *Ethics in International Relations: A Constitutive Theory*, Cambridge: Cambridge University Press.

Fukuyama, Francis (1992) *The End of History and the Last Man*, London: Hamish Hamilton.

Fukuyama, Francis (2005) '"Stateness" first', *Journal of Democracy* 16 (1): 84–88.

Gallie, W. B. (1956) 'Essentially contested concepts', *Proceedings of the Aristotelian Society*, 183–187.

Gastil, Raymond Duncan (1991) 'The comparative survey of freedom: experiences and suggestions', in Alex Inkeles (ed.) *On Measuring Democracies: Its Consequences and Concomitants*, New Brunswick: Transaction Publishers.

Gaventa, John, (2006) 'Triumph, Deficit or Contestation? Deepening the "Deepening Democracy Debate"', IDS Working Paper 264, Brighton: Institute of Development Studies.

Giddens, Anthony (1996) 'T. H. Marshall, the state and democracy', in Martin Bulmer and Anthony M. Rees (eds.) *Citizenship Today. The Contemporary Relevance of T. H. Marshall*, London: UCL Press.

Giddens, Anthony (1998) *The Third Way: The Renewal of Social Democracy*, Cambridge: Polity Press.

Ginsberg, Benjamin (1982) *The Consequences of Consent*, Reading, MA: Addison-Wesley.

Ginsberg, Benjamin and Alan Stone (eds.) (1991) *Do Elections Matter?*, second edition, Armonk, NY: M.E. Sharpe Inc..

Goldmann, Kjell (1994) *The Logic of Internationalism*, London: Routledge.

Goodhand, Jonathan and David Hulme (1999) 'From wars to complex political emergencies: understanding conflict in the new world disorder', *Third World Quarterly* 20 (1): 13–26.

Goodrich, Leland M., Edvard Hambro, and Anne Patricia Simons (1969) *Charter of the United Nations: Commentary and Documents*, third edition, New York, NY: Columbia University Press.

Gordenker, Leon (1967) *The UN Secretary-General and the Maintenance of Peace*, New York, NY: Columbia University Press.

Gordenker, Leon (2005) *The UN Secretary-General and Secretariat*, London: Routledge.

Gould, Carol (1988) *Rethinking Democracy: Freedom and Social Cooperation in Politics, Economy, and Society*, Cambridge: Cambridge University Press.

Grewe, Wilhelm G. (2000) *The Epochs of International Law*, Berlin: DeGruyter.

Griffin, Matthew (2000) 'Accrediting democracies: does the Credentials Committee of the United Nations promote democracy through its accreditation process, and should it?', *International Law and Politics* 32 (3): 725–785.

Griffin, Michele (2003) 'The helmet and the hoe: linkages between United Nations development assistance and conflict management', *Global Governance* 9 (2): 199–217.

Haas, Peter M. (1992) 'Introduction: Epistemic communities and international policy coordination', *International Organization* 46 (1): 1–35.

Hanson, Russell L. (1989) 'Democracy', in Terence Ball, James Farr, and Russell L. Hanson (eds.), *Political Innovation and Conceptual Change*, Cambridge: Cambridge University Press.

Harrop, Martin and William L. Miller (1987) *Elections and Voters: A Comparative Introduction*, Basingstoke: Macmillan.

Haynes, Jeff (2001) *Democracy in the Developing World: Africa, Asia, Latin America and the Middle East*, Cambridge: Polity Press.

Heater, Derek (1996) *World Citizenship and Government: Cosmopolitan Ideas in the History of Western Political Thought*, Basingstoke: Macmillan.

Heater, Derek (2004) *Citizenship: The Civic Ideal in World History, Politics and Education*, third edition, Manchester: Manchester University Press.

Held, David (1996) *Models of Democracy*, second edition, Cambridge: Polity Press.

Henkel, Heiko and Roderick Stirrat (2001) 'Participation as spiritual duty; empowerment as secular subjection', in Bill Cooke and Uma Kothari (eds.) *Participation. The New Tyranny?*, London: ZED Books.

Heraclides, Alexis (1991) *The Self-determination of Minorities in International Politics*, Totowa, NJ: Frank Cass.

Heywood, Andrew (1999) *Political Theory: An Introduction*, second edition, Basingstoke: Palgrave.

Hill, Charles (ed.), (2003) *The Papers of United Nations Secretary-General Boutros Boutros-Ghali, Volumes 1–3*, New Haven, CT: Yale University Press.

Huntington, Samuel P. (1991) *The Third Wave: Democratization in the Late Twentieth Century*, Norman: University of Oklahoma Press.

Huth, Paul K. and Todd L. Allee (2002) *The Democratic Peace and Territorial Conflict in the Twentieth Century*, Cambridge: Cambridge University Press.

ICISS (2001) *The Responsibility to Protect*, Ottawa: International Development Research Centre.

Johnstone, Ian (2003) 'The role of the UN Secretary-General: the power of persuasion based on law', *Global Governance* 9 (4): 441–458.

Jolly, Richard, Louis Emmerij, Dharam Ghai, and Frédéric Lapeyre (2004) *UN Contributions to Development Thinking and Practice*, Bloomington: Indiana University Press.

Kaldor, Mary (2001) *New & Old Wars: Organized Violence in a Global Era*, Cambridge: Polity Press.

Karatnycky, Adrian (2002) 'The 2001–2002 Freedom House survey of freedom. The Democracy Gap', in Freedom House (ed.), *Freedom in the World 2001–2002: The Annual Survey of Political Rights and Civil Liberties*, http://www.freedomhouse.org/research/freeworld/2002/index.htm, accessed 26 October 2004.

Kelsen, Hans (1951) *The Law of the United Nations*, London: Stevens & Sons.

Kille, Kent J. (2006) *From Manager to Visionary: The Secretary-General of the United Nations*, Basingstoke: Palgrave Macmillan.

Kingdon, John W. (2003) *Agendas, Alternatives and Public Policies*, second edition, New York, NY: Longman.

Kjaer, Anne Mette (2004) *Governance*, Cambridge: Polity Press.

Koselleck, Reinhart (1985) *Futures Past: on the semantics of historical time*, Cambridge, MA: MIT Press.

Kumar, Krishna and Jeroen de Zeeuw (2006) 'Democracy assistance to postconflict societies', in ibid. (eds.) *Promoting Democracy in Postconflict Societies*, Boulder, CO: Lynne Rienner.

Lane, Jan-Erik and Svante Ersson (2003) *Democracy. A Comparative Approach*, London: Routledge.

Layne, Christopher (1994) 'Kant or Cant: The myth of the democratic peace', *International Security* 19 (2): 5–49.

Leftwich, Adrian (1996) 'Two cheers for democracy? Democracy and the developmental state', in Adrian Leftwich (ed.) *Democracy and Development: Theory and Practice*, Cambridge: Polity Press.

Leftwich, Adrian (2000) *States of Development: On the Primacy of Politics in Development*, Cambridge: Polity Press.

Levy, Jack (1988) 'Domestic politics and war', *Journal of Interdisciplinary History* 18 (Spring): 653–673.

Lijphart, Arend (1999) *Patterns of Democracy*, New Haven, CT: Yale University Press.

Linz, Juan J. and Alfred Stepan (1996) *Problems of Democratic Transition and Consolidation. Southern Europe, South America, and Post-communist Europe*, Baltimore: Johns Hopkins University Press.

Lipset, Seymour Martin (1959) 'Some social requisites of democracy: economic development and political legitimacy', *American Political Science Review* 53 (1): 69–105.

Ljungman, Cecilia M. (2004) 'Applying a Rights-Based Approach to development: concepts and principles', paper given at The Winners and Losers from Rights-Based Approaches to Development Conference, Manchester, 21–22 February 2005.

Lombardo, Caroline E. (2001) 'The making of *An Agenda for Democratization*: a speechwriter's view', *Chicago Journal of International Law* 2 (1): 253–266.

Long, David and Peter Wilson (eds.) (1995) *Thinkers of the Twenty Years' Crisis: Inter-war Idealism Reassessed*, Oxford: Clarendon Press.

Luard, Evan (1982) *A History of the United Nations, Volume 1: The Years of Western Domination, 1945–1955*, London: Macmillan.

Luard, Evan (1989) *A History of the United Nations, Volume 2: The Age of Decolonization, 1955–1965*, London: Macmillan.

Luck, Edward C. (1999) *Mixed Messages: American Politics and International Organization 1919–1999*, Washington, DC: Brookings Institute.

Luckham, Robin, Anne Marie Goetz, and Mary Kaldor (2000) *Democratic Institutions and Politics in Contexts of Inequality, Poverty, and Conflict*, IDS Working Paper 104, Brighton: Institute for Development Studies.

Macfarlane, S. Neil, Carolin J. Thielking, and Thomas G. Weiss (2004) 'The Responsibility to Protect: is anyone interested in humanitarian intervention?', *Third World Quarterly* 25 (5): 977–992.

Macpherson, C.B. (1977) *The Life and Times of Liberal Democracy*, Oxford: Oxford University Press.

Mani, Rama (2002) *Beyond Retribution: Seeking Justice in the Shadows of War*, Cambridge: Polity Press.

Mansfield, Edward and Jack Snyder (2005) *Electing to Fight: Why Democracies Go to War*, Cambridge, MA: MIT Press.

Manzo, Kate (2003) 'Africa in the rise of rights-based development', *Geoforum* 34: 437–456.

Maoz, Zeev and Bruce Russett (1992) 'Alliance, contiguity, wealth, and political stability: is the lack of conflict among democracies a statistical artefact?', *International Interactions* 17 (3): 245–267.

Marshall, T.H. (1992) 'Class, citizenship and social development', in T.H. Marshall and Tom Bottomore (eds.) *Citizenship and Social Class*, London: Pluto Press.

Martinez, Elena (2005) *Democracy, Citizenship and Social Cohesion in Latin America*, UNDP-European Commission International Seminar, Brussels, 15 February, http://democracyreport.undp.org/Downloads/DiscursoElenaMartinez-Bruselas.pdf, accessed 4 March 2010.

Martinussen, John (1996) *Introduction to the concept of Human Development*, Integrated Farming in Human Development Workshop, 25–29 March, Danish Agricultural and Rural Development Advisors' Forum (ARDAF), http://www.ardaf.org/NR/rdonlyres/8138D5C7-B2E9-4673-9576-90E9BB99BF6D/0/19961Martinussen.pdf, accessed 26 August 2010.

Marx, Karl (2008) *The Communist Manifesto*, Ware: Wordsworth Editions.

McCormack, Tara (2005) 'Human security and sovereignty', paper given at BISA working group Sovereignty and Its Discontent seminar series, King's College, London, 19 May.

McDonald, Matt (2002) 'Human security and the construction of security', *Global Society* 16 (3), 277–295.

Mohan Das, Sukanya (2005) Building Peace in Timor-Leste: A Critical Analysis, PhD thesis, Victoria University of Wellington.

Moore, Mick (1993) 'Introduction', *IDS Bulletin* 24: 1–7.

Morsink, Johannes (1999) *The Universal Declaration of Human Rights: Origins, Drafting, and Intent*, Philadelphia, PA: University of Pennsylvania Press.

Newman, Edward (1995) *International Civil Servants and International Power Structures: The Secretaryship-General and Perez de Cuellar*, Kent Papers in Politics and International Relations, Canterbury: University of Kent.

Newman, Edward (1998) *The UN Secretary-General from the Cold War to the New Era: A Global Peace and Security Mandate?*, Basingstoke: Macmillan Press.

Newman, Edward (2001) 'Human security and constructivism', *International Studies Perspectives* 2 (3): 239–251.

Newman, Edward (2004) 'A normatively attractive but analytically weak concept', *Security Dialogue* 35 (3): 358–359.

Newman, Edward (2009) '"Liberal" peacebuilding debates', in Edward Newman, Roland Paris and Oliver P. Richmond (eds.) *New Perspectives on Liberal Peacebuilding*, Tokyo: UN University Press.

Newman, Edward, Roland Paris and Oliver P. Richmond (eds.) (2009) *New Perspectives on Liberal Peacebuilding*, Tokyo: UN University Press.

Nicholas, H.G. (1959) *The United Nations as a Political Institution*, London: OUP.

Nielinger, Olaf (1998) *Demokratie und Good Governance in Afrika*, Hamburg: LIT.

Olson, William C. and A.J.R. Groom (1991) *International Relations Then and Now: Origins and Trends in Interpretation*, London: Harper Collins Academic.

Oppenheim, Felix E. (1971) 'Democracy – characteristics included and excluded', *The Monist* 55 (1): 29–50.

Ottaway, Marina (2004) *Democracy Challenged: The Rise of Semi-authoritarianism*, Washington, DC: Carnegie Endowment for International Peace.

Parfitt, Trevor (2004) 'The ambiguity of participation: a qualified defence of participatory development', *Third World Quarterly* 25 (3): 537–556.

Paris, Roland (2004) *At War's End: Building Peace after Conflict*, Cambridge: Cambridge University Press.

Pateman, Carol (1970) *Participation and Democratic Theory*, Cambridge: Cambridge University Press.

Peou, Sorpong (2002) 'The UN, peacekeeping and collective human security: from An Agenda for Peace to the Brahimi Report', *International Peacekeeping* 9 (2): 51–68.

Perez de Cuellar, Javier (1997) *Pilgrimage for Peace: A Secretary-General's Memoir*, New York: St Martin's Press.

Plant, Raymond (2002) 'Social democracy today', in April Carter and Geoffrey Stokes (eds.) *Democratic Theory Today: Challenges for the 21st Century*, Cambridge: Polity Press.

Ponzio, Richard (2004) 'UNDP experience in long-term democracy assistance', in Edward Newman and Roland Rich (eds.) *The UN Role in Promoting Democracy: Between Ideals and Reality*, Tokyo: UN University Press.

Prunier, Gérard (1997) 'Somaliland, a forgotten country', *Le Monde Diplomatique (English edition online)*, October.

Pugh, Michael (2010) 'Welfare in war-torn societies: nemesis of the liberal peace?' in Oliver P. Richmond (ed.) *Palgrave Advances in Peacebuilding: Critical Developments and Approaches*, Basingstoke: Palgrave Macmillan.

Radan, Peter (1997) 'The Badinter Arbitration Commission and the partition of Yugoslavia', *Nationalities Papers* 25 (3): 382–382.

Rady, Martyn (1996) 'Self-determination and the dissolution of Yugoslavia', *Ethnic and Racial Studies* 19 (2): 379–390.

Rapley, John (1996) *Understanding Development: Theory and Practice in the Third World*, Boulder, CO: Lynne Rienner.

Rapoport, David C. and Leonard Weinberg (eds.) (2001) *The Democratic Experience and Political Violence*, London/Portland OR: Frank Cass.

Ratner, Steven R. (2000) 'Democracy and accountability: the criss-crossing paths of two emerging norms', in Gregory H. Fox and Brad R. Roth (eds.) *Democratic Governance and International Law*, Cambridge: Cambridge University Press.

Ray, James Lee (1995) *Democracy and International Conflict: An Evaluation of the Democratic Peace Proposition*, Columbia, SC: University of South Carolina Press.

Rich, Roland (2004) 'Crafting Security Council mandates', in Edward Newman and Roland Rich (eds.) *The UN Role in Promoting Democracy: Between Ideals and Reality*, Tokyo: UN University Press.

Richmond, Oliver P. (2009) 'Beyond liberal peace? Responses to "backsliding"', in Edward Newman, Roland Paris and Oliver P. Richmond (eds.) *New Perspectives on Liberal Peacebuilding*, Tokyo: UN University Press.

Richmond, Oliver P. (2010a) 'Introduction', in ibid. (ed.) *Palgrave Advances in Peacebuilding: Critical Developments and Approaches*, Basingstoke: Palgrave Macmillan.

Richmond, Oliver P. (2010b) 'A genealogy of peace and conflict theory', ibid. (ed.) *Palgrave Advances in Peacebuilding: Critical Developments and Approaches*, Basingstoke: Palgrave Macmillan.

Rittberger, Volker and Bernhard Zangl (2006) *International Organization: Polity, Politics and Policies*, Basingstoke: Palgrave Macmillan.

Rivlin, Benjamin (1996) 'Boutros-Ghali's ordeal: leading the United Nations in an age of uncertainty', in Dimitris Bourantonis and Marios Evriviades (eds.) *A United Nations for the Twenty-first Century: Peace, Security and Development*, The Hague: Kluwer Law International.

Roth, Brad R. (2000) *Governmental Illegitimacy in International Law*, Oxford: Oxford University Press.

Rushton, Simon (2008) 'The UN Secretary-General and norm entrepreneurship: Boutros Boutros-Ghali and democracy promotion', *Global Governance* 14 (1): 95–110.

Russell, Ruth B. (1958) *A History of the United Nations Charter*, Washington, DC: Brookings Institute.

Russett, Bruce (1993) *Grasping the Democratic Peace: Principles for a Post-Cold War World*, Princeton, NJ: Princeton University Press.

Russett, Bruce (2003) 'Afterword', in Charles Hill (ed.) *The Papers of United Nations Secretary-General Boutros Boutros-Ghali*, New Haven, CT: Yale University Press.

Salter, Mark B. (2002) *Barbarians & Civilization in International Relations*, London: Pluto Press.

Saward, Michael (1998) *The Terms of Democracy*, Cambridge: Polity Press.

Saward, Michael (2003) *Democracy*, Cambridge: Polity Press.

Schneider, Cornelia (2005) 'Striking a balance in post-conflict constitution-making: lessons from Afghanistan for the international community', *Peace, Conflict and Development* 7 (7): 174–216.

Schumpeter, Joseph A. (1976) *Capitalism, Socialism and Democracy*, fifth edition, London: George Allen & Unwin.

Schwartz, Thomas and Kiron K. Skinner (2002) 'The myth of the democratic peace', *Orbis* 46 (1): 159–172.

Sen, Amartya (1999a) 'Democracy as a universal value', *Journal of Democracy* 10 (3): 3–17.

Sen, Amartya (1999b) *Development as Freedom*, Oxford: Oxford University Press.

Simma, Bruno (2002) *The Charter of the United Nations: A Commentary*, second edition, Oxford: Oxford University Press.

Singh, Anita Inder (2000) 'Democracy as conflict prevention', *UN Chronicle* 37 (3): 14–16.

Sirowy, Larry and Alex Inkeles (1991) 'The effects of democracy on economic growth and inequality: a review', in Alex Inkeles (ed.) *On Measuring Democracy: Its Consequences and Concomitants*, New Brunswick, NJ: Transaction Publisher.

Skjelsbaek, Kjell (1991) 'The UN Secretary-General and the Mediation of International Disputes', *Journal of Peace Research* 28 (1): 99–115.

Sklar, Richard L. (1996) 'Towards a theory of developmental democracy', in Adrian Leftwich (ed.) *Democracy and Development: Theory and Practice*, Cambridge: Polity Press.

Smith, B.C. (2003) *Understanding Third World Politics: Theories of Political Change & Development*, Basingstoke: Palgrave Macmillan.

Smith, Tony (1994) *America's Mission: the United States and the Worldwide Struggle for Democracy in the Twentieth Century*, Princeton, NJ: Princeton University Press.

Snyder, Jack (2000) *From Voting to Violence: Democratization and Nationalist Conflict*, New York, NY: W.W. Norton.

Somaliland Forum (2001) *Somaliland. Ten years of freedom*, Press Release, 18 May, http://www.hartford-hwp.com/archives/33/109.html, accessed 23 December 2005.

Stokes, Geoffrey (2002) 'Democracy and Citizenship', in April Carter and Geoffrey Stokes (eds.) *Democratic Theory Today. Challenges for the 21st Century*, Cambridge: Polity Press.

Streit, Clarence K. (1939) *Union Now*, London: Jonathan Cape.

Taylor, Paul (1999) 'The United Nations in the 1990s: proactive cosmopolitanism and the issue of sovereignty', *Political Studies* 47 (3): 538–565.

Thakur, Ramesh (2005a) 'Intervention, sovereignty, and the responsibility to protect', in Ramesh Thakur, Andrew Cooper, and John English (eds.) *International Commissions and the Power of Ideas*, Tokyo: UN University Press.

Thakur, Ramesh (2005b) 'In defence of The Responsibility to Protect', *The International Journal of Human Rights* 7 (3): 160–178.

Thomas, Caroline (2001) 'Global governance, development and human security: exploring the links', *Third World Quarterly* 22 (2): 159–175.

Thornberry, Patrick (1994) 'The principle of self-determination', in Vaughan Lowe and Colin Warbrick (eds.) *The United Nations and the Principles of International Law*, London: Routledge.

Truman, Harry (1949) *Inaugural Address*, http://avalon.law.yale.edu/20th_century/truman.asp, accessed December 2009.

UN (1994) *Yearbook of the United Nations*, New York, NY: UN Department of Public Information.

UN (1999) *Yearbook of the United Nations*, New York, NY: UN Department of Public Information.

UN (21 August 2000) *Report of the Panel on United Nations Peace Operations [Brahimi Report]*, UN doc. A/55/305-S/2000/809.

UN (2000) *ACC Matrix of Governance*, New York: UN, http://hlcp.unsystemceb.org/reference/03/D15_2.

UN (2004) *A more secure world: our shared responsibility, Report of the Secretary-General's High-level Panel on Threats, Challenges and Change*, New York, NY: UN Department of Public Information.

UN (2006) *Requests for electoral assistance, 1989–2005*, http://www.un.org/Depts/dpa/ead/overview.html #Statistics.

UNDP (1993) *People's Participation*, Oxford: Oxford University Press.

UNDP (1995) *Public Sector Management, Governance and Sustainable Human Development*, New York: UNDP.

UNDP (1997) *Reconceptualising Governance*, Discussion Paper 2, New York: UNDP.

UNDP (2002) *Deepening Democracy in a Fragmented World*, Oxford: Oxford University Press.

UNDP (2004a) *Democracy in Latin America: Towards a Citizens' Democracy*, New York: UNDP.

UNDP (2004b) *Ideas and Contributions. Democracy in Latin America: Towards a Citizen's Democracy*, New York: UNDP.

UNDP Management and Governance Division (undated) *UNDP and Governance, Experiences and Lessons Learned*, Management and Governance Division, Lessons Learned Series 1 (269), http://magnet .undp.org/docs/gov/Lessons1.htm, accessed 1 November 2004.

UNGA (16 August 1988) *Letter dated 15 August 1988 from the Chargé d'affaires of the Permanent Mission of the Philipines to the United Nations addressed to the Secretary General [Manila Declaration]*, UN doc. A/43/538.

UNGA (8 December 1988) *Enhancing the Effectiveness of the Principle of Periodic and Genuine Elections*, Resolution adopted by the General Assembly, UN doc. A/RES/43/157.

UNGA (21 February 1990), *Enhancing the Effectiveness of the Principle of Periodic and Genuine Elections*, Resolution adopted by the General Assembly, A/RES/45/150.

UNGA (18 December 1990) *Respect for the Principles of National Sovereignty and Non-interference in the Internal Affairs of States in their Electoral Processes*, Resolution adopted by the General Assembly, UN doc. A/RES/45/151.

UNGA (22 February 1993) *Respect for the Principles of National Sovereignty and Non-interference in the Internal Affairs of States in their Electoral Processes*, Resolution adopted by the General Assembly, A/RES/47/130.

UNGA (22 December 1994) *Support by the United Nations System for the Efforts of Governments to Promote and Consolidate New or Restored Democracies*, Resolution adopted by the General Assembly, UN doc. A/RES/49/30.

UNGA (23 November 1999) *Code of Democratic Conduct (draft resolution)*, UN doc. A/54/L.23.

UNGA (18 September 2000) *United Nations Millennium Declaration*, Resolution adopted by the General Assembly, UN doc. A/RES/55/2.

UNGA (24 October 2005) *2005 World Summit Outcome*, Resolution adopted by the General Assembly, A/RES/60/1.

UNGA (25 April 2000) *Promoting and Consolidating Democracy*, Resolution of the Commission of Human Rights, Res. 2000/47.

UNHCHR (27 April 1999) *Promotion of the Right to Democracy*, Resolution of the Commission on Human Rights, Res. 1999/57

UN Information Centre (2002) Rebuilding Afghanistan: peace and stability, press conference, Conference of Foreign Ministers, Petersberg, Germany, http://www.uno.de, accessed on 29 May 2005.

UNSC (27 March 2003) *Lack of Security in Afghanistan Threatens Peace Process at all Levels, Security Council Told. Assistant Secretary-General for Peacekeeping Operations introduces Fourth Report of Secretary-General on Afghan Situation*, Press Release, SC/7708.

UNSG (19 November 1991) *Enhancing the Effectiveness of the Principle of Periodic and Genuine Elections*, Report of the Secretary-General, UN doc. A/46/609.

UNSG (18 November 1993) *Enhancing the Effectiveness of the Principle of Periodic and Genuine Elections*, Report of the Secretary-General, UN doc. A/48/590.

UNSG (17 November 1994) *Enhancing the Effectiveness of the Principle of Periodic and Genuine Elections*, Report of the Secretary-General, UN doc. A/49/675.

UNSG (25 January 1995) *Supplement to An Agenda for Peace*, Position Paper of the Secretary-General on the Occasion of the Fiftieth Anniversary of the United Nations, UN doc. A/50/60-S/1995/1.

UNSG (7 August 1995) *Support by the United Nations System of the Efforts of Governments to Promote and Consolidate New or Restored Democracies*, Report of the Secretary-General, UN doc. A/50/332.

UNSG (8 November 1995) *Enhancing the Effectiveness of the Principle of Periodic and Genuine Elections*, Report of the Secretary-General, UN doc. A/50/736.

UNSG (18 October 1996) *Support by the United Nations System of the Efforts of Governments to Promote and Consolidate New or Restored Democracies*, Report of the Secretary-General, UN doc. A/51/512.

UNSG (2 June 1997) *Secretary-General calls for efforts to unleash African 'Third Wave' based on democracy, human rights, and sustainable development*, Address given by Secretary-General Kofi Annan to the Annual Assembly of Heads of State and Government of the Organization of African Unity (OAU), Harare, SG/SM/6245/Rev.1*.

UNSG (21 October 1997) *Support by the United Nations system of the efforts of Governments to promote and consolidate new or restored democracies*, Report of the Secretary-General, UN doc. A/52/513.

UNSG (29 June 1999) *Good Governance essential for Africa to reject conflict, realize potential says Secretary-General to Third Africa Governance Forum*, Message of Secretary-General Kofi Annan to the Third Annual Africa Governance Forum in Bamako, Mali, SG/SM/7054, AFR/150UNSG (22 October 1999) *Support by the United Nations system of the efforts of Governments to promote and consolidate new or restored democracies*, Report of the Secretary-General, UN doc. A/54/492.

UNSG (13 October 2000) *Support by the United Nations system of the efforts of Governments to promote and consolidate new or restored democracies*, Report of the Secretary-General, UN doc. A/55/489.

UNSG (19 June 2001) *War less likely between mature democracies, says Secretary-General*, Press Release, SG/SM/7850.

UNSG (23 October 2001) *Support by the United Nations system of the efforts of Governments to promote and consolidate new or restored democracies*, Report of the Secretary-General, UN doc. A/56/499.

UNSG (29 November 2001) *Solution to Afghan crisis must come from women and men of Afghanistan itself, Secretary-General says in Washington address*, Press Release, SG/SM/8049- AFG/171.

UNSG (11 September 2003) *Democracy cannot be imposed from abroad, but international efforts can encourage, assist says Secretary-General to Mongolia Conference*, Press release, SG/SM8860.

UNSG (26 September 2003) *Support by the United Nations system of the efforts of Governments to promote and consolidate new or restored democracies*, Report of the Secretary-General, UN doc. A/58/392.

UNSG (21 March 2005) *In larger Freedom: towards development, security and human rights for all*, Report of the Secretary General, A/59/2005.

UNSG (12 October 2005) *World summit achieved concrete, significant gains in human rights, rule of law, Secretary-General says in address to Universidade Nova de Lisboa*, Press Release, SG/SM/10161.

Weiss, Thomas G. and Tatiana Carayannis (2001) 'Whither United Nations economic and social ideas?' *Global Social Policy* 1 (1): 25–47.

Weiss, Thomas G., David P. Forsythe, and Roger A. Coate (1994) *The United Nations and Changing World Politics*, Boulder, CO: Westview Press.

Williams, Andrew (1999) *Failed Imaginations? New World Orders of the Twentieth Century*, Manchester: Manchester University Press.

Williams, David and Tom Young (1994) 'Governance, the World Bank and liberal theory', *Political Studies* 42: 84–100.

Williams, Glyn (2004) 'Evaluating participatory development: tyranny, power and (re)politicisation', *Third World Quarterly* 25 (3): 557–578.

Williams, Raymond (1983), *Keywords. A Vocabulary of Culture and Society*, London: Fontana Press.

World Bank (1989) *Sub-Saharan Africa: From Crisis to Sustainable Growth*, Washington, DC: World Bank.

World Bank (1992) *Governance and Development*, Washington, DC: World Bank.

World Bank (1994a) *Governance: the World Bank's Experience*, Washington, DC: World Bank.

World Bank (1994b) *The World Bank and Participation*, Washington, DC: World Bank.

World Bank (1997) *The State in a Changing World*, Oxford: Oxford University Press.

World Bank (2001) *Précis*, Washington, DC: World Bank.

Young, Iris Marion (2000) *Inclusion and Democracy*, Oxford: Oxford University Press.

Zacher, Mark W. (1966) 'The Secretary-General and the United Nations' Function of Peaceful Settlement', *International Organization* 20 (4): 724–749.

Index